Corpus Processing for Lexical Acquisition

Language, Speech, and Communication

Statistical Language Learning
Eugene Charniak, 1994

The Development of Speech Perception
edited by Judith Goodman and Howard C. Nusbaum, 1994

Construal
Lyn Frazier and Charles Clifton, Jr., 1995

The Generative Lexicon
James Pustejovsky, 1995

The Origins of Grammar: Evidence from Early Language Comprehension
Kathy Hirsh-Pasek and Roberta Michnick Golinkoff, 1996

Language and Space
edited by Paul Bloom, Mary A. Peterson, Merrill F. Garrett, and Lynn Nadel, 1996

Corpus Processing for Lexical Acquisition
edited by Branimir Boguraev and James Pustejovsky, 1996

Corpus Processing for Lexical Acquisition

edited by
Branimir Boguraev and James Pustejovsky

A Bradford Book
The MIT Press
Cambridge, Massachusetts
London, England

This book was set in Adobe Palatino and Computer Modern by the editors and was printed and bound in the United States of America.

Library of Congress Cataloging-in-Publication Data

Corpus processing for lexical acquisition / edited by Branimir Boguraev and
    James Pustejovsky.
        p.   cm.—(Language, speech, and communication)
    "A Bradford book"
    Includes bibliographical references and index.
    ISBN 0-262-02392-X (hc: alk. paper)
    1. Natural language processing (Computer science). I. Boguraev, Bran,
1950–   . II. Pustejovsky, J. (James)
QA76.9.N38C68 1995
006.3′5—dc20   95-26557
                                                               CIP

to Boswell, and Pasha and Lucca . . .

Contents

Contributors   xiii

Preface   xv

Acknowledgments   xvii

I   INTRODUCTION

1   Issues in Text-based Lexicon Acquisition
Branimir Boguraev, James Pustejovsky   3
1.1   The Problem of Lexical Knowledge Acquisition   4
1.2   Text-based Lexicon Acquisition   14

II   COPING WITH UNKNOWN LEXICALIZATIONS

2   Internal and External Evidence in the Identification and Semantic Categorization of Proper Names
David D. McDonald   21
2.1   Introduction   21
2.2   Internal versus External Evidence   22
2.3   Procedure Overview: Delimit, Classify, Record   24
2.4   The Setting for the Process   30
2.5   Walking through an Example   33
2.6   Conclusions   37

3   Identifying Unknown Proper Names in Newswire Text
Inderjeet Mani, T. Richard MacMillan   41
3.1   Introduction   41
3.2   Approaches to Name Identification   41
3.3   Proper Names — Syntax and Semantics   45

3.4   Overall Algorithm   46

3.5   Mention Generator   48

3.6   Knowledge Sources   48

3.7   Representation of Uncertainty   50

3.8   Appositives   50

3.9   Coreference   51

3.10 Evaluation   57

3.11 Conclusion   58

4   Categorizing and Standardizing Proper Nouns
      for Efficient Information Retrieval
      *Woojin Paik, Elizabeth D. Liddy, Edmund Yu, Mary
      McKenna*   61

4.1   Introduction   61

4.2   Proper Noun Boundary Identification   61

4.3   Proper Noun Classification Scheme   62

4.4   Use of Proper Nouns in Matching   67

4.5   Performance Evaluation   68

4.6   System Comparisons   72

4.7   Future Directions   73

III   TASK-DRIVEN LEXICON INDUCTION

5   Customizing a Lexicon to Better Suit a Com-
      putational Task
      Marti A. Hearst, Hinrich Schütze   77

5.1   Introduction   77

5.2   Creating Categories from WORDNET   79

5.3   A Topic Labeler   82

5.4   Augmenting Categories with Relevant Terms   84

5.5   Combining Distant Categories   89

5.6   Conclusions   94

**6   Towards Building Contextual Representations
of Word Senses Using Statistical Models**
Claudia Leacock, Geoffrey Towell, Ellen M. Voorhees   97

6.1   Contextual Representations   97

6.2   Acquiring Topical Context   97

6.3   An Upper Bound for Classifier Performance   107

6.4   Acquiring Local Context   109

6.5   Conclusion   113

IV   CATEGORIZATION OF LEXICAL UNITS

**7   A Context Driven Conceptual Clustering Method
for Verb Classification**
Roberto Basili, Maria-Teresa Pazienza, Paola Velardi   117

7.1   Introduction   117

7.2   CIAULA: An Algorithm to Acquire Word Clusters   125

7.3   Basic Level Categories   135

7.4   Summary   140

8   Distinguished Usage
Scott A. Waterman   143

8.1   Introduction   143

8.2   Information Extraction   146

8.3   Functionality in Lexical Semantics   147

8.4   Integrating Syntactic with Semantic Constraints   151

8.5   Patterns   152

8.6   The Current State of Pattern Acquisition   155

8.7   Structural Similarity Clustering   156

8.8   Lexical Clustering Using Edit Distance   162

8.9   Context Clustering   165

8.10 Context Method Results   167

8.11 Conclusion   171

V   LEXICAL SEMANTICS FROM CORPUS ANALYSIS

9   Detecting Dependencies between Semantic Verb Subclasses and Subcategorization Frames in Text Corpora
Victor Poznański, Antonio Sanfilippo   175

9.1   Introduction   175

9.2   Background   176

9.3   Semantic Acquisition Programs   178

9.4   Using CorPSE: Trends and Limitations   186

9.5   Conclusions   190

10   Acquiring Predicate-Argument Mapping Information from Multilingual Texts
Chinatsu Aone, Douglas McKee   191

10.1   Introduction   191

10.2   Predicate-Argument Mapping Representation   191

10.3   Automatic Acquisition from Corpora   196

10.4   Conclusion   200

VI   MEASURING LEXICAL ACQUISITION

11   Evaluation Techniques for Automatic Semantic Extraction: Comparing Syntactic and Window Based Approaches
Gregory Grefenstette   205

11.1   Introduction   205

11.2   Gold Standards Evaluation   206

11.3   Corpus   209

11.4   Semantic Extraction Techniques   210

11.5   Results   212

11.6   Conclusion   215

Bibliography   217

Author Index   229

Subject Index   233

Contributors

Branimir Boguraev	Apple Computer
Chinatsu Aone	Systems Research and Applications
Roberto Basili	University of Rome
Gregory Grefenstette	Rank Xerox Research Centre
Marti A. Hearst	Xerox PARC
Claudia Leacock	Princeton University
Elizabeth D. Liddy	Syracuse University
T. Richard MacMillan	The MITRE Corporation
Inderjeet Mani	The MITRE Corporation
David McDonald	Brandeis University
Douglas McKee	Systems Research and Applications
Mary McKenna	Syracuse University
Woojin Paik	Syracuse University
Maria-Teresa Pazienza	University of Rome
Victor Poznański	Sharp Laboratories of Europe
James Pustejovsky	Brandeis University
Antonio Sanfilippo	Sharp Laboratories of Europe
Hinrich Schütze	CSLI, Stanford University
Geoffrey Towell	Siemens Corporate Research
Paola Velardi	University of Ancona
Ellen M. Voorhees	Siemens Corporate Research
Scott A. Waterman	Brandeis University
Edmund Yu	Syracuse University

Preface

The massive re-awakening, during the recent years, of interest in empirical and statistical methods of language analysis is already evidenced in a pattern reflected in the major conferences of the field. As it has grown stronger over the past five years, specialized workshops on corpus-based linguistics have been organized and over-subscribed, and recently the major journal of the field, *Computational Linguistics*, has dedicated two issues to the theme of "Using Large Corpora."

This volume contains revised versions of a selection of the papers presented at the ACL/SIGLEX Workshop on Acquisition of Lexical Knowledge from Text, held in June, 1993, at the annual meeting of the *Association for Computational Linguistics* in Columbus, Ohio. This volume falls within the broad category of corpus-based work, but also complements it by addressing a closely related, core issue in the field, namely acquisition of lexicons for realistic—i.e., large, scalable, robust, and transportable—natural language systems.

Acknowledgments

The concept of this book emerged from the discussions at a very productive workshop; it was made real by the support of everyone who contributed to it. Special thanks are due to our editor at MIT Press, Amy Pierce, who believed in the project throughout its (occasionally meandering) life cycle.

The collation, editing, typesetting and printing of this book was done entirely on an Apple Macintosh notebook system, and thanks are due not only to the great Donald Knuth, for his TEX system, but to Wilfried Ricken, for his particulalry clean and functional port, DirectTEX for the Macintosh. Wonderful as portable computing may be, fine-tuning page masters while grappling with the ugly side effects of arcane "patch me, and forget about me" programming style tends to make even unobtrusive laptops extremely obtrusive; thanks are due to our families for effectively, and quietly, dealing with the stress. We also gratefully acknowledge the support of our respective work environments, the Advanced Technology Group at Apple Computer, and the Computer Science Department at Brandeis University. This work was supported in part by a grant from the National Science Foundation and the Advanced Research Projects Agency (IRI-93-14955).

While this book would never have happened without the Workshop on Acquisition of Lexical Knowledge from Text, the workshop itself was rooted in an idea by Robert Amsler, who has been a long-standing pioneer in all aspects of lexical research. Always looking beyond the current state-of-the-art in lexicon acquisition, he had the vision, many years ago, to "learn" a lexicon for real texts from the texts themselves — the workshop, and this book, are a proof of that vision.

Corpus Processing for Lexical Acquisition

I INTRODUCTION

1 Issues in Text-based Lexicon Acquisition

Branimir Boguraev, James Pustejovsky

In computational linguistics research, it has become clear that, regardless of a system's sophistication or breadth, its performance must be measured in large part by the resources provided by the computational lexicon associated with it. The fundamental resource that go into a lexical item enable a wide range of morphological, lexical, syntactic, semantic and pragmatic processes to operate in the course of tasks such as language analysis, text processing, content extraction, document summarization, or machine translation. Lexical acquisition, therefore, has emerged as an essential phase in getting any realistic natural language processing system off the ground. This work began approximately 10-13 years ago with research aimed at leveraging the information compiled by lexicographers, which was then becoming available in the form of machine-readable dictionaries. We are now at a point where it is clear that, even with the lexical data available in those resources, there is a large number of different word classes which remain outside the coverage of a "conventional" dictionary; furthermore, there is information required by current computational systems, which is unavailable in machine-readable dictionaries in any case.

The fundamental problem of lexical acquisition, then, is how to provide, fully and adequately, the systems with the lexical knowledge they need to operate with the proper degree of efficiency. The answer, to which the community is converging today, is to extract the lexicon from texts themselves.

It has always been trivial to generate word lists by extracting isolated word forms in a text. Then, corpora with these forms tagged and syntactically annotated became available, giving us the basis for a new class of stochastic parsers. Corpus processing techniques demonstrated, among other things, how certain categories of lexical properties could be identified by means of empirical studies of word occurrences in large bodies of text. For instance, paired corpora in two languages provide evidence that a lexicon could be induced from alignment of texts which are translations of each other; word collocations can be distinguished from coincidental co-occurrences; semantic analysis of phrasal segments points to evidence for regular behavior of certain word classes; conversely, analysis of patterns of parsed (or otherwise structurally annotated) texts revealed the potential for deducing semantic information about lexical classes.

The collection of papers in this volume is the most recent "snapshot" of lexical acquisition techniques and practices, including contributions in the general areas of:

- recognition of text objects as lexical entities;
- identification of the properties of such lexical entities;
- identification and recognition of the most informative piece of text which is characteristic of these properties of the lexical entity.

More specifically (but not exhaustively), topics addressed by the individual papers range over: recognition of open compounds; incremental acquisition of meanings from sentence usages; recognition of new senses of existing words; sense disambiguation (relative to a sense-annotated dictionary, or as warranted by the given text); recognition of specific classes of words; recognition and annotation of patterns of word use (e.g., subcategorization, selectional restrictions, syntactic and semantic shifts relative to a given corpus, and so forth; linguistic- and text structure-driven identification of lexical/semantic relations (e.g., use of appositives to generate definitions, or concept refinement from list syntax).

1.1   The Problem of Lexical Knowledge Acquisition

One of the significant bottlenecks in natural language technology comes from having to populate a computational lexicon with entries for tens, and even hundreds, of thousands of words. A great number of language processing systems are strikingly limited in their range of application. This lack of versatility is to a large extent due to the typically small number of lexical entries available to them. A further problem concerns the fragility of most experimental systems in the face of serious attempts to "scale up" laboratory prototypes or application programs carefully tuned for particular domains, because so much of the information contained in lexical entries is specific to the particular system in its current state. For this reason, we will briefly define the problem of knowledge acquisition for large lexicons. There are several approaches to this problem, falling into two general categories of manual crafting of (lexical) knowledge bases and automatic acquisition from on-line textual resources.

There are two types of text resource used for lexical data acquisition: machine-readable dictionaries (MRDs) and text corpora. Dictionaries are, by definition, repositories of lexical information pertaining to a large number of words; most, if not all of this could be used for natural language processing. Text corpora reflect language as it is used and as it evolves; by studying regularities of use and patterns of behavior of words, which only emerge from analysis of very large samples of text and/or speech, it is possible to induce (among other things) lexical properties and thus populate a computational lexicon.

While certainly representative of lexical behavior of words, both dictionaries and corpora have their drawbacks. At best, a computational lexicon derived from MRD sources tends to be incomplete, both with respect to coverage (words) and content (lexical properties). At worst, such a lexicon leaves much to be desired as far as consistency and organization of data is concerned. The question of organizing the lexical knowledge extracted from a text resource is equally pressing in the case of using text corpora; furthermore, until issues like what constitutes the right kind of corpus given certain lexical properties, how to balance it, and how to abstract the information acquired through "learning" from the learning mechanism itself, the transition from corpus to lexicon will remain in need of streamlining.

For reasons like these, at least, there is a view in the field that time and effort notwithstanding, a substantial fragment of lexical knowledge can only be, and therefore should be, crafted by hand. This applies not only to building application- and domain-specific lexicons, but to general-purpose lexical knowledge and data bases. In the first section below, we examine the three major trends of lexical knowledge acquisition, and what success has been achieved with each approach to date.

1.1.1   Manual acquisition

The most labor intensive method of populating a lexicon with syntactic, morphological, and semantic information is manual entry. However, this method is probably still the most frequently used, for a number of reasons. First, the startup costs are low. No corpora or existing dictionaries or lexicons need to be obtained and no automatic analysis programs need to be written. Minimally, all that is needed is a text editor. Second, as was already noted, the lexicons of most natural language systems, excluding Machine Translation, are typically small—on the order of tens of words. Even when domains—such as the Resource Management database query task [Price *et al.*, 1988] and the ATIS air travel task [Hemphill *et al.*, 1990] —have had significantly larger vocabularies (approximately 1,000 words), typically the vocabulary has remained at a fixed size over a long period, rather than requiring continual massive increases in size.

In addition to system and domain specific tools, there are projects totally devoted to knowledge acquisition for natural language processing. One project worth mentioning is the CYC project ([Lenat and Guha, 1990]) underway at MCC. CYC has the goal of capturing all human commonsense knowledge in a very large knowledge base. The CYC approach is to manually enter all knowledge relevant to making commonsense inferences. Thus, the task for language analysis and, in particular, for lexicon design, is to hand-code all syntactic, morphological, semantic, and pragmatic information associated with a word. The representation language used for encoding knowledge in CYC is CYCL. Associated with every element in the ontology is a lexical item or perhaps a phrase. The set of these associations can essentially be seen as the lexicon within the CYC system.

Another example of a large effort to manually enter lexical knowledge into a knowledge base is the ONTOS project at CMU's Center for Machine Translation (CMT) (see [Nirenburg, 1989]). This effort is aimed at providing the concept lexicon for a language independent conceptual representation between languages for translation purposes. ONTOS provides an interactive environment for acquiring knowledge associated with the words in a language. This information is embedded within a frame network representation of objects, events, and situations.

The methodological point assumed by ONTOS is that the information needed for robust machine translation (or for that matter, analysis or generation in isolation) is not to be found in any systematic form in dictionaries or corpora alone. Thus, tools are required for interactively entering, and updating, knowledge about words and meanings.

1.1.2 Machine-readable dictionaries

Computational lexicons are unlike human dictionaries in many respects; it is certainly the case that a computer cannot just make a reference to a dictionary, even if it is available on-line, since the form and content of lexical entries "designed" for people are substantially different from those required by computers. Still, dictionaries are the largest available repositories of organized knowledge about words, and it is only natural for computational linguists to turn to them in the hope that this knowledge can be extracted, formalized, and made available to NLP systems.

The appeal of using on-line dictionaries in the construction of formal computational lexicons is intuitively obvious: dictionaries contain information about words, and lexicons need such information. If automated procedures could be developed for extracting and formalizing lexical data, on a large scale, from existing on-line resources, NLP systems would have ways of capitalizing on much of the lexicographic effort embodied in the production of reference materials for human consumption.

Not surprisingly, then, one approach to scaling up the lexical components of natural language systems prototypes to enable them to handle realistic texts has been to turn to existing machine-readable forms of published dictionaries. On the assumption that they not only represent a convenient source of words, but also contain (in a less obvious, and more interesting way) a significant amount of lexical data, recent research efforts have shown that automated procedures can be developed for extracting and formalizing explicitly available, as well as implicitly encoded, information—phonological, syntactic and semantic—from machine-readable dictionaries (MRDs).

Such work reflects a change in view: whereas early efforts for utilizing dictionary data were aimed primarily at what had been explicitly stated in the entries (see, for instance, [Walker *et al.*, 1995] and articles therein), comparatively recent developments have focused on carrying out much more detailed analysis of the sources, with a view of uncovering information which turns out to be systematically, albeit implicitly, represented by dictionary entry content, dictionary structure, and lexicographic conventions ([Boguraev and Briscoe, 1989a] is a representative collection).

To a large extent, such approaches to the acquisition problem are motivated by the desire to make maximal use of the information in dictionaries; they are also, however, necessary in order to overcome some major disadvantages to the use of MRDs in natural language processing. Firstly, since these are produced with the human user in mind, there is a strong assumption about the nature of understanding and interpretation available to make use of a dictionary entry; secondly, due to the very nature of the process of (human) lexicography, present day dictionaries are far from complete, consistent, and coherent, certainly with respect to virtually any of the numerous kinds of lexical data they choose to represent and encode. An important question then becomes: where is the line between useful and relevant data to be extracted from existing machine-readable sources, and the inconsistencies, mis-representations, omissions, and so forth inherent in such sources and detrimental to the enterprise of deriving computational lexicons by (semi-)automatic means?

Issues like these are at the core of computational analysis of language on the basis of information available in dictionaries. More specifically, they highlight questions pertaining to the infra-structure for any research effort whose ultimate goal is to develop a general purpose computational lexicon and instantiate this—at least in part—with derived lexical data. For instance:

- how to make dictionary sources available to extraction procedures, in a way which allows flexible access to an arbitrary depth of detail of (source) lexical description;
- how to make such procedures attuned to lexical demands of NLP systems, and keep them "open" as language processing frameworks become better understood and more elaborate;
- how to satisfy these demands by suitably constrained search through on-line MRD sources; and
- how the relationship between natural language processing, formal syntax, and lexical semantic theories is reflected in the kind of information sought in dictionaries for incorporation into a computational lexicon.

A number of arguments have been put forward in support of a claim that, in effect, a dictionary is only as good as its worst (or least experienced) lexicographer and/or user—and by that token, it is not much good for developing systematic procedures for extraction of lexical data. For instance, in reference to recent work with MRDs in the field of computational linguistics, [Atkins, 1991] not only summarizes the process of building a large-scale lexicon as "trawling" a machine-readable dictionary in search for lexical facts, but points out at an imbalance between the kinds of syntactic and semantic information that can be identified by "minutely examining" existing dictionaries: "the useful semantic information which may be extracted at present is more restricted in scope, and virtually limited to the construction of semantic taxonomies."

It is the interplay of lexical needs of current language processing frameworks and contemporary lexical semantic theories that very much influences the direction of computational dictionary analysis research for lexical acquisition. Given the increasingly more prominent place the lexicon is assigned—in linguistic theories, in language processing technology, and in domain description—it is no accident, nor is it mere rhetoric, that the term "lexical knowledge base" has become a widely accepted one. Researchers use it to refer to a large-scale repository of lexical information, which incorporates more than just static descriptions of words, e.g., by means of clusters of properties and associated values. A lexical knowledge base would state

- constraints on word behavior,
- dependence of word interpretation on context, and
- distribution of linguistic generalizations (see, for instance, [Byrd, 1989] and [Boguraev and Levin, 1990]).

It is essentially a dynamic object, as it incorporates, in addition to its information types, the ability to perform inference over them and thus induce word meaning in context. This is the sense of "computational lexicon," the population of which is giving new meaning to lexical acquisition from MRDs.

Recent research critically examines the notion of building a lexicon on the basis of existing dictionaries. A common feature is a certain amount of scepticism towards attempts to fully instantiate such a lexicon by automatic means. However, there is a shared attitude that while there are many ways in which dictionaries fail as sources for a computational lexicon (infelicity, inconsistency, incompleteness, to name a few), there are also ways to maximize the value of the information found in them. The particular strategies developed (see, for instance, [Boguraev, 1991b] and articles therein) follow from a mix of:

- critical assessment of the nature of facts in dictionaries and the ways they are presented;
- analysis of the lexical requirements of natural language processing frameworks, especially as such frameworks evolve towards generality and domain-independence;
- elaboration of the intersection between available and required data, which might take the form of, e.g., a generic "lexical template";
- linguistically-motivated justification for the utility of such templates, both as a holding device for data extracted from dictionaries, and as an underlying knowledge structure for NLP; and
- proposals for instantiating lexical templates: these are based on borrowing methods from lexicography and corpus studies, as well as applying special-purpose computational tools for dictionary analysis.

Overall, there is far more in a dictionary than meets the eye; however, this wealth of information typically cannot be observed, nor extracted, without reference to a formal linguistic theory with very precise lexical requirements, and without a set of tools capable of making very explicit the highly compacted and codified information typical of dictionary sources.

1.1.3   Text corpora

One of the arguments brought against using dictionaries for lexical knowledge acquisition is that they are static objects, representing, at best, a "frozen" snapshot of language. Given that language is a dynamic and rapidly evolving object, there is a sense in which, by the time a dictionary makes it through the compilation and publication process, it has grown out of date. To a certain extent, this argument is used to motivate more recent efforts for manual crafting of lexicons. More importantly, however, it brings in focus the value of text corpora as alternative (or complementary)[1] source of lexical information.

---

[1] Opinions in the field differ on whether to use, exclusively, one type of resource, or to complement sources and merge information acquired from either type.

This is a comparatively recent development, brought on by several factors. The field has its own "canonical" corpora, which have been in existence for many years: the Brown corpus ([Francis and Kučera, 1982]), the Lancaster-Oslo-Bergen (LOB) corpus ([Garside *et al.*, 1987]), the London-Lund corpus ([Svartvik and Quirk, 1980]), are perhaps the best known examples for this category. They suffer from the same drawback as dictionaries, namely, they have been in existence for so long, that a whole fragment of language, as it has evolved over the last twenty-odd years, is not reflected in them at all. However, recent technological developments in gathering, publishing and distributing information have made it possible to have—more or less as a side product—immediate access to very large volumes of text as it is being created. Through services like news wires, transcripts, electronic publishing, and so forth, text is available on a scale unmatched by any static language sample. Furthermore, developments in computer technology make it possible to handle such sizable samples without running into operational difficulties due to the limited processing power of earlier generation computers.

The combination of *size of corpora* (as word count climbs up into tens and hundreds of million, the value of a corpus as comprehensive and representative sample of language increases), their *dynamic nature, wider availability* (the ACL/Data Collection Initiative is just one channel through which large text samples are made generally available [Liberman and Walker, 1989]), and the *ability to process* them computationally accounts for a noticeable revival of empiricism. From the perspective of (applied) computational linguistics, this has taken the shape of making very prominent a long and established tradition of quantificational analysis of language; a representative example is a line of work which uses corpora as the basis from which to induce stochastic models of language (see, for instance, [Garside *et al.*, 1987]).

Clearly, the term "language model," while typically associated with notions like probabilistic part-of-speech taggers (such as those developed by [Garside *et al.*, 1987], [Church, 1988], [DeRose, 1988]) and parsers (e.g. [Atwell, 1987], [Ejerhed, 1988]), has a substantial lexical component to it. A tagger assigns syntactic categories to lexical items; thus the output of such a program can be used to annotate a word list with part-of-speech labels. Similarly, the very existence of a parse tree would enable further enhancement of items in a word list by adding e.g. subcategorization information. It is just a matter of emphasis whether essentially the same operational mechanisms are applied for language analysis per se, or for language processing with a view of further integration of (aspects of) the output into a permanent lexical structure. In this vein, more recent—and explicitly of lexical acquisition nature—work includes, for instance, frequency-based elicitation of word distribution patterns, concordance-driven definition of context and word behavior, extracting and representing word collocations, acquisition of lexical semantics of verbs from sentence frames, and even derivation of transfer lexicons for machine translation (see, for instance, [van Berkel and DeSmedt, 1988], [Slator, 1992], [Smadja, 1992], [Webster and Marcus, 1989], [Brown *et al.*, 1990]).

The final, and a particularly strong, argument for using text corpora rather than machine-readable dictionaries for lexical knowledge acquisition comes from a relatively recent trend in (human) lexicography, which interleaves several basic principles in applied linguistics and dictionary compilation. Since language is a constantly changing dynamic system, no existing reference materials (including other dictionary sources) should be used in the process of compiling a new dictionary. Rather, the analysis of words—from decisions concerning the make-up of the word list to the specific content of individual entries—should be carried out entirely on the basis of studies of a large representative corpus, both of spoken and written text. This is not just a matter of "keeping up" with language as it evolves: lexicographers "have learned what happens when [they] sit an intuit how words are used — [they] are likely to get it wrong" ([Sinclair, 1987b]).

This is the difference in method between "armchair lexicography" and "corpus lexicography": rigorous applications of a set of principles for measuring hard evidence of lexical behavior of words is, arguably, going to result in a representative, coherent and consistent—altogether a more faithful—object than the dictionaries produced by conventional means and/or the lexicons crafted on the basis of (computational) linguists' intuition. [Atkins, 1987] Atkins argues this point in detail; the COBUILD dictionary ([Sinclair, 1987a]) stands as an example the corpus-based methodology for dictionary construction, and [Sinclair, 1987b] addresses the issues behind the principles, the motivations, and the realization of this methodology.

From such a perspective, there are obvious questions like: why use existing dictionaries for lexical acquisition, when even the lexicographers who created them agree that they are inadequate; why wait for better dictionaries, when the source they will eventually be created from can now be tapped directly? A strong relation is being forged between computational methods for quantificational analysis of language and corpus lexicography (see, for instance, [Church and Hanks, 1990], [Justeson and Katz, 1991], [Church *et al.*, 1992]), and this is certain to influence lexical knowledge acquisition.

There is no clear answer to these questions. If anything, the field has tended to associate lexicon construction on the basis of MRD sources with the AI-influenced tradition of using semantic networks, knowledge representation mechanisms and inference techniques to address questions of lexical representation and organization. Likewise, the contrastive association has been that of corpus analysis with probabilistically-based approaches to language processing, which require (seemingly) different lexicon models. This is, in fact, a very interesting, and relevant to whole the practice of computational linguistics, issue concerning the potential conflict between the two paradigms in NLP.

On the one hand, there is the "traditional" approach which aims to model the human cognitive mechanism and is implemented via a (complex) set of symbol manipulating inference procedures which make use of an extensive body of world, in addition to linguistic, knowledge. On the other hand, a paradigm based entirely on quantificational analysis of language relies heavily on the gathering and use of probabilistic measures for word collocations.

We argue that the two approaches are complementary. In this, we follow a particularly important reference ([Hindle, 1990]), which argues for a synergy between the two approaches, in favor of a framework using large corpora of naturally occurring text *together with* rule-based systems, in an attempt to build more effective linguistic processors.

> It is important to emphasize that the question whether we can acquire linguistic information from text is independent of whether the model is probabilistic, categorical, or some combination of the two. The issue is not [...] symbolic versus probabilistic rules, but rather whether we can acquire the necessary linguistic information instead of building systems completely by hand.

More recent work supports this view. [Wilks *et al.*, 1992] have applied statistical measures to a dictionary, treating it as a (highly representative) text sample. [Boguraev, 1991a] instantiates aspects of the lexical semantics of nominals and verbs on the basis of fine-grained analysis of dictionary sources, and argues for the need to complement the extraction results with corpus-derived data. [Hindle, 1990] acquires semantic data of very similar nature, on the basis of studying distributional patterns over syntactic structures associated with the sentences in a large text corpus. [Anick and Pustejovsky, 1990] argue for the value of a theory of lexical semantics as a constraining agent for purely statistical collocational analysis, aimed at populating lexical semantic templates. The field seems to have finally both acknowledged the weakness of dictionary extraction techniques, and admitted the utility of corpus-based research for lexical acquisition. In the next section, we describe the progress made towards this marriage of approaches as presented in the papers in this volume.

1.2   Text-based Lexicon Acquisition

Having reviewed the basic issues in lexical acquisition, we turn now to the specific approaches reported in this volume. The first part of the book concentrates on the problem of "unknown lexicalizations," i.e., words that are not recognized as part of the language by the system. All three papers in this section address the difficult problem of identifying proper names in unrestricted text, and their subsequent classification according to semantic type. McDonald's paper, "Internal and External Evidence in the Identification and Semantic Categorization of Proper Names," makes use of two sources of information for solving this task: *internal evidence* refers to how the structure of the word sequence itself identifies it as a proper name, and perhaps even its semantic class; *external evidence*, on the other hand, refers to the use of the surrounding context of a proper name to classify it within a particular semantic class. These two types of contextual information are encoded in context-sensitive rules which label word sequences with the appropriate part-of-speech tags and semantic classifiers. A similar approach is taken by Mani and Macmillan in their contribution, "Identifying Unknown Proper Names in Newswire Text," where the goal is to provide profiles of people, companies, products, and places for subsequent information retrieval purposes. Mani and Macmillan also exploit the information available in text from multiple mentions of the same entity in order to build a stronger semantic model of the entity. Paik *et al.*'s paper, "Categorization and Standardizing Proper Nouns for Efficient Information Retrieval," focuses on the utility of proper name identification for information retrieval (IR) tasks. Taking advantage of various heuristic methods, including similar to those discussed by Mc-Donald and Mani and Macmillan, the authors address the contribution of proper name identification to overall precision and recall statistics in the service of IR within TIPSTER and MUC-style tasks.

The second group of papers in the volume deals with the problem of "task-driven lexicon induction." The first paper in this section, "Customizing a Lexicon to Better Suit a Computational Task", by Hearst and Schüetze, shows how statistical methods operating over corpora can improve existing semantic classifications and relations in structured lexicons, and in particular, WORDNET. They describe how inducing semantic representations for a large number of words from lexical co-occurrence statistics allows them to augment and rearrange the elements of a lexicon to make it more suitable or appropriate to a domain-specific task. This work can be seen as combining manually-entered lexical information with statistically-derived corpus sensitive usage knowledge. Leacock, Towell, and Voorhees address a related topic in their paper "Towards Building Contextual Representations of Word Senses Using Statistical Models." Specifically, they investigate automatic techniques that perform word sense resolution by encoding rich contextual representations for the word sense. These contextual representations are automatically extracted from a text corpus by using both *topical* and *local* information. Topical context can be seen as related semantic field knowledge for a particular word, while local context refers to syntactic and morphological information surrounding the word being investigated. Their results from both human and computational experiments show that both topical and local context are necessary to perform robust word sense disambiguation.

The next section, "Categorization of Lexical Units," discusses the progress made with the automatic clustering of words into syntactic and semantic classes. The first paper, "Hierarchical Clustering of Verbs," by Basili, Pazienza, and Velardi, argues that *thematic* information is the most important factor in determining verb categorization from a corpus. This view is consistent with psychological and psycholinguistic findings suggesting that characteristic features between objects helps categorize the verbs relating them. The authors present an unsupervised clustering algorithm which groups verbs according to their thematic roles as discovered by corpus analysis techniques. Using a fairly different metric of clustering, Waterman's contribution, "Structural Methods for Lexical/Semantic Patterns" describes experiments towards inducing hierarchical lexical classifications from structural cues in text corpora. Using localized "edit distance" as a measure of similarity, Waterman was able to create initial hierarchical descriptions of context and predicate types associated with lexical items. The method described is interesting for how far it is able to get without semantic information associated with the patterns.

The next section deal with deriving lexical semantics from corpus analysis. Poznanski and Sanfilippo's paper, "Detecting Dependencies between Semantic Verb Subclasses and Subcategorization Frames in Text Corpora," present a method for inducing semantically tagged subcategorization frames from free-text in a corpus. Their method exploits the systematic regularities that exist in the syntax-semantics interface in language, as well as corpus analysis techniques which help determine which semantic tags are most likely associated with a particular verb. Related work, Aone and McKee's paper "Acquiring Predicate-Argument Mapping Information from Multilingual Texts," approaches the same problem, but from multilingual text sources. Predicate-argument mapping information that is specific to a particular language is associated with the core meaning of a verb. Cross-linguistic generalized mappings called *situation types* are then used to associate the word senses for one language text to those of another.

Finally, the last paper in the volume deals with measuring the success of lexical acquisition techniques. Grefenstette's paper, "Evaluation Techniques for Automatic Semantic Extraction: Comparing Syntactic and Window-Based Approaches," proposes using an evaluation technique with gold standards (pre-existing manually compiled resources) for comparing the different extraction techniques. The results suggested that no single statistical technique is appropriate for all ranges of frequency of words in a corpus. Different methods might be usefully applied for distinguishing the more frequent words, using finer-grained context discrimination, while rare words might require examination of fairly large windows or contexts in order to correctly classify them.

The work presented here points to many exciting new directions in the areas of corpus-based language processing and lexicon construction. It is clear from reading these articles that, although these extraction methods are state-of-the-art, in some sense this is only the beginning of a new research programme combining linguistically inspired language analysis and statistically-based corpus research.

II COPING WITH UNKNOWN LEXICALIZATIONS

2 Internal and External Evidence in the Identification and Semantic Categorization of Proper Names

David D. McDonald

> Proper names are the Rodney Dangerfield of linguistics.
> They don't get no respect.

2.1 Introduction

Within theoretical linguistics, proper names are relegated to the 'periphery' of the language. Unlike the 'core' phenomena of long-distance movement, case marking, argument structure, and the like, there is an assumption that the study of proper names will yield no deep insights into the nature of language or illustrate principles with broad application. When thought about at all, proper names, like numbers, dates, ages, etc. are imagined to be easy to analyze, or, in a computational context, to generate or understand.

People who actually work with proper names know better. The accurate identification and semantic categorization of names has proved to be anything but easy, yet understanding names, and their patterns of initial and subsequent reference, is central to the analysis of the extended, unrestricted texts that have become the focus of research in the natural language processing community.

From the study of these texts (principally newspaper articles or specialized sets of messages) we know that proper names exhibit an enormous diversity, but that they also have a systematic and compositional structure that can be captured in a grammar. This grammar is more lexical and less syntactic, and its links to semantics are far tighter than is the case for the so-called core grammar, but it is still a principled structure with a generative capacity that allows never-before-seen instances of proper names to be reliably recognized and semantically understood.

This paper will argue that this grammar must be context sensitive, and that the semantic interpretation of proper names should be mediated by semantic structures that denote names, per se, with only an indirect link to the individuals being named. In the next section we introduce this notion of context sensitive analysis for proper names and the motivations behind it. In section three we go through our procedure for analyzing names and provide examples of the kinds of complexities that can be encountered. In section four we discuss the setting for this analysis as part of the SPARSER language understanding system, and finally in section five we step through a fairly complex example.

2.2 Internal versus External Evidence

The requirement that a grammar of proper names must be context-sensitive derives from the fact that the classification of a name involves two complementary kinds of evidence, which we will term 'internal' and 'external.' *Internal evidence* is taken from within the sequence of words that comprise the name. This can be definitive criteria, such as the presence of known 'incorporation terms' that indicate companies ("Ltd.," "G.m.b.H."); or it can be heuristic criteria such as abbreviations or known first names, which often indicate people. Name-internal evidence is the only criteria considered in virtually all of the name recognition systems that are reported as part of state of the art information extraction systems (see e.g., [Rau, 1991], [Alshawi, 1991], [Cowie *et al.*, 1992]), most of which depend on large (~20,000 word) gazetteers and lists of known names for their relatively high performance.

By contrast, *external evidence* is provided by the context in which a name appears. The basis for this evidence is the obvious observation that names are just ways to refer to individuals of specific types (people, churches, rock groups, etc.), and that these types have characteristic properties and participate in characteristic events. The presence of these properties or events in in syntactic relation with a proper name can be used to provide confirming or criterial evidence for a name's category. External evidence is analyzed in PNF in terms of substitution contexts, and operationalized in terms of context-sensitive rewrite rules.

External evidence is necessary for high accuracy performance. One obvious reason is that the predefined word lists so often used as internal evidence can never be complete. Another is that in many instances, especially those involving subsequent references, external evidence will override internal evidence. In the final analysis it is always the way a phrase is used—the attributions and predications it is part of—that make it a proper name of a given sort. Without the consideration of external evidence, this definitive criteria is missed, resulting in mistakes and confusion in the state of the parser.[1]

An additional reason for using external evidence, and one with considerable engineering utility from the point of view of the grammar writer, is that the inclusion of external evidence into the mix of available analysis tools reduces the demands on the judgements one requires of internal evidence. The internal analysis can get away with a weaker (less specific) categorization about which it can be more certain, and the categorization can then be refined as external evidence becomes available. Lacking definitive internal evidence, one can initially label a segment simply as a 'name,' and then later strengthen the judgement when, e.g., the segment is found to be adjacent to an age phrase or a title, whereupon context-sensitive rewrite rules are triggered to re-label it as a person and to initiate the appropriate semantic processes.

This kind of staged analysis is a requirement when the conclusions from internal evidence are ambiguous. It is not uncommon, for example, for the names of a person and of a company in the same news article to share a word, as when the company is named after its founder. A subsequent reference using just that word cannot be definitively categorized on internal evidence alone, and must wait for the application of external evidence from the context. In the event that the context is inadequate, as when it involves a predication not in the grammar, the further analysis of such 'name' segments can be left to default judgements by statistical heuristics operating after a first pass by the parser, and the stronger categorizations then tested for coherency as the parse is resumed.[2]

To make this discussion concrete, we will ground the remainder of this paper in a description of "PNF," the proper name facility of the SPARSER

---

[1] Relying solely on name lists has led to some funny errors, for example mistaking the food company Sara Lee for a person. Even some external evidence such as a title can be inadequate if it is considered apart from the wider context of use, as in General Mills—both of which are actual mistakes made by an otherwise quite reasonable program some years ago ([Masand and Duffey, 1985]).

[2] In the case of a company and a person with the same name, a well edited publication is very unlikely to use the ambiguous word to refer to the founder without prefixing it with "Mr." or "Ms." as needs be, so a word with both person and company denotations but without external evidence can be assumed to be referring to the company.

natural language understanding system, paying particular attention to how PNF uses external evidence and deploys its semantic model of names and their referents to handle ambiguities such as the one noted just above. In a blind test of an earlier implementation on "Who's News" articles from the the Wall Street Journal, PNF performed at nearly 100% when the name appeared in a sentence in the sublanguage for which a full grammar had been prepared. We are currently testing a new implementation on a more diverse set of texts.

Space will not permit a comparison of this algorithm with other approaches to proper names beyond occasional remarks and references. As far as we know this is the only treatment of proper names that uses context-sensitive rewrite rules for the analysis of external evidence, however the FUNES system of [Coates-Stephens, 1992b] is very similar to this work in making essential use of external evidence, and Coates-Stephens' extensive research into proper names is an important contribution to the field; we have adopted some of his terminology as noted below.

2.3   Procedure Overview: Delimit, Classify, Record

The goal of the Proper Name Facility in SPARSER is to form and interpret full phrasal constituents—noun phrases—that fit into the rest of a text's parse and contribute to the analysis of the entire text just like any other kind of constituent. That is to say that PNF is a component in a larger natural language comprehension system, and not a stand-alone facility intended for name spotting, indexing, or other tasks based on skimming. This integration is essential to the way the PNF makes its decisions; it would not operate with anything like the same level of performance if it were independent, since there would then be no source of external evidence.

To analyze an instance of a proper name for use by a full natural language comprehension system we must

1. *delimit* the sequence of words that make up the name, i.e. identify its boundaries;
2. *classify* the resulting constituent based on the kind of individual it names; and
3. *record* the name and the individual it denotes in the discourse model

as our interpretation of the constituent's meaning.

For other parts of SPARSER's grammar, these three actions are done with one integrated mechanism much as they would be in most any other system. Constituents are initiated bottom up by the terminal rules of the lexicalized grammar, and compositions of adjacent constituents are checked for and nonterminal nodes introduced as the grammar dictates.[3] The grammar's production rules delimit and classify (label) constituents in one action: the classifications are given by the productions' lefthand sides, and the new constituents' boundaries by the sequence of daughter constituents on the rules' righthand sides, with the new constituent's denotation given by an interpretation function included directly with the rule and applied as the rule completes.

This normal mode of operation, however, has not proved workable for proper names. The reason has to do with the central problem with names from the point of view of a grammar, namely that in unrestricted texts the total set of words that names can be comprised of can not be known in advance. The set is unbounded, growing at an apparently constant rate with the size of the corpus, while the growth of other classes of content words tapers off asymptotically ([Liberman, 1989]). This means that we cannot have a lexicalized grammar for proper names since the bulk of the names we will encounter will be based on words that are unknown at the time the grammar is written.

Complicating this picture is the fact that virtually any normal word can do double duty as part of a name: " ... *Her name was equally preposterous. April Wednesday, she called herself, and her press card bore this out.*" [MacLean, 1976, p. 68]. This means that one either introduces a massive and arbitrary ambiguity into the normal vocabulary, allowing any word to be part of a name, or one looks for another means of parsing proper names, which is the course that was taken with PNF. For PNF we have separated the three action—delimiting, classifying, and recording—into distinct and largely independent operations.

---

[3] SPARSER uses a moderately complex control structure to ensure that the grammar is applied deterministically (each span of text only ever receives one analysis) and that the semantic interpretation is monotonic and indelible. The grammar—the rules of constituent combination—is specified by a set of phrase structure rules, but its runtime operations are more like those of a categorial grammar where the identity of each constituent label determines its possibilities for combination; the original rules are not a material part of the process as they would be in a conventional phrase-structure based parsing algorithm.

2.3.1 Delimit

The delimit operation is based on a simple state machine rather than on the application of rewrite rules. This reflects that fact that the internal constituent structure of a proper name is typically a sequence of an indefinite number of elements with local groupings into embedded names that are sisters in the name as a whole. Because of the indefinite length of the subsequences, a phrase structure account would impose a tree structure on the components of the name that was just an artifact of the rule application machinery rather than a reflection of the actual constituency.

PNF's delimitation algorithm simply groups any contiguous sequence of capitalized words (including 'sequences' of length one).[4] This is virtually always the correct thing to do as the example below illustrates, though the exceptions have to be treated carefully as discussed later.

> *"The Del The Del Fuegos, O Positive, and We Saw the Wolf will perform acoustic sets in Amnesty International USA Group 133's Seventh Annual Benefit Concert at 8 p.m. on Friday, March 19, at the First Parish Unitarian Universalist Church in Arlington Center."* (Arlington Advocate, 3/18/93)

A sequence is terminated at the first non-capitalized word or comma; other punctuation is handled case by case, e.g., "&" is taken to extend sequences, and periods are taken as terminators unless they are part of an abbreviation.

2.3.2 Classification

Classifying a proper name is a two-step process. First, the regular parsing routines are applied within the delimited word sequence. This embedded parsing process introduces any information the grammar

---

[4] It is reasonable to depend upon the existence of mixed-case text, since the number of online sources that use only uppercase is rapidly diminishing and will probably disappear once all of the Model-33 Teletypes and other 6-bit data entry terminals in the world are finally junked. In any event, to handle all-uppercase texts within PNF it is only the delimitation algorithm that must be changed. A good approximation of the needed segmentation is independently available from the distribution of function words and punctuation in any text. In this example these are the commas, the apostrophe-s, "in," "at," and "on." A mistake would be made in "We Saw the Wolf" [sic] which in any event will be problematic without external context.

has about known words or phrases. Such information is the basis for the most of the structure within a proper name, and provides the name-internal evidence on which the classification will be based at this stage. For PNF this includes:

- embedded references to cities or countries, e.g., *"Cambridge Savings Bank."*
- open class 'keywords' like *"Church"* or *"Bank"* (following the terminology of Coates-Stephens), and the incorporation-terms used by companies of various countries when giving their full legal names (*"Inc."* in the U.S.A., *"P.T."* in Indonesia, *"G.m.b.H."* in Germany, etc.).
- the relatively closed class of stylized modifiers used with people like *"Jr.,"* *"Sir,"* *"Mr.,"* *"Dr."*
- items used for heuristic classification judgements (the items above are definitive) such as including initials (a strong indicator that the name refers to a person or a company based on a person's name), punctuation like *"&"* (a company marker), or ambiguous modifiers like "II" (which invariably means 'the second,' but may be used with Limited Partnerships as well as people).

The parsing stage will reveal when the capitalized word based delimitation process has included too much. One such case is of course when a proper name appears just after the capitalized word at the start of a sentence: *"An Abitibi spokesman said ... "* This is handled by recognizing closed-class grammatical functional words as such during the embedded parse, and resegmenting the word sequence to exclude them.

Another, more interesting case is where we have a sequence of modifiers prefixed to a proper name that are themselves proper names, e.g., *"Giant Group said [it is] seeking to block a group led by Giant Chairman Burt Sugarman from acquiring ... "* In this situation there is no hope for correctly separating the names unless the grammar includes rules for such references to companies and titles, in which case they will appear to the classification process as successive edges (parse nodes) with the appropriate labels ('company,' 'title') so that they can be appreciated for what they are and left out of the person's name.[5] It is important to

---

[5] It is perhaps a matter of judgement to hold that a person's title is not a part of their name, but that policy appears to be the most consistent overall since it permits

appreciate that all of these considerations only make sense when one is analyzing proper names in the context of a larger system that already has grammars and semantic models for titles and employment status and such; they are hard to justify in an application that is simply name spotting.

In practice, the operations of delimiting and classifying are often interleaved, since the classification of an initially delimited segment can aid in the determination of whether the segment needs to be extended, as when distinguishing between a list of names and a compound name incorporating commas, e.g., " ... *a string of companies — including Bosch, Continental and Varta — have announced co-operative agreements ...* " (The Financial Times, 5/16/90) versus "HEALTH-CARE FIRM FOLDS: *Wood, Lucksinger & Epstein is dissolving its practice.*" (*Wall Street Journal* 2/26/91). We will describe this process in the extended example at the end of the paper.

Once the words of the sequence have been parsed and edges introduced into the chart reflecting the grammar's analysis, the second part of the classification process is initiated and a state machine is passed over that region of the chart to arrive at the most certain classification possible given just this name-internal evidence. If no specific conclusion can be reached, the sequence will be covered with an edge that is simply given the category 'name,' and it will be up to external evidence to improve on that judgement as will be described later. If a conclusion is made as to the kind of entity being named, then the edge will be labeled with the appropriate semantic category such as 'person,' 'company,' 'newspaper,' etc.

2.3.3   Recording

The recording process now takes over to determine what the new edge should have as its denotation in the discourse model. Before this denotation is established, PNF's representation of the name is just a label and the sequence of words and edges (parse nodes) internal to the name (e.g., edges over an embedded reference to a city or region). What we are providing now via the recording process is a structured representa-

---

the capitalized premodifier version of a title of employment (e.g., "Chairman") and its predicative lowercase version (as in an appositive) to be understood as the same kind of relationship semantically—a different relationship than the one between a person and her conventional title such as "Dr.".

tion of the name qua 'name'—a unique instance of one of the defined classes of names that reifies this specific pattern of words and embedded references.

Including names as actual entities in the semantic model, rather than just treating them as ephemeral pointers to the individuals they name and only using them momentarily during the interpretation process, provides us with an elegant treatment of the ambiguity that is intrinsic to names as representational devices. Real names, unlike the hypothetical 'rigid designators' entertained by philosophers, may refer to any number of individuals according to the contingent facts of the actual world. We capture this by making the denotation of the lexico-syntactic name—the edge in SPARSER's chart—be a semantic individual of type 'name' rather than (the representation of) a concrete individual. The name object in turn may be then associated in the discourse model with any number of particular individuals of various types: people, companies, places, etc. according to the facts in the world. The ambiguity of names is thus taken not to be a linguistic fact but a pragmatic fact involving different individuals having the same name.

The structure that the semantic model imposes on names is designed to facilitate understanding subsequent references to the individuals that the names name. The type of name structure used predicts the kinds of reduced forms of the name that one can expect to be used. This design criteria was adopted because, again, the overarching purpose of PNF is to contribute to the thorough understanding of extended unrestricted texts. This means that it is not enough just to notice that a given name has occurred somewhere in an article, something that is easy to do by looking for just those cases where the full company name is given with the 'incorporation term' that well edited newspapers will always provide when a company is introduced into a text, e.g., "*Sumitomo Electric Industries, Ltd.*".

The model PNF constructs for the name must be rich enough to be able to recognize that that same individual is being talked about later when it sees, e.g., "*Sumitomo Electric*" (or "*the company*"). In addition, PNF must be able to distinguish that individual from subsequent references to other companies that share part of its name: "*Sumitomo Wiring Systems*," or to correctly deduce a subsidiary relationship "*Sumitomo Electric International (Singapore)*." By the same token, people and companies or locations that share name elements should be appreciated as such: *"the Suzuki Motors Company ... Osamu Suzuki, the president of the company."*

To facilitate such subsequent references, not only does each proper name receive a denotation as an entirety, but the words that comprise it are also given denotations which are related, semantically, to the roles the words each played in that name and in the names of other individuals. Thus the word *"Suzuki,"* for example, is taken to always denote the same semantic object, identified by the prosaic print form `#<name-word "suzuki">`. In turn this object is related to (at least) two individuals—to the car company by way of the relation 'first-word-in-name,' and to its president by the relation 'family-name.'

2.4   The Setting for the Process

In order to supply the external evidence needed to accurately categorize proper names and understand them semantically, a language understanding system must include grammars (and their attendant semantic models) for properties and event-types that are characteristically associated with the kinds of individuals that the names name, and these grammars should have as broad a coverage as possible.

SPARSER has been applied to understanding news articles about people changing their jobs (particularly the *Wall Street Journal*'s "Who's News" column), and with a lesser competence to articles on corporate joint ventures and quarterly earnings. As a result, it has quite strong semantic grammars for some of the very most frequent properties of companies and people in business news texts: the parent–subsidiary relationship between companies, age, titles, and for a few of the more common event-types.

A complementary consideration is what approach will be taken to such relatively mundane things as punctuation, capitalization, or abbreviations. For SPARSER, since it is designed to work with well-edited news text written by professional journalists, punctuation is retained and there are grammar rules that appreciate the (sometimes heuristic) information that it can provide. The whitespace between words is also noted (newlines, tabs, different numbers of spaces) since it provides relatively reliable evidence for paragraphs, tables, header fields, etc., which in turn can provide useful external evidence.

Additionally, SPARSER is designed to handle a constant, unrestricted stream of text, day after day, and this has led to a way to treat unknown words that allows it to look at their properties without being required to give them a long-term representation which would eventually cause the program to run out of memory.

To illustrate how these work, and at the same time establish the setting in which proper name processing takes place, we will now describe the lower levels of SPARSER's operation, starting with its tokenizer and populating the terminal positions of the chart.

2.4.1 Tokenizing

The tokenizer transduces characters into objects representing words, punctuation, digit sequences, or numbers of spaces. It is conservatively designed, just grouping contiguous sequences of alphabetic characters or digits and punctuation, and passing them them all through to be the terminals of the chart. Even the simplest compounds are assembled at the chart level by sets of rules that are easily changed and experimented with. For example, rather than conclude within the tokenizer that the character sequence "$47.2 million" is an instance of money, the tokenizer just passes through six tokens, including the space.

A word is 'known' if it is mentioned in any of the grammar rules.[6] A known word has a permanent representation, and the tokenizer finds and returns this object when it delimits the designated sequence of characters. The 'token-hood' of any given instance of the word type is represented by the word filling a particular location in the chart.

The tokenizer separates the identity of a word from its capitalization. A word is defined by the identity of its characters. The pattern of upper and lowercase letters that happens to occur in a given instance is a separate matter, and is represented in the chart rather than with the word.[7] When the chart is populated with terminals, each position records the word that starts there, its capitalization, and the kind of

---

[6] Note that since SPARSER uses a lexicalized semantic grammar, words have pre-terminal categories like 'title' or 'head-of-Co-phrase' (e.g., "company," "firm," "enterprise"), or are often treated just as literals as with prepositions or with words like "ago" in "44 years ago."

[7] One can deliberately define a capitalization-sensitive version of a word, e.g., to syntactically distinguish titles in pre-head position from those in appositives or elsewhere. In such cases there is a distinct word object for the capitalized version, with a link to the case-neutral version of the word.

whitespace that preceded it, all given as separate fields of the position object. The token scan is done incrementally in step with the rest of the SPARSER's actions.

2.4.2 Word-triggered operations

SPARSER's processing is organized into layers. Tokenizing and populating the terminals of the chart is the first level, then comes a set of special operations that are triggered by words or their properties (e.g., the property of ending in "*ed*" or of consisting solely of digits). The the next layer is the application of phrase structure rules, and finally there is the application of heuristics in order to spanning the gaps caused by unknown words. Semantic interpretation is done continuously as part of what happens when a rule completes and an edge is formed. We will not describe the last two layers (see [McDonald, 1992] for a description of the phrase structure algorithm), but will briefly describe the word-level operations since they include triggering PNF.

Actions triggered just by the identity of a word include forming initials and known abbreviations, and particularly the recognition of multi-word fixed phrases which we call "polywords" following [Becker, 1975]. Polywords are immutable sequences of words that are not subject to syntactically imposed morphological changes (plurals, tense) and that can only be defined as a group. Polywords are a natural way of predefining entities that have fixed, multi-word names such as the countries of the world, the states of the US, major cities, etc. Instances of this relatively closed class of individuals are a valuable kind of evidence in the classification of proper names.

When PNF finishes the recognition and classification of a new name, it adds to the grammar a polyword rule for that sequence of words, with the recorded name-object as the polyword's denotation. This permits the process to be short-circuited the next time the name is seen. Note that this does not stop PNF from running its delimiting operation the next time that sequence is seen; it only speeds up the classification and recording. If we allowed the polyword operation to take complete precedence, we would never see the longer word sequences that embed known names ("*New York Port Authority*").

There are also special rules that allow paired punctuation (parentheses, quotation marks, etc.) to be grouped even if the words separating them are not all known. This is particularly useful for picking up nicknames embedded within a person's name since that nickname will often be given as a word in parentheses embedded within the person's name ("Justice Byron (Whizzer) White"). Subsidiaries of companies are often marked for their geographical area in the same way, e.g., "*manufactured by* UNIVERSAL FLUID HEADS *(Aust.)* PTY. LTD." (taken from the name plate on a camera tripod).

The first check at the word-level is for actions triggered by a word's properties, particularly here the properties of its characters. This is how compound numbers are formed ("42,357.25"), triggering off words that consist of sequences of digits ("42"), and it is how PNF is triggered. Every time a chart position is reached that indicates that the following word is capitalized, PNF is called. PNF then takes over the process of scanning the successive terminals of the chart until it scans a word that is not capitalized, calling other SPARSER mechanisms like polyword recognition or phrase structure rewrite rules as needed.

When PNF is finished, its results are given in the edge it constructs over the sequence of capitalized words and selected punctuation that comprise the name. Since SPARSER uses a semantic grammar, the label on the edge is the constituent's classification—a semantic category like 'person.' There is also conventional label (always NP for a name) included with the edge for default or heuristic rules of phrasal formation; see [McDonald, 1993b] for the details of this two label system.

2.5   Walking through an Example

In this final section of this paper we will look at the processing of the following paragraph-initial noun phrase from the *Wall Street Journal* of 10/27/89, article #34:

> "*An industry analyst, Robert B. Morris III in Goldman, Sachs & Co.'s San Francisco office, said ... *"

The capitalization of the very first word "*An*" triggers PNF, but the delimitation process stops immediately with the next word since it is lowercase. The classification pass through the (one word) sequence shows it to be a grammatical function word, and classification applies the heuristic 'single word sequences consisting solely of a non-preposition function word are not to be treated as names' and takes no further action. PNF is then finished; the article reading of "*An*" will have been introduced into the chart during classification; and the scan moves on.[8]

As the parse moves forward, the title phrase "an industrial analyst" is recognized and the comma after it is marked as possibly indicating an appositive (or also a list of titles, though this is less likely).

PNF is triggered again by the capitalization of "*Robert*," and the delimitation process takes it up to the word "*in.*" Running the regular rules of the grammar within that sequence uncovers the initial and the generation-indicator "III" for 'the third.' We do not maintain any lists of the common first names of people or such, so consequently both "*Robert*" and "*Morris*" are seen as unknown words. The initial and generation-indicator are enough, however, to allow the sequence to be reliably classified as the name of a person.

Given that classification, an edge is constructed over the sequence and given the label 'person,' and the recording process constructs a name object for the edge's denotation. The pattern given by the classifier is 'name – initial – name – generation-indicator,' from which the name subtype 'person's name with generation' can be instantiated. This type of name object takes a sequence of first names or initials, a last name (the word before "III"), and then the "III" in a slot that also gets words like "*Junior.*" Let us call this new name-individual Name-1.[9]

Part of the recording process is the creation of denotations for the words "*Robert*" and "*Morris.*" Discourse model objects are created for them of type 'single word element of a name,' and rules are added to the grammar so that the next time PNF sees them in a text, the embedded parse during classification will immediately recover those same objects. In addition, we attribute properties to the names (the semantic objects)

---

[8] We have yet to see a company whose name was "The," though an ad running in the *Boston Phoenix* during May of 1993 included a graphic for an upcoming entertainer named "the The." Of course there are companies like Next Inc. and On Technology, which, like the names of race horses or boats, add spice to the grammarian's life by overloading the interpretations of closed-class words. The only consistent treatment we have arrived at for these ("On" referring to the company does occur in sentence-initial position) is to treat the words as ambiguous and to introduce two edges into the chart, one for each reading. We only do this if the full name of the company appeared earlier in the article, however, at which time the preposition will have received its denotation as an element of a name and the basis of the ambiguity can be established.

[9] There is no interesting limit on the number of 'first names' a person can have, so we have not yet found it profitable to have any more structure in that field than simply an ordered sequence; consider "M.A.K. Halliday" or "(Prince) Charles Philip Arthur George."

'Robert' and 'Morris'—'Robert' is the first name of Name-1 and 'Morris' is its last name.

This policy of letting words like *"Morris"* denote single-word name objects with semantic links to the full names they are part of (with those names in turn linked to the people or other types of individual whose names they are) provides a very direct way to understand subsequent references involving just part of the original name (e.g., *"Mr. Morris"*), as we can trace the abbreviated name directly to the person just by following those links. (Of course the links will also take us to anyone else the who has been recorded in the world model who has that same last name, hence the need for a good discourse model that appreciates the context set up by the article being processed.)

Moving on, the rest of this example text is *"in Goldman, Sachs & Co.'s San Francisco office"* and the PNF is triggered again at the word *"Goldman."* This is seen as a one word sequence because the conservative delimitation process takes the comma just following as a reason to stop, and, again, it is an unknown word. Not being a function word and not including any reliable internal evidence, *"Goldman"* is spanned with an edge labeled just 'name' and just a new single-word name is recorded as its denotation. Given the significance of commas for name patterns, PNF also makes a note (sets a flag) that this comma was preceded by a name.

PNF immediately resumes with *"Sachs & Co.,"* stopping the delimitation process when it recognizes the *"ı"* and *"s"* tokens as constituting an apostrophe-s, which is a definitive marker for the end of a noun phrase. During the delimitation process, the abbreviation *"Co."* will also have been recognized and expanded to *"Company,"* and the *"&"* noted and appreciated as being a punctuation mark that can appear in names. Punctuation is always handled during the course of delimitation, since the identify of the punctuation is crucial to whether the name sequence should be continued beyond the punctuation or stopped.

The presence of the *"&"* and the word *"Company"* are definitive markers of companies and the classification process will start the assembly of a pattern to send off to be recorded. In this case however, as noted earlier, there is what amounts to an interaction between classification and delimitation. Part of what the classifier knows about companies is that there is a profusion of cases where the name of the company is a sequence of words separated by commas (law firms, advertising agencies, etc.; any sort of partnership tends to use this name pattern). Appreciating this, the process looks for the contextual note about the preceding comma. Finding it, it observes that the name in front of the comma is not itself classified as a company (which would have indicated a list of companies rather than a single name), and it proceeds to assimilate the edge over *"Goldman"* and the comma into the name it is already assembling. Had there been still more 'stranded' elements of the name followed by commas, this would have been noted as well and those elements added in.

Occasionally the name of a company like this is given with *"and"* instead of the special punctuation character. Had that happened here, the fact that the *"and"* preceded the word *"company"* would have been sufficient evidence to take the whole sequence as the name of a single company, however if there had been no such internal evidence within any of the elements of the conjunction, they would have been grouped together as unconnected names spanned by a single edge labeled 'name,' leaving it to external evidence from the context to supply a stronger categorization (both as to what category of name was involved and whether they were one name or several).

We can see this use of external evidence in operation with the next capitalized word sequence that PNF delimits, *"San Francisco."* With access to a good gazetteer we could have already defined San Francisco as the name of a city using a polyword. However, just by using external evidence and without needing any word list, we can conclude that it is a location, and probably a city, just by looking at its context: the word *"office."*

As said earlier, the availability of mechanisms that use external evidence like this allows PNF to make a weak analysis that can be strengthened later. In this case it will see *"San Francisco"* as a sequence of two unknown words. Without any internal evidence to base its judgement on, it can only (1) accept the sequence as a phrase and span it with an edge, indicating thereby that the words have a stronger relationship to each other than either has to its neighbors, and (2) give this edge the neutral label 'name.'

After PNF is done with *"San Francisco,"* the phrase structure component of SPARSER takes over. SPARSER's rewrite rule facility includes context-sensitive as well as context-free productions, including for this case the rule

```
name -> location / __ ''office''
```

This says that an edge labeled 'name' can be re-spanned with a new edge with the label 'location' when the name edge appears just in front of the word "office." Context sensitive rules are handled in SPARSER with the same machinery as context free rules, the only difference is what happens when the rule is completed. The context sensitive rule is coded as though it had a righthand side like a context free rule, in this case the pair of labels 'name' + "*office*." The only difference is that when this pattern is matched, instead of covering the whole righthand side with a new edge as would be done for a context free rule, with a context sensitive rule we just re-span the one indicated constituent. In this case the 'name' is re-spanned by an edge labeled 'location.'

Similarly, if the name of the person in this example had been just "*Robert Morris*," where there would have been no available internal evidence to indicate its classification (rather than "*Robert B. Morris III*"), we could later have applied either of two context free rules: one working forwards from the definitively recognized title, the other backwards from the prepositional phrase 'in-company.'

```
name -> person / title '','' ___
name -> person / ___ in-company
```

A repertoire of such context-sensitive rules or their equivalent is needed if a proper name classification facility is expected to work well with the open-ended set of name words found in actual texts; SPARSER used a set of roughly 30 rules to handle the names in the blind test on the "Who's News" column mentioned earlier.

2.6   Conclusions

The combination of the internal evidence provided by PNF's delimit, classify, and record processes with the external evidence provided by the context in which a name appears as operationalized in a set of context-sensitive rewrite rules has proved nearly one hundred percent effective in identifying and semantically characterizing the names of people and companies that occurred in the specific, relatively small sublanguage where we originally developed and tested it.

As we have begun to move beyond this sublanguage to look at the wider range of proper names and capitalized sequences that occur in, e.g., an entire issue of the *Wall Street Journal*—deliberately staying within the register of carefully edited, largely informative, presentations of current events—we have found two things. The first is that the vocabulary of what Coates-Stephens calls "keywords," words that provide internal evidence about how a name is to be classified such as 'newspaper,' '(cruise) liner,' etc. is enormous and will require semi-autonomous "corpus mining" techniques or similar mass methods if it is to be dealt with adequately. That this should be so is not particularly surprising, since what these keywords typically are is just the common noun naming a kind of thing, but it is sobering to be reminded when working for a long time in just one sublanguage how many kinds of things there are.

The second is that the range of kinds of things that are conventionally represented in English using proper nouns and capitalization far exceeds what is seen in short articles on restricted subjects. A vast array of things have names: movies, books, legislation, parks, astronomical phenomena ("the Milky Way"), etc. To a certain extent this wider set of classes of individuals comes accompanied by keywords that serve to identify the class (e.g., "Act," "Park"), but equally often it is not, especially for things that are named by the use of titles or that are forced by law to have all different names (boats, race horses) and so tend to use ordinary words in unordinary ways.

The goal of our continuing work is less to assimilate this much extended space of possibilities into our proper name grammar (though for keywords that is not being neglected) than to refine our techniques for ensuring that the semantic classifications that are made are made accurately—that no guess work is incorporated into PNF on the basis of a few instances of what appears to be good heuristic internal evidence. The largest factor in achieving this goal has turned out to be having a complete set of the context sensitive rules that are used to render observations about the context in which a given class of named individual occurs into a useful form. This is leading to the development, some of it foreshadowed in [McDonald, 1993b], of a system of what amount to rule-definition macros that take on the work of automatically constructing the set of context sensitive rules implied by each new predicate or attribute that is added to the grammar and semantic model. Human grammar writers too often forget to include even obvious cases, and the more that the knowledge of the grammar writer can be encoded in a system of automatic rule-writing facilities, the more successful the grammars will be in the long run.

3 Identifying Unknown Proper Names in Newswire Text

Inderjeet Mani, T. Richard MacMillan

3.1 Introduction

The identification of unknown proper names in text is a significant challenge for natural language processing systems operating on unrestricted text. A system which indexes documents according to name references can be useful for information retrieval or as a pre-processor for more knowledge intensive tasks such as database extraction. With the growing use of tagged corpora in a variety of language-related research areas, being able to reliably tag proper names is an obvious advantage. In addition, the development of practical techniques for name identification helps to shed light on the various uses of proper names in text.

The goal of name identification is to identify names of various kinds occurring in text, especially new names. In our case, the entities of interest are people, products, organizations, and locations. The extent of identification depends on what kind of information one wants to retrieve. A user may want documents which mention a particular entity, where some part of the entity's name is known, or the user may want any entity which satisfies some semantic description. Our goal is to extract from text the salient attributes of these entities, for example a person's occupation and associated organization, or an organization's type and location. Once extracted, this information can be used in retrieval. An example of a simple input-output pair for name identification is shown below in Figure 3.1[1].

3.2 Traditional and Non-traditional Approaches to Name Identification

Traditional approaches to unknown proper name identification involve, broadly speaking, the lexical lookup of names or name fragments in a

---
[1] Source: *Wall Street Journal* 10/31/1989.

```
Input:

Gen-Probe Inc., a biotechnology concern, said it signed a
definitive agreement to be acquired by Chugai Pharmaceutical Co.
of Tokyo for about $100 million, or almost double the market
price of Gen-Probe's stock. ... Osamu Nagayama, deputy
president of Chugai, which spends 15% of its sales on research
and development, was unable to pinpoint how much more money
Chugai would pump into Gen-Probe.

Output:

<org name="Gen-Probe Inc." type=company
  business=biotechnology index=1>
<org name= "Chugai Pharmaceutical Co." type=company
  business=pharmaceuticals located-in=3 index=2>
<loc name="Tokyo" type=city located-in=Japan index=3>
<person name="Osamu Nagayama" occupation=corporate-officer
  title=deputy-president org=1 index=4>
```

Figure 3.1
Example Input and Output of Name Identification

name database. For example, approaches such as [Aone *et al.*, 1992], [Aberdeen *et al.*, 1992], and [Cowie *et al.*, 1992], identify person names by marking off phrases which contain unknown words close to known name elements like first or last names, and (in [Cowie *et al.*, 1992]) unknown words close to specific title words. As the above studies show, name databases such as cross-cultural listings of common first and last names as well as geographical gazetteers and the like, are obviously helpful in name recognition. However, they require a pre-existing name element database. Creating such databases and keeping them up-to-date can be a labor intensive task. The fact that proper names form, lexically speaking, an open class and the fact that they often contain other open-class elements, makes the incompleteness of such databases an obvious problem.

There are two further problems with approaches based exclusively on unknown words and known name elements. First, they can be easily confused by known common nouns (or other parts of speech) which occur in proper names, even person names. For example, the company "General Mills" might be missed since "mills" is a dictionary word, or mistaken for a person based on the title word, while the person

"General Mills" might be mistaken for a company based on a company name list. Second, as name databases grow increasingly large, there is the increased possibility of ambiguity. For example, "Paris" is the name not only of the capital of France, but also of several small towns in the United States. Clearly, a system should entertain multiple hypotheses about a name, preferably disambiguating them based on additional information from context.

Our approach aims at deriving proper names and their semantic attributes automatically from large corpora, without relying on any listing of name elements. The overall approach is based on two main ideas. Firstly, we hypothesize that for certain genres of text, for example, *Wall Street Journal* (WSJ) news stories, new references are introduced by information occurring in the immediate syntactic environment of the proper name. Many of these local contextual clues reflect felicity conventions for introducing new names. New names of people (as well as organization names, and to some extent location names) are generally accompanied by honorifics and various appositive phrases which help anchor the new name reference to mutually assumed knowledge. Further contextual clues come from selectional restrictions, for example, given "*Kambomambo murdered Zombaluma*" (from [Radford, 1988]), the verb is the main clue to the hypothesis that the two names are those of people.

Although the idea of exploiting local context to identify semantic attributes in new names is in itself not new (e.g., [Coates-Stephens, 1992a], [Paik *et al.*, 1993b], [McDonald, 1993a]), little attention has been paid in name identification work to the discourse properties of names. Our second, and more general idea is to view proper names as linguistic expressions whose interpretation often depends on the discourse context. For example, in the discourse "*U.S. President Bill Clinton ... Clinton ... Mr. Clinton ... President Clinton*," the interpretations of "Clinton," "Mr. Clinton" and "President Clinton" are dependent on the prior reference to "U.S. President Bill Clinton," much as "the president," "he" and "himself" are dependent on prior context in the discourse "*U.S. President Bill Clinton$_i$ ... the president$_i$ ... he$_i$ ... himself$_i$.*" The need for text-driven identification of names presupposes in turn a computational model of discourse which identifies individuals based on the way they are described in the text, instead of relying on their description in a pre-existing knowledge base. The overall discourse representation framework which we use is LuperFoy's three-tiered model [Luperfoy, 1991], which in turn is a computational adaptation of Landman's pegs model of NP semantics [Landman, 1986].

The idea of the three-tiered model is that there are three significant levels of representation: linguistic expressions, Discourse Pegs, and knowledge base objects. A distinctive feature of Discourse Pegs (hereafter referred to as Pegs) as opposed to similar constructs in the literature, like File Cards [Heim, 1981], Database Objects [Sidner, 1979], Discourse Referents [Karttunen, 1968], and Discourse Entities [Webber, 1978], [Dahl and Ball, 1987], is that they describe unique objects with respect to the current discourse, rather than with respect to the underlying belief system or world model. Thus, in an article mentioning Bill Clinton there may be two guises in which he may appear, as Governor Clinton and President Clinton; these would correspond to two distinct pegs. It is important to stress that pegs, as a result, do not correspond to equivalence classes of coreferential mentions; rather, there is one peg for each distinct object under discussion, irrespective of the number of entities in the world of reference. Objects which are distinct in the text may still need to be related to each other for their interpretation; for example, in the discourse "*President Bill Clinton . . . the Clintons . . . Hilary,*" the expressions "President Bill Clinton," "the Clintons" and "Hilary" each introduce new pegs, but these pegs are each linked, as partial dependents, to the previous one. An interesting subcase of this involves name mergers, for example, an article describing a joint venture between two companies may use the two individual company names followed by a merged name for the joint venture.

In applying this framework to the unknown name problem, we first distinguish three types of entities: (i) Mentions — these are text segments which are tokens of proper names in text; (ii) Contexts — these are text segments which provide information about syntactic and semantic properties associated with a name; and (iii) Hypotheses — these are hypotheses about individuals and their semantic attributes, associated with a Mention. Given this framework, the goal of unknown name identification is to use the text itself to generate Hypotheses about possible individuals distinguished by a Mention. In a given text context, descriptions from earlier Mentions of a name may be further specified by new information associated with subsequent Mentions of the name (which may take a somewhat different form from previous Mentions).

In general, two Hypotheses, each associated with a different Mention, are linked together (by means of a common Peg) whenever they are mutually compatible. Thus, two Mentions, Mention 1 and Mention 2, can be considered to be indirectly anchored together to a common Peg whenever the hypothetical information associated with each is mutually compatible. For ease of presentation, we may speak of these coanchored mentions as *coreferential* (when what we really mean is this more specific sense of coanchoring); also, we will use the capitalized word *Coreference* for the process of computing pegs for a mention, a process which may result in either the coanchoring of the mention to one or more existing pegs, or the allocation of a new peg. We describe the Coreference process in more detail in Section 3.9.

3.3   Proper Names — Syntactic Forms and Semantic Function

We first need to describe more precisely what we mean by proper names. In terms of syntactic categories, proper names are commonly identified as lexical NPs. In the examples in this paper, we use [] to identify an internal proper name constituent of interest. Proper names often occur inside definite NPs, where the proper name can function as the syntactic head ("the [President of France]," "the [Gulf of California]," "the Reagan [White House]," "Iraq's president [Saddam Hussein]," "Lake [George]"), a complement ("the president of [France]"), or an adjunct or attributive NP ("the [Reagan] White House," "the [Bush] administration"). They can also occur with indefinite determiners ("an [Arnold Schwartzenegger]," "a [Washington Redskin]," "an [IBM]"). As lexical NPs, proper names have substantial internal structure: they can be formed out of primitive proper name elements ("Oliver North," "Gramm-Rudman," "Villa-Lobos"), other proper names ("Lake George," "the [President of France]," "the [Reagan White House]," "Anne of a Thousand Days") and also out of non-proper names ("the [Savings and Loan] crisis," "General Electric Co.," "Federal Savings and Loan Insurance Corporation," "Committee for the Protection of Public Welfare"). A common resulting form is the open compound proper name ("the [Carter Administration National Energy Conservation Committee]").

As can be seen from the above examples, the issue of what constitutes a name is not entirely clear. In general, theoretical investigation of names has not, as far as we know, identified a set of linguistic tests which could distinguish names from definite descriptions. For example, expressions like "The Society for Prevention of Cruelty to Animals" seem akin to definite noun phrases.[2] In his seminal study of name forms in newswire text, [Coates-Stephens, 1992a] (p. 85) observed that "as with place names, or perhaps even to a greater degree, with corp PN's [proper names] we find an intermingling of the name and its description." That names contain descriptions should not come as a surprise.[3] For one thing, many names like family names and place names, which may seem non-descriptive today, originated historically as definite descriptions or titles. Secondly, such descriptions seem to function at the very least to encode additional information into the name (a similar point is brought out by [Carroll, 1985], who speaks of "name packing"). The descriptions in names can, of course, be quite useful in name identification. In the case of organization names ("Microelectronics and Computer Technology Corporation") and geographical location names ("Easter Island"), the internal structure of the name can be used to hypothesize various semantic attributes. A study reported in [Amsler, 1989] on proper names in the *New York Times* containing the word "Center" as in "Grand Forks Energy Research Center" and "Boston University's Center for Adaptive Systems") is suggestive of the scope of such techniques. Identifying idiomatic uses is obviously a problem: as [Amsler, 1989] points out, "Grand Funk Railroad" is the name of a rock group.

3.4   Overall Algorithm

As [McDonald, 1993a] points out, there are two kinds of evidence which can be used to infer a sequence of words to be a name: *internal evidence* and *external evidence*. Internal evidence has to do with the internal form of the name; for example the name may be (in its entirety) in the database (e.g., "New York"), it may contain a common first name, an

---

[2]Strawson was one of the first to single out "the class of quasi-names, of substantial phrases which grow capital letters" [Strawson, 1985].

[3]It is not clear what role such descriptions should play in a semantic theory of name reference.

incorporation term (like "Inc." or "Co.") or a specific title word. External evidence comes from the context around the name, for example, "Osamu Nagayama, *deputy president of Chugai.*"

Our approach aims at deriving proper names and their semantic attributes automatically from large corpora, by combining multiple sources of evidence. While our approach can exploit the use of name lists, it does not rely on the use of these. (In essence, name lists, as they grow in size, tend to increase the possibility of ambiguity, which information from context can help disambiguate.) In this respect our approach is similar to other recent approaches [Coates-Stephens, 1992a], [Paik *et al.*, 1993b], [McDonald, 1993a], which exploit both kinds of evidence. However, since the evidence is often partial and we can rarely be certain about the rules which infer the evidence, it is important to represent uncertainty in the system. Where there is ambiguity, we need to rank alternatives based on the strength of evidence. Our approach, therefore, differs from the others in that it represents uncertainty explicitly (this is discussed in Section 3.7). It also tackles the problem of coreference, both within and across documents. Finally, it addresses some of the problems of attachment of complex names. All this is carried out within the confines of a text skimming approach, based on partial natural language analysis.

The processing of a document begins with a tokenization process, which segments the text into the appropriate units (including sentences and words) based on the type of document we are dealing with. A mention generator then proposes certain sequences of words as candidate name mentions, allowing various knowledge sources (KSs) to vote on and propose hypotheses about a given mention. Each KS can generate multiple scored interpretations (hypotheses) about a given mention. When a new mention is generated, applicable KSs fire on that mention, with each KS refining the interpretations (hypotheses) generated by the previous KSes. Hypotheses which score above a certain confidence level (which is a system parameter specifying a variable recall/precision threshold) are output by the system. These names, together with their semantic information, can be added to a database after checking with the user. Over time, learnt names (or name elements) increase the likelihood of recognizing a name mention.

Both the original name mentions, and the subsequent interpretations of them proposed by the different KSs, are obviously units of text, linked

to other text-units by *subtype* and *part-of* links. In addition, text units at
the sentence level and below are threaded together in a chart. The chart
here functions as a blackboard similar to the one described in [Barnett
et al., 1990], [Cohen *et al.*, 1989], with the appearance of information of
a specific type of chart edge triggering an appropriate set of KSs.

3.5   Mention Generator

The mention generator proposes contiguous capitalized words as candidate names. When a mention is sentence initial, its beginning word
is excluded if it happens to be a function word. Thus, given *"Royal
Bank of Scotland,"* it would propose "Royal Bank" and "Scotland"; given
"Bank of Credit and Commerce International," it would propose "Bank,"
"Credit," and "Commerce International." This philosophy of minimal
attachment (of prepositional phrases and noun phrase conjuncts) allows one to delay attachment decisions until a later stage of processing,
when more semantic information is available to group partial names
into longer names.

In languages where orthography does not distinguish names or in
situations where mixed case text is not available, the problem of mention generation is harder. Syntax alone is often insufficient to tell you
whether something is a name (consider phrases like "the budget committee', or "friends of Bill"). We have not focused on this aspect of
the problem. However, we are currently experimenting with a strategy which combines noun phrase identification (with unknown words
guessed as names) with pushing some of the semantic tests used by the
KSs into the mention generator.

3.6   Knowledge Sources

The approach of text skimming is associated with much recent work
on data extraction from text (e.g., [Mauldin, 1989], [Jacobs, 1988], and
many others). In general, this means that different parts of the text
can be processed to different depths, with some parts being skipped
over lightly. The text skimming approach also implies, in our case, that
we lighten the burden of lexical semantics: in contrast to approaches
like [Coates-Stephens, 1992a], we need only represent word meanings

for words closely related in meaning to the semantic attributes we are attempting to extract.

The knowledge sources which tag organizations use well-tried techniques (e.g., [Rau, 1991]), such as looking for suffixes (like "Inc."), prefixes followed by specific function words (e.g., "Bank of"), patterns involving "&", and exploiting organization lexicons. Some of these lexicons are simply name lists, e.g., a list of company names available from [CLR, 1994]. The suffixes and prefixes themselves were derived semi-automatically from analysis of such name lists. Other lexicons have semantic information associated with them, e.g., a MITRE corporate database specifying internal organizations, their abbreviations, and their area of expertise. Other organization KSs look for appositive phrases, e.g., "X, a machine-tool supplier."

The KSs which tag people include one which looks for honorifics (like "Mr.", "His Holiness", "Lt. Col.") to make inferences about personhood, as well as gender and job occupation. Other person KSs look for external evidence in premodifying adjective phrases and noun compounds, as well appositive constructions, e.g., "P, O's top managing director", "a top Japanese executive, P." The KS Agent-of-Human-Action looks for verbs like "lead," "head," "say," "explain," "think," "admit" in the syntactic context to estimate whether a given mention could be a person; the frequent use of metonymy involving companies as agents makes this a relatively weak KS. There is also a KS which uses a cross-cultural list of first names, used for inferring gender information when not specified in the text, and also for recognizing person names that are not accompanied by external evidence in the form of honorifics, appositives, or coreferential information.

Location KSs use as their main source of internal evidence a geographic lexicon (TIPSTER gazetteer). Place names which occur in this lexicon, as well as geography-related headwords ("the Bay of Fundy") can provide strong internal evidence. Adjectives related to geography ("North Ossetia") provide weaker internal evidence. External evidence includes, for example, appositive constructions ("L, a small Bay Area town," "the L, Michigan contractor").

The KSs are all based on simple rules involving pattern matching, defined over chart elements, and using extensions to a pattern matcher developed by [Norvig, 1992]. The pattern elements include words, proximity measures (e.g., "less than two words away"), and part of speech codes, the latter generated by the MIT part-of-speech tagger [de Marcken, 1990a]. Attributes related to tags have a shallow ontology associated with them. For example, a president is either a head-of-state or a corporate-officer; a person has age, title, gender and occupation; a place may be a continent, country, state, city, etc.

Each KS can generate multiple hypotheses with different confidences. For example, the mention "General Electric Co." may trigger an initial hypothesis that it could be a person, based on interpreting "General" a title, and other hypotheses that it could be a company or a county, based on the abbreviated suffix "Co.". Each distinct set of possible attributes and values corresponds to a distinct hypothesis. When all the KSs have fired, a second pass is made through the names in the chart, grouping small partial names into longer names. The information gathered in the first pass enables certain kinds of prepositional and conjunction attachments to be resolved. For instance, if O is an organization and L is a location, then "O of L" is hypothesized as an organization, e.g., "Royal Bank of Scotland." Note that this is done based on matching the type of name, rather than matching specific words, Similarly, a Suffixless-Org-and-Org rule would combine "Bank of Credit" and "Commerce International," but would not combine "Ford Motors" and "General Motors."

3.7   Representation of Uncertainty

Early on in the project, we realized that the representation of uncertainty in the system might change. We therefore provided, as a system parameter, a *Combine-Confidence* function, through which all confidence calculations are routed. *Combine-Confidence* takes a hypothesis about a mention and returns a probability between 0 and 1 that the mention is one of the four different kinds of entities. The current implementation of the *Combine-Confidence* function uses an ad-hoc scheme that computes confidence as a weighted sum of the probability assigned to the hypothesis by each KS that contributed to it, weighted by the reliability of that KS. The KS's reliability is based on an initial global ranking followed by later calibration based on feedback from system performance. The calibration statistics contain enough information to enable us to calculate Bayesian conditional-probability matrices. We therefore expect to someday replace the current implementation of *Combine-Confidence* with one based on Bayesian reasoning.

3.8 Appositives

Appositives are important linguistic devices for introducing new mentions. We limit ourselves to constituents of the form <NP, NP>. These are of the form name-comma-appositive (e.g., "<name>, <ORG>'s top managing director," "<name>, a small Bay Area town"), and appositive-comma-name (e.g., "a top Japanese executive, <name>"). We ignore double appositives, except for simple ones involving age, as in "Osamu Nagayama, 33, senior vice president and chief financial officer of Chugai.". Therefore, given a candidate name mention, the appositive modifier is a NP to the right or the left of the name. (A <NP, NP> constituent can of course be part of an enumerated, conjoined NP; however, if one conjunct is a name, it's likely that the other one may be one too. Of course, a <NP, NP> sequence may not be a constituent in the first place).

To identify appositive boundaries, we experimented with both (a) a regular expression grammar tuned to find appositives in the training corpus, and (b) syntactic-grammar based parsing using the MIT Fast Parser [de Marcken, 1990a]. Here we found pattern matching, based on looking for left and right delimiters such as comma and certain parts of speech, to be far more accurate. For example, given *"said Chugai's senior vice president for international trade, Osamu Nagayama,"* the appositive identifier would find "Chugai's senior vice president for international trade." For extracting premodifiers, head and postmodifiers, we have found technique (b) to be somewhat more useful, though attachment errors still occur. The extracted premodifiers and head (or maximal fragment thereof) are then looked up in the semantic lexicon ontology; looking up "senior vice president" would yield corporate-officer or government-official. Hypotheses about "Chugai," based on information from Coreference linking it to a mention of "Chugai Pharmaceutical Corp.", can be used to infer that "Osamu Nagayama" is more likely to be a corporate officer than a government official.

3.9   Coreference

3.9.1   Finding previously mentioned candidates

When a new mention is processed by the Coreference KS, pegs from previous mentions seen earlier in the document are considered as candidate coanchored mentions. This is carried out by Function *Find-Candidate-Pegs*. Obviously, we wish to avoid considering the set of all previous pegs in the discourse. The use of focus information at some level can be used to constrain this set, but that would require in turn strong assumptions about the discourse structure of texts - which could severely limit our applicable domains. Given a mention of "Bill Clinton," we want to avoid considering a peg for "New York City" as a candidate antecedent. This suggests we consider only previous mentions which are similar in some way, i.e., we need a suitable technique for indexing mentions for subsequent reference.

Obviously, there can be considerable variability in the form of a name across different mentions. For example, a mention of "President Clinton" could be followed by "Bill Clinton"; one of "Georgetown University" by "Georgetown"; "the Los Angeles Lakers" by "the Lakers," "the Society for Prevention of Cruelty to Animals" by "the S.P.C.A." (See [Carroll, 1985] for a discussion of the regularities and numerous irregularities in alternations in name forms). Our strategy here is to generate multiple indexing terms for use by coreference. Thus, when a new mention is processed, it is indexed by its *normalized name*, by *name elements* in its name, and by its *abbreviations*. We now discuss each of these index types in turn.

The *normalized name* is a standard form of the name. In the training corpus, the heuristic of choosing the last name element in the surface form of a name as a normalized name works well for people. This may reflect the fact that newspapers often impose their own normalization conventions. There are obvious exceptions to the last name element heuristic; for example, in the WSJ, a mention of "Roh Tae Woo" is followed by a coreferential mention of "Mr. Roh." For organization names, our heuristic is to choose all but the corporate designator (if any) as the normalized name. Of course, at the time of invoking Coreference for a hypothesis associated with a mention, we may or may not have (depending in part on the ordering of knowledge sources) enough

```
Function Find-Candidate-Pegs (H:Hypothesis, Norm-Names-Table,
                              Abbrevs-Table, Name-Els-Table);
% Norm-Names-Table: Norm-Name X Hypotheses
% Abbrevs-Table: Abbrev X Hypotheses
% Name-Els-Table: Name-El X Hypotheses
 norm-name, name-els, abbrevs: Name; cand-hyps: Hypothesis;
 norm-name := norm-name(H);
 cand-hyps := lookup-norm-name(norm-name, Norm-Names-Table);
 if null(cand-hyps)
    then name-els :- name-els(H);
         cand-hyps:=
           Nearest-Neighbors(name-els, Name-Els-Table,
                             Num-Seq-Words-in-Common);
% Num-Seq-Words-in-Common is a similarity predicate.
 abbrevs:= abbrevs(H);
 cand-hyps:= union(cand-hyps,
                   lookup-abbrevs(abbrevs, Abbrevs-Table));
 Return cand-hyps.
```

Figure 3.2
Algorithm *Find-Candidate-Pegs*

information to decide which normalized name heuristic to invoke, in which case we use the last name as a default. *Name elements* are individual words within the name. *Abbreviations* for each name are generated by rule, except when the name is present in some lexicon along with an abbreviation. If the type of an object is known, type-specific rules are used to generate all plausible abbreviations of the object's name, which are used to index the object as a candidate for subsequent coreference. These rules strip off function words in some cases, and use various formats for abbreviating person names, company names, and place names.

Given a new name mention, *Find-Candidate-Pegs* (Figure 3.2) collects as candidate mentions (the union of) those previous mentions which have the same normalized name as the new mention, or which have the same abbreviation as the new mention (the new mention itself may or may not be an abbreviation). If no previous mentions with the same normalized names can be found, then the nearest neighboring names are added to the set of candidate mentions. The search space for the nearest neighbor procedure is the set of all names with name elements in common with the new mention, and the similarity predicate involves having a high percentage of sequential words in common. Thus "IBM Inc." would be a candidate for "IBM" (normalized name), "Bank of Credit and Commerce International" for "BCCI" and vice versa (ab-

```
Function Coreferential? (h:Hypothesis, P:Pegs);
   co-anchored?: boolean; new-peg: peg;
   for each p in P
         if Match?(h, p)
               then link(h,p);
                          co-anchored? := true;
   if co-anchored? = nil
         then new-peg := make-new-peg(P);   % updates P
                  link(h, new-peg);
   Return P.
```

Figure 3.3
Algorithm *Coreferential?*

breviation), "Leaseway Transportation Corp." for "Leaseway" (nearest neighbors), and "Kim Il Sung" for "Mr. Kim" (nearest neighbors). Note that once the candidate mentions have been found, they become candidates for the separate procedure of matching, which is described in Section 3.9.2.

In practice the generation of candidates by these techniques works well, except for spelling errors. If necessary, the system can use a strategy of iterative widening; if the system fails to find a candidate mention, in iterative widening mode it attempts to search through the space of all other previous mentions. In this mode, the system can also separately collect and warn about mentions whose names are close to but not identical in spelling to the current mention, using the Damerau-Levenshtein [Damerau, 1964] "spelling distance" metric.[4]

3.9.2   Matching candidates

When a new mention is processed by the Coreference KS, pegs from previous candidate mentions seen earlier in the document (and collected by *Find-Candidate-Pegs*) are considered as candidate coanchored mentions. At each peg site, the system collects information (significant slots and values) from hypotheses associated with the new mention, and unifies it with information accumulated from the other mentions anchored at the peg site. Algorithm *Coreferential?* (Figure 3.3) outlines the algorithm.

The unification (Function *Match?*) itself is sensitive to abbreviations. For example, the unifier for the slot First-Name comparing the hy-

---

[4] The system does not as such deal with the problem of multiple transliterations of names, for example, the numerous English spellings of "Muhammad Ghaddafi."

potheses for "W. Newman" and "William A. Newman" would succeed. *Coreferential?* terminates when all the candidate previous pegs have been considered. As a rule, successful unification results in coanchoring. A failure of unification (due, for example, to a conflict on the Occupation slot) may also result in co-anchoring, if the new information has high confidence and the old information has low confidence, or if all the other evidence at the peg strongly supports the new mention's hypothesis. Conflicting elements which have the same confidence (e.g., the names "W. Newman" vs. "G. Newman," or a conflict on the Gender slot triggered by evidence from the honorific "Mr." vs. "Mrs.") prevent co-anchoring, and in that case the new mention is matched against the other peg sites. If the new mention cannot be anchored to any existing peg, a new peg is created for it.

The partitioning of hypotheses does not perform any merger operations on co-anchored hypotheses. However, once all the KSs have fired, the best surviving super-threshold hypothesis of each mention is output as a final name tag. At this stage information from hypotheses of coreferential mentions are merged into the final tag. For example, given "*Osamu Nagayama, deputy president ... Mr. Nagayama ...* ", the final tag for each mention would include occupation derived from the first mention and gender derived from the second.

As indicated by the evaluation below, this general model of coreference performs well, splitting and merging appropriately in fairly complex test cases. As an illustration, Figure 3.4 shows an example of Coreference and ambiguity resolution. To simplify the presentation, only one hypothesis is shown per mention, appositives are ignored, and each attribute of each hypothesis is assumed to have the same confidence. (Each Mention is presented as a string, with its hypothesis directly below it).Given the one-to-one mapping, in the discussion below each hypothesis will be referred to by the name of its Mention.

Assume Mention 1 is discourse-initial; assume further that the Person-Name and Age KSs have fired. The Coreference KS on Mention 1 leads to the creation of a new peg, Peg 1, representing the hypothetical entity Bill Clinton. In applying Coreference to Mention 2, *Find-Candidate-Pegs* looks first for hypotheses with the same normalized name as Mention 2. This leads to Mention 1 being selected as a candidate. The system unifies the properties associated with Mention 2 with Mention 1's properties. In this case, since there is no conflict, both mentions are

```
MENTIONS AND HYPOTHESES              PEGS

1. "Bill Clinton, 45"                [1. Bill.Clinton]
   Name: Bill.Clinton
   Age: 45
   Norm: Clinton

2. "Mr. Clinton"                     [1]
   Name: .Clinton
   Gender: Male
   Norm: Clinton

3. "Ms. Hilary Clinton"             [2. Hilary.Clinton]
   Name: Hilary.Clinton
   Gender: Female
   Norm: Clinton

4. "U.S. President Clinton"         [2, 1]
   Name: .Clinton
   Occupation: HeadofState
   Norm: Clinton

5. "First Lady Hilary Clinton"      [2]
   Name: Hilary.Clinton              Leads to breaking of link from
   Gender: Female                    Mention 4 to Peg 2.
   Occupation: FirstLady
   Norm: Clinton
```

Figure 3.4
Coreference and disambiguation

anchored to Peg 1. Mention 3 results in Coreference attempting a link to Peg 1. This leads to a conflict in unification with the properties from one of the other links to Mention 1, arising specifically from the full name and gender information of Mention 1. These are conflicts because they violate a single-valued constraint for these attributes. The conflict with Mention 3 is honored, since there is no disparity in confidence measures. This results in Mention 3 being anchored to a new peg Peg 2, representing a hypothetical entity Hilary Clinton. Mention 4's properties are compatible with both pegs, hence it is coanchored to both, making it ambiguous. Mention 5 leads to a conflict on name at Peg 1. There is no confidence disparity at Peg 1, so the conflict is honored, resulting in a search for some other peg. At Peg 2, there is a conflict on occupation. Since all the other evidence at the peg (from Mention 3) strongly supports Mention 5's hypothesis, Mention 5 is anchored to Peg 2. This leads to breaking of the link of the conflicting Mention 4 with Peg 2, disambiguating Mention 4.

3.9.3   Coreference across documents

The coreference linking between names can be extended across documents, even though the documents may not have been authored as a single discourse. The technique here involves merging each new document's final tags (partitioned under coreference) with a cumulative set of final tags from previous documents (also partitioned under coreference). The merger operation takes the two partitions, and builds a new merged partition (under the same coreference relation).

3.10   Evaluation

A general problem in evaluating information retrieval systems is the difficulty of obtaining relevance data identifying which documents are judged relevant to a given set of queries. Furthermore, different tasks have different information needs. For example, the topics constructed for the TREC (Text Retrieval Conference) [Harman, 1993] conference data set may or may not have something in common with the name-tracking needs of an analyst responding to a crisis. Our strategy here is two-fold: firstly, using a standard test set of queries and documents, to evaluate how well a combination of keywords and our name tags compares to retrieval by keywords. This effort is currently underway. Second, we decided to evaluate the automated name tagging against human tagging of names, as described below.

An initial evaluation was carried out in mid-1993 on a test set of 42 hand-tagged *Wall Street Journal* articles, containing 2075 names. The hand-tagging marked only the type of the tag (person, organization, or location), ignoring attributes. Precision (a measure of how many retrieved documents are relevant) was calculated as the number of correct program tags divided by the number of program tags. Recall (a measure of how many relevant documents were retrieved) was calculated as the number of correct program tags divided by the number of hand tags. At a threshold setting where Precision was 85%, Recall was 67%. This figure was obtained without the aforementioned cross-cultural list of first names and list of company names, both of which were made available to us at a later stage.

Subsequent evaluations were carried out on other varieties of text, including news sources like the *New York Times*, Clarinet email news feed, some subcollections from the TIPSTER corpus, as well as other sources such as miscellaneous electronic reports [Kahaner, 1991], and a wide variety of MITRE documents, such as memos, letters, working papers, and technical reports. These allowed us to measure the accuracy on different genres. At the same parameter setting as was used in the *Wall Street Journal* evaluation, again in the absence of the two aforementioned name lists, we obtained similar measures for precision, but on the MITRE and [Kahaner, 1991] documents, recall was somewhat lowered. The vast majority of the recall errors were due to formats which were not handled by our system, for example tabular formats, names in bibliographic citations, addresses and glossaries, various styles of name enumeration that were new to the system (e.g., last name-comma-first name). Format handling is therefore a critical factor in maintaining accuracy over a wide variety of genres. Interestingly, some of the Clarinet documents were written relatively informally, with fewer name-external clues to help identify person names. In due course, when the two name lists were added to the system, we were able to obtain higher recall, without loss of precision for the Clarinet sources by configuring the system to give a higher strength for name list based heuristics for this genre of text.

A more recent evaluation was carried out in March 1994 on a smaller sample of 546 names from news sources, but with the two additional name lists. At the same setting as earlier, where Precision was 88%, Recall was 73%. The absence of standard test sets for names makes it difficult to compare these figures with other researchers' results. Furthermore, many of the researchers (see [Paik *et al.*, 1993b] for a summary of such results) measured only precision, not recall. However, an informal survey of the literature suggests that our numbers are comparable to those obtained by systems which use substantially larger name lists and name alias lists than we used in the evaluation. We expect that incorporating such name lists will lead to further improvement in the accuracy measures.

3.11   Conclusion

In conclusion, then, we have found that a treatment of proper names as potentially context-dependent linguistic expressions can be effectively applied to the problem of unknown name identification in newswire text, especially when combined with local-context based text skimming. In addition to determining more precisely the limitations of such an approach, one future direction would be to consider porting the system to another natural language such as Spanish. We have also embedded the name tagger in an information retrieval system currently being tested at MITRE for searching and browsing on-line news sources and MITRE documents.

Acknowledgments

We are grateful to the following colleagues who collaborated with us on these ideas and their implementation at various times: Stephen Glanowski, Sharon Laskowski, Susann LuperFoy, and Elaine Lusher.

4 Categorizing and Standardizing Proper Nouns for Efficient Information Retrieval

Woojin Paik, Elizabeth D. Liddy, Edmund Yu, Mary McKenna

4.1 Introduction

In information retrieval, proper nouns, group proper nouns, and group common nouns present unique problems. Proper nouns are recognized as important sources of information for detecting relevant documents in information retrieval and extracting contents from a text [Rau, 1991]). Yet most of the unknown words in texts, which degrade the performance of natural language processing information retrieval systems, are proper nouns. Group proper nouns (e.g., "Middle East") and group common nouns (e.g., "third world") will not match on their constituents unless the group entity is mentioned in the document. The proper noun processor herein described is a module in the DR-LINK system [Liddy et al., 1993b] for document detection whose initial development was funded under the auspices of ARPA's TIPSTER program.

Our approach to solving the group common noun and the group proper noun problem has been to expand the appropriate terms in a query, such as "third world," to all possible names and variants of third world entities. For all proper nouns, our system assigns categories from a proper noun classification scheme to every proper noun in both documents and queries, to permit proper noun matching at the category level. Category matching is more efficient than keyword matching if the query requires entities of a particular type. Standardization provides a means of efficiently categorizing proper nouns and retrieving documents containing variant forms of a proper noun.

4.2 Proper Noun Boundary Identification

In our most recent implementation, which has improved from our initial attempt [Paik et al., 1993a], documents are first processed using a probabilistic part of speech tagger [Meteer et al., 1991a]. Then a proper noun boundary identifier utilizes the proper noun part-of-speech tags from the previous stage to bracket adjacent proper nouns. Additionally, heuristics developed through corpus analysis are applied to bracket proper noun phrases with embedded conjunctions and prepositions as one unit. For example, a specified list of proper nouns will be bracketed with non-adjacent proper nouns if "of" is an embedded preposition. Proper nouns in this list include Council, Ministry, Secretary, and University.

The success of ratio of our proper noun boundary identification module is approximately 96% in comparison to our initial system's 95% [Paik *et al.*, 1993a]. This improvement was achieved by re-ordering the data flow. A general-purpose phrase bracketer, previously applied before the proper noun boundary identification heuristics for non-adjacent proper nouns, is now applied to texts after all proper noun categorization and standardization steps. Thus, we have eliminated one major source of error: the conflict between the general-purpose noun phrase bracketer and the proper noun boundary identification heuristics. For example, embedded prepositions in a proper noun phrase are sometimes recognized as the beginnings of prepositional phrases by the general-purpose phrase bracketer. The remaining 4% of error is due mainly to incorrect proper noun tags assigned to the uncommon first word of a sentence by the part of speech tagger and wrongly identified sentence boundaries.

4.3   Proper Noun Classification Scheme

Our proper noun classification scheme, which was developed through corpus analysis of newspaper texts, is organized as a hierarchy consisting of 9 branching nodes and 30 terminal nodes. Currently, we use only the terminal nodes to assign categories to proper nouns in queries and documents. Based on an analysis of 589 proper nouns from a set of randomly selected documents from the *Wall Street Journal*, we found that our 29 meaningful categories correctly accounted for 89% of all proper nouns in the documents. We reserve the last category as a miscellaneous category. Figure 4.1 shows a hierarchical view of our proper noun categorization scheme.

The system categorizes all identified proper nouns using several methods. The first approach is to compare the proper noun with a list of all identified prefixes, infixes and suffixes for possible categorization based

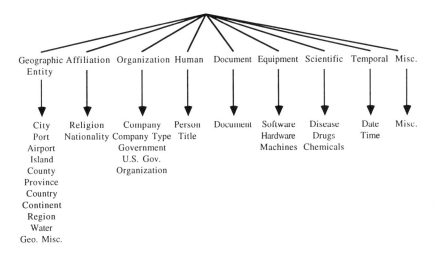

Figure 4.1
Proper Noun Categorization Scheme

on these lexical clues. If the system cannot identify a category in this stage, the proper noun is passed to an alias database to determine if the proper noun has an alternate name form. If this is the case, the proper noun is standardized and categorized at this point. If there is no match in the alias database, the proper noun moves to the knowledge-base look up, constructed using online lexical resources such as *the TIPSTER Gazetteer, the 1992 CIA World Factbase,* and *the Executive Desk Reference.* If the knowledge-base look up is not successful, the proper noun is run through a context heuristics application developed from corpus analysis, which suggests certain categories of proper nouns. For example, if a proper noun is followed by a comma and another proper noun, which has been identified as a state, we will label the proper noun as a city name, e.g., "Time, Illinois." Finally, if the proper noun still has not been categorized, it is compared against a list of first names generated from corpora for a final personal name categorization check. If the proper noun is not categorized in this stage, it will be labeled with the 'miscellaneous' category code.

For the categorization system to work efficiently, variant terms must be standardized. This procedure is performed at three levels, with the prefixes, infixes and suffixes standardized first. Next, the proper nouns in alias forms are standardized to official forms. Using the standardized form of a proper noun reduces the number of possible variants which the system would otherwise need to search, improving both retrieval efficiency and performance. Finally, if a proper noun was mentioned at least twice in a document, for instance, Analog Devices, Inc. and later as "Analog Devices," a partial string match of a proper noun is co-indexed for reference resolution. This technique allows for a full representation of a proper noun entity. Figure 4.2 illustrates the flow of the proper noun categorization system within the first stages of DR-LINK processing.

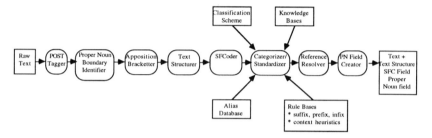

Figure 4.2
DR-LINK Proper Noun Categorizer

When standardization and categorization have been completed, a new field is added to both the query and the document containing the proper noun and the corresponding category code. These fields are then used for matching and representation.

Figures 4.3 and 4.4 show a proper noun categorized and standardized newspaper story. In the proper noun field marked by < PN> and < / PN> pseudo-SGML tags: the first column represents index numbers of standardized proper nouns; the second column represents proper noun categories; and the third column represents the standardized forms of the proper nouns. If a proper noun in text is composed of more than one category of proper noun (e.g., "Judge Lawrence Ollason" consisting of Title and Personal Name category proper nouns), each constituent proper noun is assigned its appropriate category but shares the same index number. In addition, we try to identify locational attributes of categorized proper nouns. Locational attributes can be extracted either through context clues in texts (e.g., it is plausible to assume "Van Nuys" is located in California from the following piece of text, " ... Van Nuys, Calif. ... ") or by a pre-constructed knowledge base (e.g., we know

```
<DOC>
<DOCNO> WSJ920102-0151 </DOCNO>
<HL> Tucson Electric Power's Creditors Fail In Bid to Force
Utility Into Chapter 11 </HL>
<TEXT>
<PN>
0    Company       Tucson Electric Power CO
1    Date          Tuesday
2    Person        Lawrence Ollason
     Title         Judge
3    Government    U.S.Bankruptcy Court
4    Government    Arizona Corporation Commission
5    Province      Arizona
     Country       United States
6    Misc.         Chapter 11
7    Person        Ira R. Adler
8    Organization New York Stock Exchange
     Country       United States
9    Date          July
10   Company       Century Power CO
11   Company       Catalyst Energy CO
12   City          New York City
     Country       United States
13   Person        Adler
     Title         Mr.
14   Date          Oct. 11
15   Date          Dec. 31
</PN>
........
```

Figure 4.3
Proper Nouns from a News Story (4.4), Categorized

Arizona is a state in the United States.) The locational attributes are added in the proper noun field with an appropriate category; the attribute shares the index identification of the proper noun that actually occurred in the text. This type of added information is used for certain types of queries in information retrieval tasks. For example, for a query such as "find documents which mention bankrupted companies in a certain country," the system can find documents which discuss a bankrupted company even though only a city name is mentioned in the text.

Proper noun boundaries are maintained through underscores between constituent words within each text. Index numbers are attached at the end of bounded proper nouns in text using '|' as a separator. This feature allows the system to track the same proper noun across one document. Part-of-speech tags are removed from the text in Figure 4.4 for readability.

There is one error in the classification and standardization in Figure 4.4. The proper noun, "Tucson" in the second sentence is categorized as a company and standardized as "Tucson Electric Power CO" while the context reveals that "Tucson" in this sentence is meant is a name of a city in Arizona. This mistake is due to our aggressive use of sub-string matching to standardize a partial form of a proper noun a to previously introduced fully named proper noun. Currently, we are working toward using multiple sources of evidences for better categorization and the standardization.

```
  Tucson_Electric_Power_Co.|0 retreated from the brink of insolvency proceedings when a federal judge
Tuesday|1 dismissed a call by creditors for involuntary bankruptcy .
  Immediately following the decision by Judge_Lawrence_Ollason|2 of U.S._Bankruptcy_Court|3 in Tucson|0 ,
the Arizona_Corporation_Commission|4 confirmed as permanent a 7% net rate increase and other interim
orders granted earlier contingent on the company 's release from bankruptcy proceedings .
  The troubled electrical utility , which serves most of southern Arizona|5 , has tottered from one
financial problem to another since 1989 , when it posted an $_82.1_million loss and slashed its dividend
. Tucson_Electric|0 , among other things , invested heavily through the 1980s in unneeded generating
capacity and ill-starred financial services ventures .
  Though the court dismissed creditors' calls to force the utility into Chapter_11|6 proceedings , " it
will be several years before the company will be on a strong financial footing , " said Ira_R._Adler|7 ,
senior vice president and chief financial officer , shortly after the bankruptcy court 's dismissal .
  He added that " it will be years before the company is strong enough to pay dividends . "
  Tucson_Electric|0 stock climbed 12.5 cents a share to close at $_4.50 Tuesday|1 in composite trading on
the New_York_Stock_Exchange|8 .
  In July|9 , six large creditors began the effort to force Tucson_Electric|0 into Chapter_11|6
proceedings . In succeeding months , the utility worked out|RP arrangements with each of them . The
last to be reached was concluded with Century_Power_Co.|10 , a unit of closely-held Catalyst_Energy_Co.|11
of New_York|12. With the agreements , creditors dropped their demands for bankruptcy proceedings .
  But the pacts submitted to the court are preliminary and in outline
form only . " We now face the task of documentation of the terms and of soliciting shareholder approval
, " Mr._Adler|13 said . That process will take three to six months , he said .
  If the proposed restructuring is accomplished , current stock holdings will be sharply diluted .
Plans call for about 60_million new common shares to be issued in addition to the roughly 26_million
currently outstanding . Creditors and preferred stock holders thus will own about 70% of the company 's
stock outstanding .
  The agreement with Century_Power|10 , whose generating assets once were part of Tucson_Electric|0 but
were spun off|RP to shareholders some years ago , calls in part for Tucson_Electric|0 to lease directly
and to operate a giant generating unit that had been leased by Century|10 , which then sold the power to
Tucson_Electric|0 . The agreement would terminate an onerous contract that called for Tucson_Electric|0
to buy much of the plant 's power through 2014 . It is hoped that such arrangements will cut costs for
Tucson_Electric|0 .
  Losses at the utility in the first nine months of 1991 totaled $_483.9_million , or $_18.82 a share ,
including about $_350_million in one-time charges . Revenue totaled $_442.4_million .
  The Arizona_Corporation_Commission|4 's order Tuesday|1 made permanent an Oct._11|14 interim order
permitting the utility to boost rates 15% but also terminating temporary fuel surcharges that
had equaled about 8% of prior rates . The resulting net 7% increase was considered vital to the company
. But in a clear signal for creditors to settle with the utility , the Arizona|5 regulators said the
interim order would expire Dec._31|15 if the company were n't removed from bankruptcy proceedings .
  The commission 's order also barred Tucson_Electric|0 from recovering $_250_million of expenditures on
two generating facilities ,
which were deemed in excess of the utility 's needs . The disallowances , together with a provision for
possible default by Century_Power|10 on $_100_million of bonds guaranteed by Tucson_Electric|0 , were
reflected in the one-time charges against the utilities latest nine-month results .

</TEXT>

</DOC>
```

Figure 4.4
Standardized News Story, after Proper Noun Categorization

4.4   Use of Proper Nouns in Matching

Both the lexical entry for a proper noun or a category code may be used for matching documents to queries. For example, if a query is about a boarder incursion, we can limit the potentially relevant documents to those documents which contain at least two different country names, flagged by the two country category codes in the proper noun field.

While the category matching strategy is useful in many cases, the expansion of a group proper noun such as "European Community" to member country names is also beneficial. For example, relevant documents for a query requiring sanctions against Japan by European Community countries, are likely to mention the group proper noun's constituents, rather than the group proper noun specified in the query. We are currently using a proper noun expansion database with 168 expandable entries for query processing. In addition, certain common nouns or noun phrases in queries such as "socialist countries" need to be expanded to the names of the countries which satisfy the definition of the term to improve performance in detecting relevant documents. The system consults a list of common nouns and noun phrases which can be expanded into proper nouns and actively searches for these terms during the query processing stage. Currently, the common noun expansion database has 37 entries.

The creation and use of proper noun information is first utilized in the DR-LINK system as an addition to the subject-content based filtering module, which uses a scheme of 122 subject field codes (SFCs) from a machine-readable dictionary, rather than keywords, to represent documents. Although SFC representation and matching provides a very good first level of document filtering, not all proper nouns reveal subject information, so some of the proper noun concepts in texts are not actually represented in the SFC vectors.

In our new implementation, categorized and standardized proper nouns are combined with Text Structure [Liddy *et al.*, 1993a] information for matching queries and documents. Text Structure is the recognition of a discernible, predictable schema of texts in a particular type. The Text Structurer module in the DR-LINK system delineates the discourse-level organization of document content. Processing at later stages can focus on components identified by the Text Structurer as being the most likely candidates for information requested in a query.

All proper nouns in a document collection are indexed in an inverted file along with the document accession number, the Text Structure component in which the proper noun was located, and the category code. For processing queries for proper noun requirements, we developed a Boolean criteria script which determines which proper nouns, or combinations of proper nouns, are needed from Text Structure components in each query. These requirements are then run against the proper noun inverted file to rank documents. The categorization information of proper nouns is also used in a later stage of the system, which extracts concepts and relations from text, to produce a more refined representation. For example, proper nouns may reveal the location of a company or the nationality of an individual.

We do not have evaluation results based on the implementation using proper noun information in conjunction with Text Structure information. Testing the system which did not utilize Text Structure information [Paik *et al.*, 1993a], reranking documents from SFC module based on the degree of proper noun requirements matching a set of queries against a document collection, resulted in placing all relevant documents within the top 28% of the ranked results. It should be noted that precision figures based on the output of the SFC module with the proper noun matching module produced very reasonable precision results (.22 for the 11-point precision average), even though the combination of these two modules was never intended to function as anything more than a filter used to pass along likely relevant documents to precision enhancement modules.

Finally, the proper noun extraction and categorization module, although developed as part of the DR-LINK system, could be used to provide improved document representation for any information retrieval system. The standardization and categorization features permit queries and documents to be matched with greater precision, while the expansion functions of group proper nouns and group common nouns improve recall.

4.5   Performance Evaluation

The evaluation of the proper noun categorizer reported here is based on 25 randomly selected *Wall Street Journal* documents. Program generated

	Total Correct	Total Incorrect	Precision
City	44	0	1.00
Port	20	2	0.83
Province	24	0	1.00
Country	67	0	1.00
Continent	1	0	1.00
Region	1	7	0.13
Geo. Misc.	0	3	0.00
Religion	2	0	1.00
Nationality	33	1	0.97
Company	88	12	0.88
Government	5	1	0.83
U.S. Government	23	5	0.92
Organization	13	0	1.00
Person	96	9	0.90
Title	44	2	0.96
Document	3	1	0.75
Machine	0	1	0.00
Date	27	0	1.00
Misc.	64	0	1.00
TOTAL	545	44	0.93
TOTAL-Misc.	481	44	0.92

Table 4.1
DR-LINK Proper Noun Categorizer Performance

proper noun categorization was compared to manual categorization. This document set was also used in evaluating our initial version of the categorizer [Paik *et al.*, 1993a]. Table 4.1 demonstrates the performance of the categorizer on 589 proper nouns occurring in the test set. Precision is calculated according to the following formula.

$$Precision = \frac{Total\ Num.\ Correct}{Total\ Num.\ Correct + Total\ Num.\ Incorrect}$$

In addition to 589 proper nouns, 14 common words were incorrectly identified as proper nouns due to errors by the part-of-speech tagger and typos in the original text. The boundaries of 11 proper nouns were incorrectly recognized due to unusual proper noun phrasing such as, "Virginia Group to Alleviate Smoking in Public," which the proper noun boundary identification heuristics failed to bracket.

64 proper nouns were correctly categorized as miscellaneous as they did not belong to any of our 29 meaningful categories. This is considered to be a coverage problem in the proper noun categorization scheme, not an error in the categorizer. Some examples of the proper nouns belonging to the miscellaneous category are: "Promised Land," "Mickey Mouse," and "IUD." The last row of Table 4.1 shows the overall precision of our categorizer based on the proper nouns which belong to the 29 meaningful categories.

In our initial implementation [Paik *et al.*, 1993a], errors in categorizing person and city names accounted for 68% of the total errors. To improve performance, we added a list of common first names, which was semi-automatically extracted from *the Associated Press* and the *Wall Street Journal* corpora, as a special lexicon to consult when there is no match using all categorization procedures. This addition improved our precision of categorizing person names from 46% in the initial implementation to 90% in the current implementation.

The errors categorizing city names in our initial system were mainly due to two problems:

1. The locational source of the news, when mentioned at the beginning of the document, is usually capitalized in the *Wall Street Journal*. This special convention caused miscategorizing of locational proper nouns (usually city names) as Miscellaneous; and
2. City names which were not in our proper noun knowledge base were categorized as Miscellaneous.

The first problem was handled in current categorizer by moving the locational information of the news story to a new field, '<DATELINE>', and normalizing capitalization (from all upper case texts to mixed case) at the document preprocessing stage before the part of speech tagging. For example, if a story is about a company in Dallas then the text is originally represented as:

```
<DOC>
DALLAS: American Medical Insurance Inc. said that ...
........
</DOC>
```

After the preprocessing module is applied, the text representation is changed:

```
<DATELINE> Dallas </DATELINE>
<DOC>
American Medical Insurance Inc. said that ...
........
</DOC>
```

For the second problem, we incorporated a context rule for identifying city names. City names are followed by a country name or a province name, from the United States and Canada, unless the name is very well known. For example, "Van Nuys," can now be categorized as a city name, as it is preceded by a valid United States province name:

```
... Van Nuys, Calif. ...
```

By adding the above new procedures to our categorization system, as well as some well known city names which are not province capitals or heavily populated places based on IDA's Gazetteer to our proper noun knowledge base, the precision of categorizing city names has improved from the initial system's 25% to 100%.

The overall precision of the new proper noun categorizer has improved from 77% [Paik *et al.*, 1993a] to 93%, including proper nouns which are correctly categorized as miscellaneous. This significant improvement was achieved by adding a few sensible context heuristics and modification of the knowledge base. These additions or modifications were based on the analysis of randomly selected documents.

We note the limitations of not manually updating the proper noun knowledge base for uncommon proper nouns when confronted with proper nouns such as "Place de la Reunion" and "Pacific Northwest." We are currently developing a strategy based on context clues using locational prepositions as well as appositional phrases to improve categorization of uncommon proper nouns.

Table 4.2 shows the overall recall figure of our categorizer which is affected by the proper noun phrase boundary identification errors caused by the general-purpose phrase bracketer. Recall is calculated as:

$$Recall = \frac{Total\ Num.\ Correct}{Total\ Num.\ Actual}$$

Total Num. Actual = Total Num. (Correct + Incorrect + Missing)

Totals:	Correct	Incorrect	Missing	Recall
With Misc. Category	545	44	11	0.91
Without Misc. Category	481	44	11	0.90

Table 4.2
DR-LINK Categorizer Overall Recall

4.6   System Comparisons

To compare our proper noun categorization results to the evaluation of a system with similar goals detailed in the literature, we chose Coates-Stephens' 1992a result on acquiring genus information of proper nouns to compare our overall precision. While his approach is to acquire information about unknown proper nouns' detailed genus and differentia description, we consider our approach of assigning a category from a classification scheme of 30 classes to an unknown proper noun generally similar in purpose to his acquisition of genus information. However, it should be noted that our method for assigning categories to proper nouns is different from Coates-Stephens' method, as we rely more on built-in knowledge bases while his approach relies more on context.

Based on 100 unseen documents containing 535 unknown proper nouns, FUNES [Coates-Stephens, 1992a] successfully acquired genus information for 340 proper nouns. Of the 195 proper nouns not acquired, 92 were due to the system's parse failure. Thus, the success ratio based on only the proper nouns which were analyzed by the system, was 77%. DR-LINK's proper noun categorizer's overall precision, which is computed with the same formula, was 93%, including proper nouns which were correctly categorized as miscellaneous (see Table 4.1).

Katoh's 1991 evaluation of his machine translation system, which was based on translating the 1,000 most frequent names in the AP news corpus, successfully analyzed 94% of the 1,000 names. Our precision figure for categorizing randomly chosen person names was 90%.

Finally, the evaluation result from Rau's 1991 company name extractor is compared to the precision figure of our company name categorization. Both systems relied heavily on company name suffixes. Rau's result showed 97.5% success ratio of the program's extraction of company names that had company name suffixes. Our system's precision figure was 88%. However, it should be noted that our result is based on all company names, including those which did not have any clear company name suffixes or prefixes.

4.7   Future Directions

In our current implementation of the DR-LINK system, the output of the proper noun categorization and standardization module is used to improve the efficiency and performance of the information retrieval task. However, we believe that there are other applications which can benefit from this research. For example, standardized proper nouns can be used to track a proper noun entity across years of news stories.

We have begun new research designed to extract background information about one proper noun over a period of time using the described proper noun categorization and standardization system as a base [Paik, 1993]. The research objective is to build an knowledge acquisition tool to be used in the automatic construction of a chronological proper noun knowledge base. Meaningful relations between information in a reported event and a proper noun which played an important role in the event will be extracted and stored in a knowledge base. The category of a proper noun predicts what types of information will co-occur with the proper noun in certain linguistic constructions and aids in the detection of these relations. The resulting knowledge base can be used in a question-answering system such as the one developed for answering general-knowledge questions using an on-line encyclopedia [Kupiec, 1993].

Acknowledgments

This work was supported by the Advanced Research Project Agency under Contract No. 91-F136100-000.

III TASK-DRIVEN LEXICON INDUCTION

5 Customizing a Lexicon to Better Suit a Computational Task

Marti A. Hearst, Hinrich Schütze

5.1 Introduction

Much effort is being applied to the creation of lexicons and the acquisition of semantic and syntactic attributes of the lexical items that comprise them, e.g., [Alshawi, 1987], [Calzolari and Bindi, 1990], [Grefenstette, 1992a], [Hearst, 1992], [Markowitz et al., 1986], [Pustejovsky, 1987], [Wilks et al., 1990a]. However, a lexicon as given may not suit the requirements of a particular computational task. Because lexicons are expensive to build, rather than create a new one from scratch, it can preferable to adjust an existing one to meet an application's needs. In this chapter we describe such an effort: we add associational information to a hierarchically structured lexicon in order to better serve a text labeling task.

For the purposes of information retrieval, we would like to assign labels to full-text documents that characterize their main topics.[1] These labels are to be used in an interface that displays the texts that have been retrieved in response to a query according to intersections of the texts' main topics (see [Hearst, 1994]).

One way to label texts, when working within a limited domain of discourse, is to start with a pre-defined set of topics and specify the word contexts that indicate the topics of interest (e.g., [Jacobs and Rau, 1990]). Another way, assuming that a large collection of pre-labeled texts exists, is to use statistics to automatically infer which lexical items indicate which labels (e.g., [Masand et al., 1992]). In contrast, we are interested in assigning labels to general, domain-independent text, without benefit of pre-classified texts. In all three cases, a lexicon that specifies which lexical items correspond to which topics is required. The topic labeling method we use is statistical and thus requires a large number of representative lexical items for each category.

---

[1] The terms "label," "topic," and "category" are used interchangeably in this chapter.

```
2 senses of bread

Sense 1:
shekels, gelt, dough, bread, dinero, lucre, loot,
     pelf, moolah, cabbage
     => money
          => tender, legal tender
               => medium of exchange, monetary system
                    => asset
                         => possession

Sense 2:
bread, breadstuff, staff of life
     => baked good, baked goods
          => aliment, nourishment, nutriment,
               sustenance, victuals
               => food, nutrient
                    => substance, matter
                         => object, inanimate object,
                              physical object, thing
                              => entity
```

Figure 5.1
The hypernyms (ancestors) of *bread* in WORDNET (Version 1.3).

The starting point for our lexicon is WORDNET [Miller *et al.*, 1990], which is readily available online and provides a large repository of English lexical items. WORDNET[2] is composed of *synsets*, structures containing sets of terms with synonymous meanings, thus allowing a distinction to be made between different senses of homographs. Associated with each synset is a list of relations that the synset participates in. One of these, in the noun dataset, is the hyponymy relation (and its inverse, hypernymy), roughly glossed as the "ISA" relation. This relation imposes a hierarchical structure on the synsets, indicating how to generalize from a subordinate term to a superordinate one, and vice versa.[3] This is a very useful kind of information for many tasks, such as word class generalization [Resnik, 1993a]. Figure 5.1 shows an example of one small piece of the lexicon.

We would like to adjust this lexicon in two ways in order to facilitate the label assignment task. The first is to collapse the fine-grained

---

[2] All work described here pertains to Version 1.3 of WORDNET.

[3] Actually, the hyponomy relation is a directed acyclic graph, in that a minority of the nodes are children of more than one parent. We will at times refer to it as a hierarchy nonetheless.

hierarchical structure into a set of coarse but semantically-related categories. These categories will provide the lexical evidence for the topic labels. (After the label is assigned, the hierarchical structure can be reintroduced.) Once the hierarchy has been converted into categories, we can augment the categories with new lexical items culled from free text corpora, in order to further improve the labeling task.

The second way we would like to adjust the lexicon is to combine categories from distant parts of the hierarchy. In particular, we are interested in finding groupings of terms that contribute to a frame or schema-like representation [Minsky, 1975]; this can be achieved by finding associational lexical relations among the existing taxonymic relations. For example, WORDNET has the following synsets: "athletic game" (hyponyms: baseball, tennis), "sports implement" (hyponyms: bat, racquet), and "tract, piece of land" (hyponyms: baseball_diamond, court), none of which are closely related in the hierarchy. We would like to automatically find relations among categories headed by synsets like these. (In Version 1.3, the WORDNET encoders have placed some associational links among these categories, but still only some of the desired connections appear.)

In other words, we would like to derive links among schematically related parts of the hierarchy, where these links reflect the text genre on which text processing is to be done. [Schütze, 1993b] describes a method called WordSpace that represents lexical items according to how semantically close they are to one another, based on evidence from a large text corpus. We propose combining this term-similarity information with the hierarchical information already available in WORDNET to create structured associational information.

In the next section we describe the algorithm for compressing the WORDNET hierarchy into a set of categories. This is followed by a discussion of how these categories are to be used and why they need to be improved. This is followed by a discussion of the first improvement technique: including new, related terms from a corpus. The next section describes the second improvement technique: bringing disparate categories together to form schematic groupings while retaining the given hierarchical structure. The final section concludes the chapter.

5.2   Creating Categories from WORDNET

We would like to decompose the WORDNET noun hierarchy into a set
of disjoint categories, each consisting of a relatively large number of
synsets. (This is necessary for the text-labeling task, because each topic
must be represented by many different terms.) The goal of creating categories of a particular average size with as small a variance as possible.
There is some limit as to how small this variance can be because there
are several synsets that have a very large number of children (there are
sixteen nodes with a branching factor greater than 100). This primarily occurs with synsets of a taxonymic flavor, i.e., mushroom species
and languages of the world. There are two other reasons why it is not
straightforward to find uniformly sized, meaningful categories:

(1) There is no explicit measure of semantic distance among the children
     of a synset.
(2) The hierarchy is not balanced, i.e., the depth from root to leaf varies
     dramatically throughout the hierarchy, as does the branching factor.
     (The hierarchy has ten root nodes; on average their maximum depth
     is 10.5 and their minimum depth is 2.)

Reason (2) rules out a strategy of traveling down a uniform depth from
the root or up a uniform height from the leaves in order to achieve
uniform category sizes.

   For the purposes of the description of this algorithm, a synset is a node
in the hierarchy, and a descendant of synset N is any synset reachable
via a hyponym link from N or any of N's descendants (recursively).
This means that intermediate, or non-leaf synsets, are also classified as
descendants. The term "child" refers to an immediate descendant, i.e.,
a synset directly linked to N via a hyponym link.

   The algorithm used here is controlled by two parameters: upper and
lower bounds on the category size (see Figure 5.2). For example, the
result of setting the lower bound to 25 and the upper bound to 60
yields categories with an average size of 58 members. An arbitrary
node N in the hierarchy is chosen, and if it has not yet been marked as a
member of a category, the algorithm checks to see how many unmarked
descendants it has. In every case, if the number of descendants is too
small, the assignment to a category is deferred until a node higher in

```
for each synset N in the noun hierarchy
  a_cat(N)

a_cat(N):
  if N is unmarked (has not been entered in a category)
      T <- #descendents(N)

      if ((T >= LOWER_BRACKET) &&
          (T <= UPPER_BRACKET))
          mark (N,NewCatNumber)

      else if (T > UPPER_BRACKET)
              for each (direct) child C of N
                  CT <- #descendents(C)
                  if ((CT >= LOWER_BRACKET) &&
                      (CT <= UPPER_BRACKET))
                      mark (C,NewCatNumber)
                  else if (CT > UPPER_BRACKET)
                      a_cat(C)

              T <- #descendents(N)
              if (T >= LOWER_BRACKET)
                  mark (N,NewCatNumber)
```

Figure 5.2
Algorithm for creating categories from WORDNET's noun hierarchy.

the hierarchy is examined (unless the node has no parents). This helps avoid extremely small categories, which are especially undesirable.

If the number of descendants of N falls within the boundaries, the node and its unmarked descendants are bundled into a new category, marked, and assigned a label which is derived from the synset at N. Thus, if N and its unmarked descendants create a category with k members, the number of unmarked descendants of the parent of N decreases by k.

If N has too many descendants, that is, the count of its unmarked descendants exceeds the upper bound, then each of its immediate children is checked in turn: if the child's descendant count falls between the boundaries, then the child and its descendants are bundled into a category. If the child and its unmarked descendants exceed the upper bound, then the procedure is called recursively on the child. Otherwise, the child is too small and is left alone. After all of N's children have been processed, the category that N will participate in has been made as small as the algorithm will allow. There is a chance that N and its unmarked descendants will now make a category that is too small, and if this is the case, N is left alone, and a higher-up node will eventually subsume it (unless N has no parents remaining). Otherwise, N and its remaining unmarked descendants are bundled into a category.

If N has more than one parent, N can end up assigned to the category of any of its parents (or none), depending on which parent was accessed first and how many unmarked children it had at any time, but each synset is assigned to only one category.

The function "mark" places the synset and all its descendents that have not yet been entered into a category into a new category. Note that #descendents is recalculated in the third-to-last line in case any of the children of N have been entered into categories.

In the end there may be isolated small pieces of hierarchy that are not stored in any category, but this can be fixed by a cleanup pass, if desired.

5.3   A Topic Labeler

We are using a version of the disambiguation algorithm described in [Yarowsky, 1992] to assign topic labels to coherent passages of text. Yarowsky defines word senses as the categories listed for a word in *Roget's Thesaurus* (Fourth Edition), where a category is something like TOOLS/MACHINERY. For each category, the algorithm

- Collects contexts that are representative of the category.
- Identifies salient words in the collective contexts and determines the weight for each word.
- Uses the resulting weights to predict the appropriate category for a word occurring in a novel context.

The proper use of this algorithm is to choose among the categories to which a particular ambiguous word can belong, based on the lexical context that surrounds a particular instance of the word.

In our implementation of the algorithm, the 726 categories derived from WORDNET, as described in the previous section, are used instead of *Roget's* categories, because these are not available publicly online. Training is performed on *Grolier's American Academic Encyclopedia* ($\approx$ 8.7M words).

The labeling is done as follows: instead of using the algorithm in the intended way, we are placing probes in the text at evenly-spaced intervals and accumulating the scores for each category all the way

	United States Constitution	*Genesis*
0	assembly (court, legislature)	deity divinity god
1	due_process_of_law	relative relation (mother, aunt)
2	legal_document	worship
3	administrative_unit	man adult_male
4	body (legislative)	professional
5	charge (taxes)	happiness gladness felicity
6	administrator decision_maker	woman adult_female
7	document written_document	evildoing transgression
8	approval (sanction, pass)	literary_composition
9	power powerfulness	religionist religious_person

Table 5.1
Output using original category set on two well-known texts.

through the text. The intention is that at the end the highest scoring categories correspond to the main topics of the text. This algorithm is described in more detail in [Hearst, 1994]. Table 5.1 shows the output of the labeler on two well-known texts (made available online by Project Gutenberg). The first column indicates the rank of the category, and the second and third columns show the words in the synset at the top-most node of the category for each text (these are not always entirely descriptive, so some glosses are provided in parentheses).

Note that although most of the categories are appropriate (with the glaring exception of "professional" in *Genesis*), there is some redundancy among them, and in some cases they are too fine-level to indicate main topic information.

In an earlier implementation of this algorithm, the categories were in general larger but less coherent than in the current set. The larger categories resulted in better-trained classifications, but the classes often conflated quite disparate terms. The current implementation produces smaller, more coherent categories. The advantage is that a more distinct meaning can be associated with a particular label, but the disadvantage is that in many cases so few of the words in the category appear in the training data that a weak model is formed. Then the categories with little distinguishing training data dominate the labeling scores inappropriately.

In the category-derivation algorithm described above, in order to increase the size of a given category, terms must be taken from nodes adjacent in the hierarchy (either descendants or siblings). However, adjacent terms are not necessarily closely related semantically, and so after a point, expanding the category via adjacent terms introduces noise. To remedy this problem, we have experimented with increasing the size of the categories in two different ways:

(1) The first approach is to retain the categories in their current form and add semantically similar terms, extracted from corpora independent of WORDNET, thus improving the training of the labeling algorithm.

(2) The second approach is to determine which categories are semantically related to one another, despite the fact that they come from quite different parts of the hierarchy, and combine them so that they form schema-like associations.

These are described in the next two sections, respectively.

5.4 Augmenting Categories with Relevant Terms

As mentioned above, one way to improve the categories is to expand them with related relevant terms. In this section we show how comparing WordSpace vectors to the derived categories allows us to expand the categories. The first subsection describes the WordSpace algorithm, and the subsequent subsections show how it can be used to augment the derived categories.

5.4.1 Creating WordSpace from free text

WordSpace [Schütze, 1993b] is a corpus-based method for inducing semantic representations for a large number of words (50,000) from lexical cooccurrence statistics. The representations are derived from free text, and therefore are highly specific to the text type in question. The medium of representation is a multi-dimensional, real-valued vector space. The cosine of the angle between two vectors in the space is a continuous measure of their semantic relatedness.

Lexical cooccurrence, which is the basis for creating the word space vectors, can be easily measured. However, for a vocabulary of 50,000 words, there are 2,500,000,000 possible cooccurrence counts, a number too high to be computationally tractable. Therefore, *letter fourgrams* are used here to bootstrap the representations. Cooccurrence statistics are collected for 5,000 selected fourgrams. The 5000-by-5000 matrix used for this purpose is manageable. A vector for a lexical item is then computed as the sum of fourgram vectors that occur close to it in the text.

The first step of the creation of WordSpace consists of deriving fourgram vectors that reflect semantic similarity in the sense of being used to describe the same contexts. Consequently, one needs to be able to pairwise compare fourgrams' contexts. For this purpose, a *collocation matrix* for fourgrams was collected such that the entry $a_{i,j}$ counts the number of times that fourgram i occurs at most 200 fourgrams to the left of fourgram j. Two columns in this matrix are similar according to the cosine measure if the contexts the corresponding fourgrams are used in are similar. The counts were determined using five months of the *New York Times* (June – October 1990). The resulting collocation matrix is dense: only 2% of entries are zeros, because almost any two fourgrams cooccur. Only 10% of entries are smaller than 10, so that culling small counts would not increase the sparseness of the matrix. Consequently, any computation that employs the fourgram vectors directly would be inefficient. For this reason, a singular value decomposition was performed and 97 singular values extracted (cf. [Deerwester *et al.*, 1990]) using an algorithm from SVDPACK [Berry, 1992]. Each fourgram can then be represented by a vector of 97 real values. Since the singular value decomposition finds the best least-square approximation of the original space in 97 dimensions, two fourgram vectors will be similar if their original vectors in the collocation matrix are similar. The reduced fourgram vectors can be efficiently used in the following computations.

Cooccurrence information was used for a second time to compute word representations from the fourgram vectors: in this case cooccurrence of a target word with any of the 5000 fourgrams. 50,000 words that occurred at least 20 times in 50,000,000 words of the *New York Times* newswire were selected. For each of the words, a context vector was computed for every position at which it occurred in the text. A context vector was defined as the sum of all defined fourgram vectors in a window of 1001 fourgrams centered around the target word. The context vectors were then normalized and summed. This sum of vectors is the vector representation of the target word. It is the *confusion* of all its uses in the corpus. More formally, if $C(w)$ is the set of positions in the corpus at which w occurs and if $\varphi(f)$ is the vector representation for fourgram

word	nearest neighbors
burglar	burglars thief rob mugging stray robbing lookout chase
disable	deter intercept repel halting surveillance shield
disenchantment	disenchanted sentiment resentment grudging mindful
domestically	domestic auto/-s importers/-ed threefold inventories
Dour	melodies/-dic Jazzie danceable reggae synthesizers Soul
grunts	heap into ragged goose neatly pulls buzzing rake odd
kid	dad kidding mom ok buddies Mom Oh Hey hey mama
S.O.B.	Confessions Jill Julie biography Judith Novak Lois
Ste.	dry oyster whisky hot filling rolls lean float bottle ice
workforce	jobs employ/-s/-ed/-ing attrition workers clerical

Table 5.2
Ten random words and their nearest neighbors.

f, then the vector representation $\tau(w)$ of w is defined as: (the dot stands for normalization)

$$\tau(w) = \sum_{i \in C(w)} \left(\sum_{f \text{ close to } i}^{\bullet} \varphi(f) \right)$$

Table 5.2 shows a random sample of 10 words and their nearest neighbors in Word Space (using the cosine measure). As can be seen from the table, proximity in the space corresponds closely to semantic similarity in the corpus. (*N'Dour* is a Senegalese jazz musician. In the 1989/90 *New York Times*, *S.O.B.* mainly occurs in the book title "Confessions of an S.O.B.," and *Ste.* in the name "Ste.-Marguerite" a Quebec river that is popular for salmon fishing.)

5.4.2 Augmenting WORDNET categories using WordSpace

We chose the following simple mapping from the derived WORDNET categories to WordSpace:

- for each word w in WordSpace
- collect the 20 nearest neighbors of w in the space
- compute the score s_i of category i for w as the number of nearest neighbors that are in i
- assign w to the highest scoring category or categories

In order to test this algorithm, we selected 1000 words from the medium frequency words in WordSpace.[4] These turned out to be the medium-frequency words from *deforestation* to *downed*. The following subsections describe the application of the assignment algorithm to classifying proper names, reassigning words in the categories, and assigning words that are not covered by the categories.

category	highest scoring proper names
artist creative_person	degas delacroix
European_country European_nation	delors dienstbier diestel
performer performing_artist; dramatic composition	deniro dennehy depalma delancey depardieu dern desi devito dey diaghilev doogie dourif
musical_organization musical_group; musician player; music	depeche(mode) deville diddley dido dire(straits) doo doobie (n')dour
athlete jock	dehere delpino demarco deleon deshaies detmer dibiaggio dinah doleman doughty doran dowis
due_process due_process_of_law	degeorge depetris devita dichiara dicicco diles dilorenzo dougan

Table 5.3
Assigning proper names to WORDNET categories.

Semantic classification of proper names   A deficiency of WORDNET for our text labeling task and for many other applications is that it omits many proper names (and since the set of important proper names changes over time, it cannot be expected to contain an exhaustive list). We tested the performance of our assignment algorithm by searching for proper names that had high scores for the categories in Table 5.3. For each category on the left-hand side we show all of the proper names that assigned high scores to those categories. The proper names assigned to "artist" are painters, the proper names assigned to "European country" are European politicians, "performer" contains actors, dancers and

---

[4] WordSpace has three parts: high-frequency, medium-frequency, and low-frequency words. The words in the test set have the internal identification numbers 26,000 through 26,999.

word	highest scoring category
dosage	medicine medication medicament
dissertation	science scientific_discipline
Derbies	horse Equus_caballus
dl	athlete jock

Table 5.4
Finding terms that characterize the senses of words better than the corresponding WORDNET assignment does (see Table 5.5).

roles, writers and titles of movies, "music" has musicians and titles of musical performances (the Pasadena Doo Dah Parade, Purcell's "Dido and Aeneas"), "athlete jock" players of various sports, and "process of law" lawyers, judges and defendants. We checked the referents of all proper names in Table 5.3 in the *New York Times* and found only one error: The President of Michigan State University, John DiBiaggio, was assigned to the "athlete" category because his name is mainly mentioned in articles dealing with a conflict he had with his athletic department. However, a few names like "DePalma" and "Delancey" had several referents only one of whom pertained to the assigned category.

Fine-tuning WORDNET **terms**   The assignment algorithm can also be employed to adjust the assignments of individual words in the WORD-NET hierarchy by matching against the derived categories. Two kinds of adjustments are possible: specializing senses and adding senses that are not covered. Two examples of each case from the 1000 word test set are given in Table 5.4.

   Dosage and *dissertation* are defined in a very general way in WORDNET (see Table 5.5). While they can be used with the general sense given in WORDNET, almost all uses of *dissertation* in the *New York Times* are for doctoral dissertations that report on scientific work. Similarly, non-medical contexts are conceivable for *dosage*, but the dosages that the *New York Times* mentions are exclusively dosages of radiation or medicine in a medical context. The automatically found labelings in Table 5.4 indicate the need for specialization and can be used as the basis for reassignment.

   In some cases, the WORDNET hierarchy is also incomplete. The two senses "horse race" and "Disabled List" for *derby* and *dl* are missing from WORDNET, although they are the dominant uses in the *New York Times*.

word	WORDNET definition
dosage	dose, dosage – (the quantity of an active agent (substance or radiation) taken in or absorbed at any one time)
dissertation	dissertation, thesis => treatise – (a formal exposition)
derby	bowler hat, bowler, derby, plug hat – (round and black and hard with a narrow brim; worn by some British businessmen)
dl	deciliter, decilitre, dl

Table 5.5
Synonym sets in WORDNET for the words in Table 5.4.

Again the classification algorithm finds the right topic area for the two words which can be used as the basis for reassignment. Unfortunately, the algorithm also labels some correctly assigned words with incorrect categories.

Assigning unknown words   We would like to be able to handle unknown words since they are often highly specific and excellent indicators for the topical structure of a document. Table 5.6 shows the automatic assignments for all words in the 1000 word test set that were not found in WORDNET.

The results are mixed. 63% (17/27) of the words are assigned to a correct topic (+), an additional 19% (5/27) are assigned to topics they are related to (0), 19% are misassigned (–). We are considering several ways of improving the assignment algorithm. For instance, there are "diluted" categories such as "speech_act" and "trait character feature" whose members are mostly words that are poorly characterized collocationally. If we ignore them in assigning categories (hoping that most unknown words will be topic-specific special terms) we can correct some of the errors, e.g., *disunity* would be assigned to "group_action interaction social_activity" which seems correct. We expect that we can improve the results in Table 5.6 as we gain more experience in combining WordSpace and WORDNET.

These results are encouraging; we have not yet tested to see if they improve the topic labeler, however.

word	score	highest scoring categories
degradable	+	compound chemical_compound
demagoguery	0	feeling emotion
deprenyl	+	infectious_disease; disease
desktop	+	memory_device storage_device
deuterium	+	chemical_element element; substance matter
(pas de) deux	+	dancing dance terpsichore
dideoxyinosine	+	medicine medication medicament; infectious_disease
(per) diem	+	commercial_document/instrument; occupation
dieters	+	foodstuff
dinnerware	+	tableware
dioxins	+	chemical_element element
dispersants	0	change alteration modification
disservice	−	cognitive_state state_of_mind
dissidence	+	leader; social_group
disunity	−	speech_act
diuretic	+	symptom
diuretics	+	disease; liquid_body_substance body_fluid
doctrinal	+	religion faith church
dogfight	+	happening occurrence; conflict struggle
doggie	−	unpleasant_person persona_non_grata
doggone	−	unit_of_measurement unit; integer whole_number
Domaine	+	wine vino
domesticity	−	person individual man mortal human soul; feeling
dopamine	+	medicine medication medicament; room
dossier	0	statement; message content subject_matter substance
doubleheaders	0	time_period period period_of_time amount_of_time
downbeat	0	message content subject_matter substance; feeling

Table 5.6
Assigning unknown words to semantically relevant categories.
Key: + correct; 0 related; − incorrect.

5.5   Combining Distant Categories

This section describes an algorithm that uses Word Space vectors to help determine which WORDNET-derived categories should be combined to create new, more schema-like categories.

5.5.1   The algorithm

To find which categories should be considered closest to one another, we first determined how close they are in WordSpace and then grouped categories together that mutually ranked one another highly.

To compute the first-degree closeness of two categories c_i and c_j we used the formula:

$$D(c_i, c_j) = \frac{1}{2} \frac{1}{|c_i||c_j|} \sum_{\vec{v} \in c_i} \sum_{\vec{w} \in c_j} d(\vec{v}, \vec{w})$$

where d is the square of the Euclidean distance:

$$d(\vec{v}, \vec{w}) = \sum_i (v_i - w_i)^2$$

The primary rank of category i for category j indicates how closely related i is to j. For instance rank 1 means that i is the closest category to j, and rank 3 means there are only two closer categories to j than i.

The second-degree closeness is computed from the rank of the primary ranks. To determine that close association is mutual between two categories, we check for mutual high ranking. Thus category i and j are grouped together if and only if i ranks j highly and j ranks i highly (where "highly" was determined by a cutoff value – i and j had to be ranked k or above with respect to each other, for a threshold k). Secondary ranking is needed because some categories are especially "popular," attracting many other categories to them; the secondary rank enables the popular categories to retain only those categories that they mutually rank highly.

The results of this algorithm are best interpreted via a graphical layout. Figure 5.3 shows a piece of a network created using a presentation tool [Amir, 1993] based on theoretical work by [Fruchtermann and Rheingold, 1990]. The underlying algorithm uses a force-directed placement model to layout complex networks (edges are modeled as springs; nodes linked by edges are attracted to each other, but all other pairs of nodes are repelled from one another).

In these networks only connectivity has meaning; distance between nodes does not connote semantic distance. The connectivity of the network is interesting also because it indicates the interconnectivity between categories. From Figure 5.3, we see that categories associated with the notion *sports*, such as *athletic_game, race, sports_equipment,* and *sports_implement,* have been grouped together. *Athletics* is linked to *competition* and *vehicle* categories; these in turn link to *weaponry* and *military_vehicles* categories, which then lead in to *legal* categories.

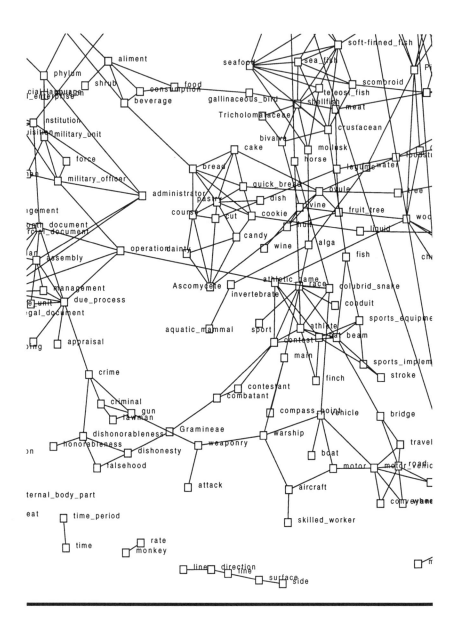

Figure 5.3
A piece of the network that results from determining which categories are mutually
close to each other using WordSpace.

The network also shows that categories that are specified to be near one another in WORDNET, such as the categories related to *bread*, are found to be closely interrelated. This is useful in case we would like to begin with smaller categories, in order to eliminate some of the large, broad categories that we are currently working with.

Most of the connectivity information suggested by the network was used to create the new categories. However, many of the desirable relationships do not appear in the network, perhaps because of the requirement for highly mutual co-ranking. If we were to relax this assumption we may find better coverage, but perhaps at the cost of more misleading links. The remaining associations where determined by hand, so that the original 726 categories were combined into 106 new super-categories. Unlike for the original categories, the names for the super-categories were chosen by the authors.

5.5.2   Revised topic assignments

The super-categories are intended to group together related categories in order to eliminate topical redundancy in the labeler and to help eliminate inappropriate labels (since the categories are larger and so have more lexical items serving as evidence). Thus the top four or five super-categories should suffice to indicate the main topics of documents. A comparison of the results of the labeling algorithm using super-categories against reader judgments appears in [Hearst, 1994]. Here we show some example output and discuss its characteristics.

Figure 5.4 compares the results of the labeler using the original categories against the super-categories. It should be kept in mind that only the top four or five labels are to be used from the super-categories; since each super-category subsumes many categories, only a few super-categories should be expected to contain the most relevant information. The first article is a 31-sentence magazine article, published in 1987, taken from [Morris, 1988]. It describes how Soviet women have little political power, discusses their role as working women, and describes the benefits of college life. The second article is a 77-sentence popular science magazine article about the Magellan space probe exploring Venus. When using the super-categories, the labeler avoids grossly inappropriate labels such as "mollusk_genus" and "goddess" in the Magellan article, and combines categories such as "layer," "natural_depression," and "rock stone" into the one super-category "land terra_firma."

Raisa Gorbachev article	
Original Categories	*Super-Categories*
0 woman adult_female	social_standing
1 status social_state	education
2 man adult_male	politics
3 political_orientation ideology	legal_system
4 force personnel	people
5 charge	psychological_state
6 relationship	socializing
7 fear	social_group
8 attitude	personal_relationship
9 educator pedagogue	government

Magellan space probe article	
Original Categories	*Super-Categories*
0 celestial_body heavenly_body	outer_space
1 mollusk_genus	light_and_energy
2 electromagnetic_radiation	atmosphere
3 layer (surface)	land terra_firma
4 atmospheric_phenomenon	physics
5 physical_phenomenon	arrangement
6 goddess	shapes
7 natural_depression depression	water_and_liquids
8 rock stone	properties
9 space (hole)	amounts

Figure 5.4
Comparison of original and super categories.

Looking again at the longer texts of the *United States Constitution* and *Genesis* we see in Figure 5.5 that the super-categories are more general and less redundant than the categories shown in Figure 5.1. (Although the high scores for the "breads" category seems incorrect, even though the term "bread" occurs 25 times in *Genesis*.) In some cases the user might desire more specific categories; this experiment suggests that the labeler can generate topic labels at multiple levels of granularity.

United States Constitution	
Original Categories	*Super-Categories*
0 assembly (court, legislature)	legal_system
1 due_process_of_law	government
2 legal_document legal_instrument	politics
3 administrative_unit	conflict
4 body (legislative)	crime
5 charge (taxes)	finance
6 administrator decision_maker	social_standing
7 document written_document	honesty
8 approval (sanction, pass)	communication

Genesis	
Original Categories	*Super-Categories*
0 deity divinity god	religion
1 relative relation (mother, aunt)	breads
2 worship	mythology
3 man adult_male	people
4 professional	social_outcasts
5 happiness gladness felicity	social_group
6 woman adult_female	psychological_state
7 evildoing transgression	personality
8 literary_composition	literature

Figure 5.5
Comparison of original and super categories for two well-known texts.

5.6   Conclusions

We have discussed two approaches to augmenting and rearranging the components of a lexicon, in effect adding new features to its members, by making use of lexical association information from a large corpus. We've used lexical cooccurrence statistics in combination with a modified lexicon to classify proper names, associate more specific senses to broadly defined terms, and classify new words into existing categories with some degree of success. We've also used these statistics to suggest how to rearrange a lexicon with a taxonymic structure into more frame-like categories, and assigned more general main-topic labels to texts based on these categories.

One conclusion that may be drawn from this work is that we have provided a mechanism for successfully combining hand-built lexicon information with knowledge-free, statistically-derived information. The combined information from the categories derived from WORDNET provided the clusters from which WordSpace centroids could be created, and these centroids in turn provided candidate words to improve the categories.

In future, in addition to expanding the evaluation of the results described here, we would like to try reversing the experiment; that is, starting with WordSpace vectors, see which parts of WORDNET should be interlinked into schematic categories.

Acknowledgments

The authors would like to thank Jan Pedersen for his help and encouragement. We are also indebted to Mike Berry for SVDPACK. The first author's research was sponsored in part by the Advanced Research Projects Agency under Grant No. MDA972-92-J-1029 with the Corporation for National Research Initiatives (CNRI), in part by an internship at Xerox Palo Alto Research Center; and this material is based in part upon work supported by the National Science Foundation under Infrastructure Grant No. CDA-8722788. The second author was supported in part by the National Center for Supercomputing Applications under grant BNS930000N.

6 Towards Building Contextual Representations of Word Senses Using Statistical Models

Claudia Leacock, Geoffrey Towell, Ellen M. Voorhees

6.1 Contextual Representations

In this chapter we investigate automatic sense resolution techniques that acquire *contextual representations* of word senses. A contextual representation, as defined by [Miller and Charles, 1991], is a characterization of the linguistic contexts in which a word can express a particular sense. We look at two components of contextual representations that can be automatically extracted from textual corpora using statistical methods. These are *topical context* and *local context*.

Topical context is comprised of substantive words that are likely to co-occur with a given sense of a target word. If, for example, the polysemous word *line* occurs in a sentence with *poetry* and *write*, it is probably being used to express a different sense of *line* than if it occurred with *stand* and *wait*. Topical context is generally insensitive to the order of words or their grammatical inflections; the focus is on the meanings of the open-class words that are used together in the same sentences.

Local context includes information on word order, distance and syntactic structure; it is not limited to open-class words. For example, 'a line from' does not suggest the same sense as 'in line for.' Unlike topical context, order and inflection are critical clues for local context.

In the next section, we examine three statistical classifiers designed for sense resolution, and show that they are effective in extracting topical context. Section 3 describes the performance of human subjects on the sense disambiguation task. We use the humans' performance as an upper bound on the effectiveness of the statistical classifiers. Section 4 describes techniques we are developing to extract local context.

6.2 Acquiring Topical Context

Of the two types of context features, topical ones seem easier to identify. The idea is simple: for any topic there is a sub-vocabulary of terms that are appropriate for discussing it. The task is to identify the topic, then to select that sense of the polysemous word that best fits the topic. For example consider the noun 'sheet': if the topic is writing, then it probably refers to a piece of paper; if the topic is sleeping, then it probably refers to bed linen; if the topic is sailing, it could refer to a sail or a rope; and so on.

Instead of using topics to discover senses, one can use senses to discover topics. That is to say, if the senses are known in advance for a textual corpus, it is possible to search for words that are likely to co-occur with each sense. This strategy requires two steps. It is necessary (1) to partition a sizeable number of occurrences of a polysemous word according to its senses, and then (2) to use the resulting sets of instances to search for co-occurring words that are diagnostic of each sense. That was the strategy followed with considerable success by [Gale et al., 1992], who used a bilingual corpus for (1), and a Bayesian decision system for (2).

To understand this and other statistical systems better, we posed a very specific problem: given a set of contexts, each containing the noun *line* in a known sense, construct a classifier that selects the correct sense of *line* for new contexts. To see how the degree of polysemy affects performance, we ran both three- and six-sense tasks. A full description of the three-sense task is reported in [Voorhees et al., 1992], and the six-sense task in [Leacock et al., 1993]. We review these experiments below for completeness.

6.2.1 Methodology

The training and testing contexts were taken from the 1987-89 *Wall Street Journal* corpus and from the APHB corpus.[1] Sentences containing *line(s)* and *Line(s)* were extracted and manually assigned a single sense from WORDNET [Miller, 1990]. Sentences with proper names containing *Line*, such as *Japan Air Lines*, were removed from the set of sentences. Sentences containing collocations that have a single sense in WORDNET, such as *product line* and *line of products*, were also excluded since these collocations are not ambiguous.

Typically, experiments have used a fixed number of words or charac-

---

[1] The 25 million word corpus, obtained from the American Printing House for the Blind, is archived at IBM's T.J. Watson Research Center; it consists of stories and articles from books and general circulation magazines.

ters on either side of the target word as the context. In these experiments, we used linguistic units—sentences—instead. Since the target word is often used anaphorically to refer back to the previous sentence, as in:

> That was the last time Bell ever talked on the *phone*. He couldn't get his wife off the *line*.

We chose to use two-sentence contexts: the sentence containing *line* and the preceding sentence. However, if the sentence containing *line* was the first sentence in the article, then the context consisted of one sentence. If the preceding sentence also contained *line* in the same sense, then an additional preceding sentence was added to the context, creating contexts three or more sentences long. The average size of the training and testing contexts was 44.5 words.

The sense resolution task used the six senses of the noun *line* shown in Figure 6.1. The figure gives both a short gloss and an example context for each sense.

The classifiers were run three times each on randomly selected training sets. The set of contexts for each sense was randomly permuted, with each permutation corresponding to one *trial*. For each trial, the first 200 contexts of each sense were selected as training contexts. The next 149 contexts were selected as test contexts. The remaining contexts were not used in that trial. The 200 training contexts for each sense were combined to form a final training set of size 1200. The final test set contained the 149 test contexts from each sense, for a total of 894 contexts.

To test the effect that the number of training examples has on classifier performance, smaller training sets of 50 and 100 contexts were extracted from the 200 context training set. The same set of 849 test contexts was used with each of the training sets in a given trial.

6.2.2   Classifiers

We tested three corpus-based statistical sense resolution methods. Each classifier attempts to infer the correct sense of a polysemous word by using knowledge about patterns of word co-occurrences. The first technique, developed by [Gale *et al.*, 1992] at AT&T Bell Laboratories, is based on Bayesian decision theory, the second is based on content vectors as used in information retrieval [Salton *et al.*, 1975], and the third

1. **text**: spoken or written text
   A local minister forbade his congregation to see "Hamlet" — presumably because of cuss words added by the company. And there were mishaps, as when Gus Watson, the grocer, forgot the **line** "how now Lord Hamlet" and settled for "Hi."

2. **formation**: a formation of people or things
   On the way to work one morning, he stops at the building to tell Mr. Arkhipov: "Don't forget the drains today." Back in his office, the **line** of people waiting to see him has dwindled, so Mr. Goncharov stops in to see the mayor, Yuri Khivrich.

3. **division**: an abstract division
   Thus, some families are probably buying take-out food from grocery stores—such as barbecued chicken—but aren't classifying it as such. The **line** between groceries and take-out food may have become blurred.

4. **phone**: a telephone connection
   "Hello, Weaver," he said and then to put her on the defensive, "what's all the gabbing on the house phones? I couldn't get an open **line** to you."

5. **cord**: a thin flexible object; cord
   The stunts performed on the rope were the most interesting to me, however. The tightly stretched **line** served as a horizontal bar; it had just enough spring to allow the contestants to combine their strength, nimbleness, and sense of timing into an astonishing array of acrobatic tricks.

6. **product**: a product
   International Business Machines Corp., seeking to raise the return on its massive research and development investments, said it will start charging more money to license its 32,000 patents around the world. In announcing the change, IBM also said that it's willing to license patents for its PS/2 **line** of personal computers.

Figure 6.1
Representative contexts for the six senses of 'line' used in the study.

is based on neural networks with back propagation [Rumelhart *et al.*, 1986]. The only information used by the three classifiers is co-occurrence of character strings in the contexts. They use no other cues, such as syntactic tags or word order, nor do they require any augmentation of the training and testing data that is not fully automatic.

Bayesian Classifier The Bayesian classifier uses Bayes' decision theory for weighting tokens that co-occur with each sense of a polysemous target. Their work is inspired by [Mosteller and Wallace, 1964], who applied Bayes' theorem to the problem of author discrimination. The main component of the model, a *token*, was defined as any character string: a word, number, symbol, punctuation or any combination. The entire token is significant, so inflected forms of a base word (*wait* vs. *waiting*) and mixed case strings (*Bush* vs. *bush*) are distinct tokens. Associated with each token is a set of *saliences*, one for each sense, calculated from the training data. The salience of a token for a given sense is $\Pr(token|sense)/\Pr(token)$. The *weight* of a token for a given sense is the log of its salience.

To select the sense of the target word in a (test) context, the classifier computes the sum of the tokens' *weights* over all tokens in the context for each sense, and selects the sense with the largest sum. In the case of author identification, Mosteller and Wallace built their models using high frequency function words. With sense resolution, the salient tokens include content words, which have much lower frequencies of occurrence. Gale, *et. al.* devised a method for estimating the required probabilities using sparse training data. In particular, they adjust their estimates for new or infrequent words by interpolating between local and global estimates of the probability.

The Bayesian classifier runs for this experiment were performed by Kenneth Church of AT&T Bell Laboratories. To remain consistent with the other classifiers, the two-sentence contexts described above are used in place of a fixed-sized window of ±50 tokens surrounding the target word that Gale, *et. al.* previously used. Since the average context size is 44.5 tokens, the classifier is using a smaller amount of context to estimate the probabilities than Gale, *et. al.* find optimal.

Content Vector Classifier The content vector approach to sense resolution is motivated by the vector-space model of information retrieval systems [Salton *et al.*, 1975], where each *concept* in a corpus defines an axis of the vector space, and a text in the corpus is represented as a point in this space. The concepts in a corpus are usually defined as the set of word stems that appear in the corpus (e.g., the strings *computer(s)*, *computing*, *computation(al)*, etc. are conflated to the concept *comput*) minus *stopwords*, a set of about 570 very high frequency words that includes function words (e.g., *the, by, you, that, who*, etc.) and content words (e.g., *be, say*, etc.). The similarity between two texts is computed as a function of the vectors representing the two texts.

For the sense resolution problem, each sense is represented by a single vector constructed from the training contexts for that sense. A vector in the space defined by the training contexts is also constructed for each test context. To select a sense for a test context, the inner product between its vector and each of the sense vectors is computed, and the sense whose inner product is the largest is chosen.

The components of the vectors are weighted to reflect the relative importance of the concepts in the text. The weighting method was designed to favor concepts that occur frequently in exactly one sense. The weight of a concept c is computed as follows:

$$\text{Let } n_s = \text{ number of times } c \text{ occurs in sense } s$$
$$p = n_s / \sum_{\text{senses}} n_s$$
$$d = \text{ difference between the two largest } n_s$$
$$\text{(if difference is 0, } d \text{ is set to 1)}$$

$$\text{then } w_s = p * \min(n_s, d)$$

For example, if a concept occurs 6 times in the training contexts of sense 1, and zero times in the other five sets of contexts, then its weights in the six vectors are $(6, 0, 0, 0, 0, 0)$. However, a concept that appears 10, 4, 7, 0, 1, and 2 times in the respective senses, has weights of $(1.25, .5, .88, 0, .04, .17)$, reflecting the fact that it is not as good an indicator for any sense. This weighting method is the most effective among several variants that were tried.

We also experimented with keeping all words in the content vectors, but performance degraded, probably because the weighting function does not handle very high frequency words well. This is evident in Table 6.1, where 'mr' is highly weighted for three different senses.

Neural Network Classifier   The neural network approach [Rumelhart *et al.*, 1986] casts sense resolution as a supervised learning paradigm. Pairs of [input features, desired response] are presented to a learning program, e.g., back propagation. The program's task is to devise some method for using the input features to partition the training contexts into non-overlapping sets corresponding to the desired responses. This is achieved by adjusting link weights so that the output unit representing the desired response has a larger activation than any other output unit.

Each context is translated into a bit-vector. As with the content vector approach, suffixes are removed to conflate related word forms to a common stem, and *stopwords* and punctuation are removed. Each stem that appears at least twice in the entire training set is assigned to a bit-vector position. The resulting vector has ones in positions corresponding to concepts in the context and zeros otherwise. This procedure creates vectors with more than 4000 positions. The vectors are, however, extremely sparse; on average they contain slightly more than 17 concepts.

Networks are trained until the output of the unit corresponding to the desired response is greater than the output of any other unit for every training example. For testing, the classification determined by the network is given by the unit with the largest output. Weights in neural networks may be either positive or negative, thereby allowing accumulation of evidence both for and against a sense.

The result of training a network until all examples are classified correctly is that infrequent tokens can acquire disproportionate importance. For example, the context *'Fine,' Henderson said, aimiably* [sic]. *'Can you get him on the line?'* clearly uses *line* in the *phone* sense. However, the only non-stopwords that are infrequent in other senses are 'henderson' and 'aimiably'; and, due to its misspelling, the latter is conflated to 'aim.' The network must raise the weight of 'henderson' so that it is sufficient to give *phone* the largest output. As a result, 'henderson' appears in Table 6.1, in spite of its infrequency in the training corpus.

To determine a good topology for the network, various network topologies were explored: networks with from 0 to 100 hidden units arranged in a single hidden layer; networks with multiple layers of hidden units; and networks with a single layer of hidden units in which the output units were connected to both the hidden and input units. In all cases, the network configuration with no hidden units was either superior or statistically indistinguishable from the more complex networks. As no network topology was significantly better than one with no hidden units, all data reported here are derived from such networks.

Product			Formation		
Bayesian	Vector	Network	Bayesian	Vector	Network
Chrysler	comput	comput	night	wait	wait
workstations	ibm	sell	checkout	long	long
Digital	produc	minicomput	wait	checkout	stand
introduced	corp	model	gasoline	park	checkout
models	sale	introduc	outside	mr	park
IBM	model	extend	waiting	airport	hour
Compaq	sell	acquir	food	shop	form
sell	introduc	launch	hours	count	short
agreement	brand	continu	long	peopl	custom
computers	mainframe	quak	driver	canad	shop

Text			Cord		
Bayesian	Vector	Network	Bayesian	Vector	Network
Biden	speech	familiar	fish	fish	hap
ad	writ	writ	fishing	boat	fish
Bush	mr	ad	bow	wat	wash
opening	bush	rememb	deck	hook	pull
famous	ad	deliv	sea	wash	boat
Dole	speak	fame	boat	float	rope
speech	read	speak	water	men	break
Dukakis	dukak	funny	clothes	dive	hook
funny	biden	movie	fastened	cage	exercis
speeches	poem	read	ship	rod	cry

Division			Phone		
Bayesian	Vector	Network	Bayesian	Vector	Network
blurred	draw	draw	phones	telephon	telephon
walking	fine	priv	toll	phon	phon
crossed	blur	hug	porn	call	dead
ethics	cross	blur	Bellsouth	access	cheer
narrow	walk	cross	gab	dial	hear
fine	narrow	fine	telephone	gab	henderson
class	mr	thin	Bell	bell	minut
between	tread	funct	billion	servic	call
walk	faction	genius	Pacific	toll	bill
draw	thin	narrow	calls	porn	silent

Table 6.1
Topical Context. The ten most heavily weighted tokens for each sense of 'line' for the
Bayesian, content vector and neural network classifiers.

6.2.3   Results

All of the classifiers performed best with the largest number (200) of training contexts, and the percent correct results reported here are averaged over the three trials with 200 training contexts. On the six-sense task, the Bayesian classifier averaged 71% correct answers, the content vector classifier 72%, and the neural networks 76%. None of these differences are statistically significant due to the limited sample size of three trials.

The ten most heavily weighted tokens for each sense for each classifier appear in Table 6.1. The words on the list seem, for the most part, indicative of the target sense and are reasonable indicators of topical context. However, there are some consistent differences among the methods. For example, while the Bayesian method is sensitive to proper nouns, the neural network appears to have no such preference. To test the hypothesis that the methods have different response patterns, we performed the χ^2 test for correlated proportions. This test measures how consistently the methods treat individual test contexts by determining whether the classifiers are making the same classification errors in each of the senses.

The results of the χ^2 test for a three-sense resolution task (*product, formation* and *text*),[2] indicate that the response pattern of the content vector classifier is significantly different from the patterns of both the Bayesian and neural network classifiers, but the Bayesian response pattern is significantly different from the neural network pattern for the *product* sense only. In the six-sense disambiguation task, the χ^2 results indicate that the Bayesian and neural network classifiers' response patterns are not significantly different for any sense. The neural network and Bayesian classifiers' response patterns are significantly different from the content vector classifier only in the *formation* and *text* senses. Therefore, with the addition of three senses, the classifiers' response patterns appear to be converging.

A pilot two-sense distinction task (between *product* and *formation*) yielded over 90% correct answers.[3] In the three-sense distinction task, the three classifiers had a mean of 76% correct, yielding a sharp degra-

---

[2] Training and test sets for these senses are identical to those in the six-sense resolution task.

[3] This task was only run with the content vector and neural network classifiers.

dation with the addition of a third sense. Therefore, we hypothesized degree of polysemy to be a major factor for performance. We were surprised to find that in the six-sense task, all three classifiers degraded only slightly from the three-sense task, with a mean of 73% correct. Although the addition of three new senses to the task caused consistent degradation, the degradation is relatively slight. Hence, we conclude that some senses are harder to resolve than others, and it appears that overall accuracy is a function of the difficulty of the sense rather than being strictly a function of the degree of polysemy. The hardest sense for all three classifiers to learn was *text*, followed by *formation*, followed by *division*. The difficulty in training for the *product*, *phone*, and *cord* senses varied among the classifiers, but they were the three 'easiest' senses across the classifiers. To test our conclusion that the difficulty involved in learning individual senses is a greater factor for performance than degree of polysemy, we ran a three-way experiment on the three 'easy' senses. On this task, the content vector classifier achieved 90% accuracy and neural network classifier 92% accuracy.

The convergence of the response patterns for the three methods suggests that each of the classifiers is extracting as much data as is available in word co-occurrences in the training contexts. If this is the case, any technique that uses only word counts will not be significantly more accurate than the techniques tested here. Although the degree of polysemy does affect the difficulty of the sense resolution task, a greater factor for performance is the difficulty of resolving individual senses. From inspection of the contexts for the various senses, it appears that the senses of *line* that were easy to learn tend to be surrounded by a lot of topical context. With the senses that were hard to learn, the crucial disambiguating information tends to be very local, so that a greater proportion of the context is noise. Although it is well known that local information is more reliable than distant information, the classifiers make no use of locality. Recall that Figure 6.1 shows some representative contexts for each sense of *line* used in the study. The *product*, *phone* and *cord* senses contain a lot of topical context, while the other senses have little or no information that is not very local.

In general, the three classifiers are doing a good job finding topical context. However, simply knowing which words are likely to co-occur in the same sentences when a particular topic is under discussion is not sufficient for accurate sense resolution.

6.3   An Upper Bound for Classifier Performance

In an effort to verify that the statistical classifiers were performing about as well as they could on the basis of the information they had to work with, we decided to see how native English speakers would perform on a sense resolution task using the same input that drives the statistical classifiers. An experiment by [Leacock *et al.*, in preparation] was designed to answer the following questions:

1. How do humans perform in a sense resolution task when given the same testing input as the statistical classifiers?
2. Are the contexts that are hard/easy for the statistical classifiers also hard/easy for people?
3. Are the senses that are hard/easy for the statistical classifiers also hard/easy for people?

The three-sense task reported in [Voorhees *et al.*, 1992] was replicated using human subjects. For each of the three senses of *line* used in the original experiment (*product, text*, and *formation*), we selected the following contexts from the original experiment: 10 *easy* contexts (contexts that were correctly classified by the three statistical methods) and 10 *hard* contexts (contexts that were misclassified by the three methods), for a total of 60 contexts. These contexts were prepared in three formats: (1) a sentential format (as they originally appeared in the corpus), (2) a *long* list format (as was used by the Bayesian classifier), and (3) a *short* list format (as was used by the content vector and neural network classifiers). The sentential format was included to verify that the senses could be resolved in the full context. The *long* list format retained inflection, upper/lower case distinctions and punctuation. In the *short* list format, words were stemmed and a stoplist of very frequent words was removed. In order to mimic the fact that the classifiers do not use word order, collocations, or syntactic structure, the *long* and *short* list format were presented to the subjects as word lists in reverse alphabetical order.

Shari Landes ran 36 subjects, each of whom saw 60 contexts, 20 in each of the three formats. The students were given definitions for each of the three senses of *line*. They were then shown the formatted contexts and asked to choose the appropriate sense of *line* for each context. The order in which the formats were presented was counter-balanced across

FORMAT			DIFFICULTY		SENSE		
Long	Short	Sentence	Hard	Easy	Product	Text	Formation
.303	.328	.026	.330	.109	.109	.303	.245

Figure 6.2
Main effects of the human subject experiment. Numbers represent the mean proportion
of errors.

subjects. No subject saw the same context twice. The subjects were
Princeton undergraduates who were paid for their participation.

As shown in Figure 6.2, there were significant main effects for format,
difficulty and sense. These effects parallel the results of the statistical
classifiers. While human subjects performed almost perfectly on the
sentential formats, they had a 31.6% error rate on the list formats. There
was no significant difference between the two list formats—indicating
that function words are of no use for sense resolution when word order
is lost. The subjects made significantly more errors on the contexts that
were hard for the statistical classifiers, and fewer errors on the contexts
that were easy for the classifiers. Finally, not all the senses were equally
difficult for human subjects to identify: there were significantly fewer
errors for the *product* sense of *line* than for the *text* and *formation* senses.

The interaction between format and difficulty is shown in Figure 6.3.
The reason for the interaction is a floor effect with the sentential format,
where the students performed almost perfectly. Error rates for the
students on the list formats were almost 50% for the hard contexts
(contexts where the classifiers performed with 100% error), so subjects
performed much better than the classifiers on these contexts. However,
on the easy contexts, where the classifiers made no errors, the students
showed an error rate of approximately 15%.

When subjects see the original sentences and therefore have access
to all cues, both topical and local, they resolve the senses of *line* with
98% accuracy. When they are given the contexts in a list format, and
are getting only topical cues, their performance drops to about 70%
accuracy. Although their performance was significantly better than
the classifiers (which all performed at 50% accuracy on this sample)
human subjects are not able to disambiguate effectively using only
topical context. In addition, the students tended to stumble over the

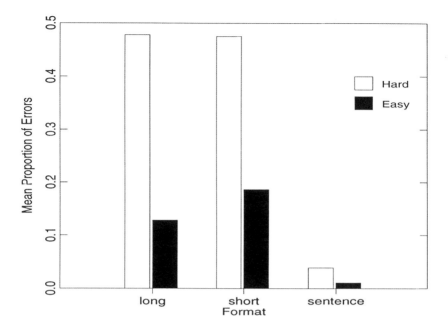

Figure 6.3
Interaction of format and difficulty. *Long* and *short* represent the two list formats.

same contexts as the classifiers (the *hard* contexts), and found the same senses (*text* and *formation*) harder to identify than the *product* sense. From this result we conclude that in order to improve the performance of automatic classifiers, we need to incorporate local information into the statistical methods.

6.4 Acquiring Local Context

Pioneering research in finding local context was carried out by [Kelly and Stone, 1975], who created algorithms for automatic sense resolution. Over a period of seven years in the early 1970s, they (and some 30 students) hand coded sets of ordered rules for disambiguating 671 words. The rules include syntactic markers (part of speech, position within the sentence, punctuation, inflection), semantic markers and selectional restrictions, and words occurring within a specified distance before and/or after the target. An obvious shortcoming of this approach is the amount of work involved.

Recently there has been much interest in automatic acquisition of local context ([Hearst, 1991], [Resnik, 1993b], [Yarowsky, 1993]). The systems that rely entirely on local context are plagued with the same problem, excellent precision but low recall. That is, if the local information that the methods learn is also present in a novel context, then that information is very reliable. However, quite frequently no local context match is found in a novel context. Given the sparseness of the local data, we hope to look for both local and topical context, and we have begun experimenting with various ways of acquiring the local context.

Local context can be derived from a variety of sources, including WORDNET. The nouns in WORDNET are organized in a hierarchical tree structure based on hypernomy/hyponomy. The hypernym of a noun is its superordinate, and the *is a kind of* relation exists between a noun and its hypernym. For example, *line* is a hypernym of *conga line*, which is to say that a *conga line* is a kind of *line*. Conversely, *conga line* is a hyponym of *line*. Polysemous words tend to have hyponyms that are monosemous collocations incorporating the polysemous word: *product line* is a monosemous hyponym of the merchandise sense of *line*; any occurrence of *product line* can be recognized immediately as an instance of that sense. Similarly, *phone line* is a hyponym of the telephone connection sense of *line*, *actor's line* is a hyponym of the text sense of *line*, etc. These collocational hyponyms provide a convenient starting point for the construction of local contexts for polysemous words.

We are also experimenting with template matching, as suggested by [Weiss, 1973], as one approach to using local context to resolve word senses. In template matching, specific word patterns recognized as being indicative of a particular sense (the templates) are used to select a sense when a template is contained in the novel context; otherwise word co-occurrence within the context (topical context) is used to select a sense. Weiss initially used templates that were created by hand, and later derived templates automatically from his dataset. Unfortunately, the datasets available to Weiss at the time were very small, and his results are inconclusive. We are investigating a similar approach using the *line* data: training contexts are used to both automatically extract indicative templates and create topical sense vectors.

To create the templates, the system extracts contiguous subsets of tokens including the target word and up to two tokens on either side

> **cord**
> *his line*
>
> **division**
> *a fine line between, fine line between, a fine line, fine line*
> *line between the, the line between, line between*
> *draw the line, over the line*
>
> **formation**
> *a long line of, long line of, a long line, long line, long lines*
> *in line for, wait in line, in line*
>
> **phone**
> *telephone lines*
> *access lines*
> *line was*
>
> **product**
> *a new line of, a new line, new line of, new line*

Figure 6.4
Templates formed for a training set of 200 contexts for each of six senses when a template must occur at least 10 times and at least 75% of the occurrences must be for one sense. No templates were learned for the *text* sense.

of the target as candidate templates.[4] The system keeps a count of the number of times each candidate template occurs in all of the training contexts. A candidate is selected as a template if it occurs in at least n of the training contexts and one sense accounts for at least $m\%$ of its total occurrences. For example, Figure 6.4 shows the templates formed when this process is used on a training set of 200 contexts for each of six senses when $n = 10$ and $m = 75$. The candidate template *blurs the line* is not selected as a template with these parameter settings because it does not occur frequently enough in the training corpus; the candidate template *line of* is not selected because it appears too frequently in both the *product line* and *formation* contexts.

With the exception of *his line* (cord) and *line was* (phone), these templates readily suggest their corresponding sense. The parameter settings of $n = 10$ and $m = 75$ are relatively stringent criteria for template

---

[4]In the template learning phase, tokens include punctuation and *stop words*. No stemming is performed and case distinctions are significant.

formation, so not many templates are formed, but those templates that are formed tend to be highly indicative of the sense.

Preliminary results show template matching improves the performance of the content vector classifier. The six-sense experiment was repeated using a simple decision tree to incorporate the templates: The sense corresponding to the longest template contained in a test context was selected for that context; if the context contained no template, the sense chosen by the vector classifier was selected. The templates were automatically created from the same training set as was used to create the content vectors. To be selected as a template, a candidate had to appear at least 3 times for the training sets that included 50 of each sense, 5 times for the 100 each training sets, and 10 times for the 200 each training sets. In all cases, a single sense had to account for at least 75% of a candidate's occurrences. This hybrid approach was more accurate than the content vector classifier alone on each of the 9 trials. The average accuracy when trained using 200 contexts of each sense was 75% for the hybrid approach compared to 72% for the content vectors alone.

Other researchers have also suggested methods for incorporating local information into a classifier. Yarowsky found templates[5] to be such powerful sense indicators that he suggests choosing a sense by matching on a set of templates and choosing the most frequent sense if no template matches [Yarowsky, 1993]. To resolve syntactic ambiguities, Resnik investigated four different methods for combining three sources of information [Resnik, 1993b]. The "backing off" strategy, in which the three sources of information were tried in order from most reliable to least reliable until some match was found (no resolution was done if no method matched), maintained high precision (81%) and produced substantially higher recall (95%) than any single method.

Our plans for incorporating templates into the content vector classifier include investigating the significance of the tradeoff between the reliability of the templates and the number of templates that are formed. When stringent criteria are used for template formation, and the templates are thought to be highly reliable sense indicators, the sense corresponding to a matched template will always be selected, and the sense vectors will be used only when no template match occurs. When the

---

[5] Yarowsky called these constructs collocations; they are similar to what we have called templates. Yarowsky's collocations differ from our templates in that they are formed using content words exclusively, passing over function words.

templates are thought to be less reliable, the choice of sense will be a function of the uniqueness of a matched template (if any) and the sense vector similarities. By varying the relative importance of a template match and sense vector similarity we will be able to incorporate different amounts of topical and local information into the template classifier.

6.5 Conclusion

The capacity to determine the intended sense of an ambiguous word is an important component of any general system for language understanding. We believe that, in order to accomplish this task, we need contextual representations of word senses containing both topical and local context. Initial experiments focused on methods that are able to extract topical context. These methods are effective, but topical context alone is not sufficient for sense resolution tasks. The human subject experiment shows that even people are not very good at resolving senses when given only topical context. Currently we are testing methods for learning local context for word senses. Preliminary results show that the addition of template matching on local context improves performance.

Acknowledgments

This work was supported in part by Grant No. N00014-91-1634 from the Defense Advanced Research Projects Agency, Information and Technology Office, by the Office of Naval Research, and by the James S. McDonnell Foundation. We are indebted to George A. Miller, Martin S. Chodorow, and Shari Landes for their help and comments.

IV CATEGORIZATION OF LEXICAL UNITS

7 A Context Driven Conceptual Clustering Method for Verb Classification

Roberto Basili, Maria-Teresa Pazienza, Paola Velardi

7.1 Introduction

The design of word-sense taxonomies is acknowledged as one of the most difficult (and frustrating) tasks in NLP systems. The decision to assign a word to a category is far from being straightforward [Nirenburg and Raskin, 1987] and often the lexicon builders do not use consistent classification principles. In the area of Artificial Intelligence, many studies are concerned with the development of models for terminological knowledge, like KL-ONE [Brachman and Schmolze, 1985], and machine learning algorithms for concept formation [Stepp and Michalski, 1986], [Fisher, 1987], [Gennari *et al.*, 1989]. These algorithms do not have however a straightforward application to the design of words ontology in NLP. First, conceptual clustering algorithms assume that a formal representation of instances is given, which is an unrealistic assumption for the case of word senses. Usually, all what is given is raw text. Second, the learning algorithms adopt a view of categorization that recent psycholinguistic theories proved to be inadequate at fully modelling the human behavior. Both these issues will be discussed later in detail.

Though psycholinguistic plausibility is not a primary concern in the design of computationally "usable" verbs (and words) ontologies, we believe that studies in this area provide valuable insights concerning issues that are critical for any automatic model of word categorization: What is the basic structure to represent the meaning of verbs? What are the principles of categorization? What type of a-priori knowledge, if any, should be available to the learner?

In this chapter we argue for a stronger tie between work on categorization in psychology and psycholinguistics, on one hand, and corpus-based linguistics and machine learning, on the other hand. We propose a lexical learning model for verbs ontology that benefit from the reciprocal contribution of these disciplines. The learning model is computational in nature, since it has been designed as a practical tool for NLP applications.

The purpose of this section is to summarize the major research trends on categorization, in the fields of psycholinguistics and computational linguistics. Section 7.1.1, in particular, presents an overview of the psycholinguistic literature, which is admittedly partial, since categorization and language learning is a matter that inspired many scientists in the past centuries. Section 7.1.2 is more closely related to our work, since it critically discusses previous computational research on classification, and in particular studies that derive clustering cues from the observation of words in corpora.

7.1.1 Psycholinguistic issues on categorization

In the design of word-sense ontology, possibly no other task is as complex as verb classification. They convey information about events, states, causality, and much more. This section summarizes, with no claim of completeness, some outstanding theories developed in the field of psycholinguistic, that we believe relevant for any "reasonable" model of automatic verb classification.

In psycholinguistics, concepts are proposed to have *defining* features, describing their internal nature, and *characteristic*, or *thematic* features, relating concepts to other external concepts within a semantic domain. Familiar examples are the IS_A relation for defining features, and the AGENT or INSTRUMENT relations for thematic features. However some feature is at the borderline, and it is very difficult to draw precise criteria. It has been experimentally observed [Keil, 1989] that some concepts, for example natural types (e.g., biological categories) are better defined in terms of defining features, whereas nominal types (e.g., verbs and social terms) are more naturally defined by their thematic features. In [Schwartz, 1989] it is claimed that "there can be no science of nominal kinds"' because these are mostly influenced by social aspects and bodily experience. Other psycholinguistic studies on verb semantics outline the relevance of thematic roles in categorization activities [Jackendoff, 1983] and *indicate the argument structure of verbs as playing a central role in language acquisition* [Pinker, 1989].

A very complex issue is that of *categorization principles*. [Lakoff, 1987] lists a number of categorization mechanisms in humans. Among these mechanisms *graded* categories are defined by a bundle of defining or characteristic features, and membership to a class is graded, i.e. "X IS_A Y with degree K." A classic example are colors and fuzzy terms such as high, near, etc... Most words are fuzzy in nature and fuzzy distributions are principled representations of the underlying concepts.

Though the *classic* model of categorization is widely adopted in Artificial Intelligence, there is a clear evidence that verbs cannot be clustered only according to necessary and sufficient conditions. *Graded* categorization seems to reflect more precisely the process of verb clustering, as emerging from the analysis of spoken and written language.

Another important issue concerns *class membership criterion*. Rosch and her followers ([Rosch, 1978]) observed that categories often have a *prototype*, i.e. a member that is commonly considered typical of that class. Accordingly, concept membership is determined by placing a criterion (graded or not) on the similarity to the prototype. Other researchers believe that the prototype effect does not influence the internal structure of a category. The very fact that "dog" in some cultural environment, say in cities, is the typical animal has little to do with the structure of the category, but rather with a more frequent exposition to the example "dog." Rosch in her later works agreed on this position. She interpreted her experiments arguing that humans create categories that are more basic than others, i.e. they bring more representative information about their members. Such *basic level* categories are neither too abstract nor too specific, and they are in general placed at an intermediate level of the ontology. For example, *dog* is more basic than *animal* or *terrier*. Basic level categories depend upon the culture of individuals. We are not aware of any experimental study that analyses basic level categories for verbs. But we attempted to define a computational model of basic level verb clusters, as discussed later in this chapter.

Verb categorization should also be analyzed in the wider context of language acquisition, since interesting insights come from the studies in this area. One fundamental issue in the study of language learning is related to the notion of *linguistic bootstrapping*. This issue involves the formalization of the dependencies existing between the type of linguistic information available to the learner (e.g., children in early stage of language acquisition) and the complex information implicit in syntax, grammatical and/or lexical categories, that are responsible for our 'natural' use of language. As Baker's paradox ([Baker, 1979]) outlines, the nature and the amount of the information available, with some evidence, to the early learner is not sufficient to justify his/her ability and speed in acquiring such a complex knowledge. This can be showed on a formal basis, since for example context-free languages (to which natural language can be assimilated) cannot be learnt only from positive evidence. Many outstanding theories ([Chomsky, 1982]) consider the acquisition of linguistic competencies as activated by basic innate components. The character and the extent of the required *a priori* knowledge is another central issue for every computational model of language learning. Some insights in this area can be directly derived from a number of psycholinguistic studies on children during linguistic exposition. The processing of errors and the role of a teacher are worth to be outlined. It is a diffused opinion that negative evidence, especially at the syntactic and lexical knowledge levels, are not available to children, at least in a way sufficient to justify some generative capabilities. Rather, there is a cross-linguistic evidence about children autonomous construction of quite general and non-linguistic syntactic, as well as semantic, categories. Furthermore unsuccessful utterances (i.e. sentences that do not trigger some expected behavior of the environment) are not systematically available, and can not be considered as true syntactic counterexamples. According to these observations, a number of authors [Pinker, 1989] agree on the existence of a form of *semantic* bootstrapping that commits large part of language development to the influence of the context. The context (i.e. what the learner perceives of it) enables the assignment of meaning to words as well as (elementary) sentence comprehension (as a map between simple syntactic structures and their semantic counterparts). In other words, there seems to be a form of *a priori semantic knowledge* that justifies the efficiency of children language development.

Modeling some notion of semantic bias seems particularly reasonable for verbs. In fact, previous works on automatic word clustering that are based only on the evidence provided by the surface structure of sentences, did not produce valuable results for verbs.

7.1.2 Categorization in computational linguistics

This section summarizes the literature on word categorization in the fields of Computational Linguistics and Natural Language Processing. In the literature, this problem is often analyzed in general, with no specific reference to verbs. But it is a common feeling that verbs are one of the major sources of difficulty.

Word ontologies are derived manually in most existing NLP systems.

Lexicon builders rely on three sources of information to guide word classification:

- introspection
- psycholinguistic experiments
- dictionaries and exemplars of word uses in contexts.

One of the most complete, and widely available, efforts in this area was produced by the WORDNET group [Miller *et al.*, 1990]. Another famous example are *Roget's* categories.

In real NLP systems, the use of domain-general categories, such as those found in thesauri like WORDNET and *Roget's*, has its evident drawbacks, namely that the categorization principles used by the linguists are inspired by a variety of philosophical concerns, while the purpose of a type hierarchy in a NLP system is more practical, for example expressing at the highest level of generality the selectional constrains of words in a given domain. For one such practical objective, the categories defined in thesauri are often inappropriate, though for example WORDNET categories rely also on a study of collocations in corpora (the *Brown* corpus). In our research, we analyzed different sublanguages and we found that, while in a given domain there are groups of words that are used almost interchangeably, the same words may have no common supertype in WORDNET. This problem is particularly apparent for verbs, that are highly characterized by the context in which they appear. For example, the verbs *simulate* and *describe* appear in identical patterns in a remote sensing domain (e.g., *simulate, describe a process, a phenomenon, etc.*), but they have no common supertype in WORDNET.

Another problem is over-ambiguity. Given a specific application, WORDNET tags create many unnecessary ambiguity. For example, we were rather surprised to find the word *high* classified as a PERSON (=*soprano*) and as an ORGANIZATION (=*high school*), though this is perfectly correct. We were initially surprised because we were biased by our knowledge of a specific domain, where this type of ambiguity was rather unexpected.

One such wide-spectrum classification is very useful on a purely linguistic ground, for example for lexicographers, but renders the classification unusable as it is, for most practical NLP applications. In a legal domain, we measured an average ambiguity of 4,76 senses per word.

In a remote-sensing domain, the average ambiguity is lower (3,25), but about 30% words (mostly technical terms) could not be classified.[1]

More recently, several studies attempted to automatically derive word classes on an extensive basis *from on-line corpora*. In [Zernik, 1989], [Webster and Marcus, 1989] it is attempted a classification of some nominal types based on the similarity of features. The features used for classification are the *syntactic frames* automatically detected for each word from on-line corpora. Syntactic frames are the lexical variants of verbs in sentences. For example, the lexical variants of *make* are: (NP,NP,AP) (e.g., *This made Mary happy*), (NP,NP,PP) (e.g., *This made her one happy woman*), etc. Both the aforementioned works are based on the strong assumption that syntactic similarity implies semantic similarity. This is questionable for several reasons:

1. verbs with similar frames may have very different meanings, e.g., "*I go to Boston,*" "*I refer to Mary.*" The problem here is that it is not possible to automatically distinguish between, say, locative and dative structures.
2. it is difficult to acquire lexical variants in presence of multiple parses (should a PP be attached to a verb or to its object?)
3. each lexical variant has optional syntactic slots:
   I left from Boston yesterday by bus
   I left from Boston
   I left yesterday by bus

To cope with problem 1), in [Webster and Marcus, 1989] syntactic information is augmented with semantic tags: AGENT, THEME, LOCATION, DATIVE and INSTRUMENT, but the authors did not confront their intuition with large scale data.

More recently [Hindle, 1990], [Pereira and Tishby, 1992],[Pereira and Tishby, 1993] proposed to cluster nouns on the basis of a metric derived from the distribution of subject, verb and object (SVO) in the texts. Both these papers use large corpora as a source of information, but differ in the type of statistical approach used to determine word similarity. These studies, though valuable, leave several open problems:

1. A metric of conceptual closeness based on mere syntactic similarity

---

[1] We used the WORDNET 4.1 version for UNIX.

is questionable, as already pointed out. Furthermore, subject and object relations do not fully characterize many verbs.

2. Many events accumulate statistical evidence only in very large corpora, even though in [Pereira and Tishby, 1992],[Pereira and Tishby, 1993] the adopted notion of distributional similarity in part avoids this problem.

3. The description of a word is an "agglomerate" of its occurrences in the corpus, and it is not possible to discriminate different senses.

4. None of the aforementioned studies provides a method to *describe* and *evaluate* the derived categories.

As a result, the acquired classifications seem of little use for a large-scale NLP system, neither they seem to provide significant guidelines to assist a linguist. In addition, all these methods admittedly[2] do not work very well with verbs.

7.1.3 An interdisciplinary perspective

Sections 7.1.1 and 7.1.2 highlighted many complex issues related to the problem of word sense categorization, in general, and verb categorization, in particular. The psycholinguistic literature (Section 7.1.1) provides a strong evidence that word sense clustering based on defining features is neither appropriate nor feasible for the majority of words in the lexicon. On the other side, non-classical models of categorization are difficult to formalize.

On the computational side, we outlined the problems that derive both from an inadequate psychological model of word classification, and from a variety of technical issues that depend upon the metric adopted for clustering words and upon the format of input observations (i.e. words in contexts) in the learning set (i.e. the corpus).

We are not here to promise the *panacea* for all this issues. More realistically, this chapter proposes a model that, in our view, is step towards a more computationally useful, theoretically sound, study of verb categorization.

It is not a case that "theoretically sound" comes after "computationally useful" in the above statement, since our emphasis is primarily on real NLP systems. We seek for classification principles that are *reason-*

---

[2] According to a personal communication of one of the authors, the surface structure of verbs is "too fuzzy" to produce stable results

able on a psycholinguistic ground, but over all they must be reasonable on the ground of automatic language processing.

- An important objective is *psycholinguistic plausibility*. Though not central to our work, psycholinguistic research summarized in Section 7.1.1 influenced the design of the word clustering algorithm that we present in this chapter, in several respects. First, our algorithm for verb clustering is based on the observation of their *thematic features*, according to the claim that thematic features (relating objects to objects), rather than solely the classical notion of defining features (such as classic IS_A hierarchies) may play an important role in verb categorization. Observations are assigned to a class according to a *graded membership* model. Second, we provide a computational definition of *basic level categories* of an acquired taxonomy, identifying the categories that bring the most predictive information about their members. Finally, the *primitive components* of the knowledge learner are semantic in nature. Linguistic bootstrapping is modelled by activating an incremental use of this knowledge, that, in turn, triggers a more refined learning.

- A second objective that we pursued is *domain appropriateness*. The purpose of a type hierarchy in a NLP system is very practical, for example expressing at the highest level of generality the thematic roles of words in a given domain. We previously demonstrated [Basili *et al.*, 1992], [Basili *et al.*, 1993a], [Basili *et al.*, 1993b], [Basili *et al.*, 1993c] that thematic roles are highly domain dependent. Hence, the word categories used in defining selectional restrictions should also be appropriate for the domain. To make an example, consider the verb *to vary*. In our studies on sublanguages, we could analyze this verb in several domains. In a commercial domain, one varies the *production*, the *supply* and the *sale* of BY_PRODUCTS and ARTIFACTS. Hence, *production, supply,* and *sale* could be good candidates for a cluster describing the direct objects of this verb. In a legal domain, the same verb would suggest *income, tax,* and *amount* as a useful category. Finally, in a remote sensing domain, one varies the *resolution*, the *altitude* and the *dependence*. Not always classification clues extracted from different domains are in contrast, though this is often the case. There is however a clear evidence that, if similarity of thematic roles should be taken as a clue for verb clustering, entirely different clusters could be obtained from different domains.

- A third objective is cluster *description*. Unlike for other corpus based methods, clusters should have a description of their instances, because this can help the evaluation of the method, and increase the "linguistic appeal" of a derived classification.

- A fourth objective is *sense discrimination*. Different senses of verbs, provided the ambiguity actually occurs in a given domain, should be assigned to different classes.

- A fifth objective is *formal evaluation*. It should be possible to measure *numerically* the utility of an acquired classification. Linguistic evaluation, though helpful at pinpointing some specific phenomenon, is not realistic. First, the intuition of the linguist is not a fully valuable criterion, as widely discussed in section 7.1.2. Second, the algorithm produces very many clusters of very many verbs (in principle, all the verbs occurring in a domain), hence a manual validation of all clusters is difficult and time consuming.

In the next sections we present CIAULA[3], a corpus-driven unsupervised learning algorithm based on a modified version of COBWEB [Fisher, 1987], [Gennari *et al.*, 1989]. The algorithm learns verb classifications through the systematic observation of verb usage's in sentences. In section 2 we highlight the advantages that concept formation algorithms, like COBWEB, have over "agglomerate" statistical approaches. However, using a Machine Learning methodology for a Natural Language Processing problem required adjustments on both sides. Raw texts representing instances of verb usage's have been processed to fit the feature-vector like representation needed for concept formation algorithms. The NL processor used for this task is briefly summarized in Section 7.2.1. Similarly, it was necessary to adapt COBWEB to the linguistic nature of the classification activity. These modifications are discussed in Sections 7.2.1 through 7.2.4. Finally, in Section 7.3 we present a method to identify the basic-level categories of a classification, i.e. those that are repository of most of the lexical information about their members.

---

[3] Ciaula stands for Concept formatIon Algorithm Used for Language Acquisition, and has been inspired by the tale *"Ciaula scopre la luna"* [Pirandello, 1992].

7.2   CIAULA: An Algorithm to Acquire Word Clusters

Problems arising from distributional methods for word clustering were summarized in Section 7.1.2. Incremental example-based learning algorithms, like COBWEB [Fisher, 1987], seem more adequate than other Machine Learning and Statistical methods to the task of acquiring word taxonomies from corpora. COBWEB has several desirable features.

a) *Incrementality*, since whenever new data are available, the system updates its classification;
b) A *formal description* of the acquired clusters;
c) The notion of *category utility*, used to select among competing classifications.

b) and c) are particularly relevant to our linguistic problem, as remarked in Section 7.1.

On the other side, applying COBWEB to verb classification is not straightforward.

First, there is a knowledge representation problem, that is common to most Machine Learning algorithms: Input instances must be pre-coded (manually) using a feature-vector like representation. This limited the use of such algorithms in many real world problems. In the specific case we are analyzing, a manual codification of verb instances is not realistic on a large scale.

Second, the algorithm does not distinguish multiple usage's of the same verb, nor different verbs that are found with the same pattern of use, since different instances with the same feature vector are considered as identical. The motivation is that concept formation algorithms as COBWEB assume the input information as being stable, unambiguous, and complete. At the opposite, our data do not exhibit a stable behavior, they are ambiguous, incomplete, and possibly misleading, since errors in codification of verb instances may well be possible.

In the following sections we will discuss the methods by which we attempted to overcome these obstacles.

7.2.1   Representing verb instances

This section describes the formal representation of verb instances and verb clusters in CIAULA.

Verb observations in contexts are represented by their thematic roles, acquired semi-automatically from corpora by the ARIOSTO_LEX system, described in detail in [Basili *et al.*, 1993c]. Though CIAULA analyses verb occurrences individually, a given verb V in a sentence is interpreted using the *global knowledge* (selectional restrictions) on that verb, acquired by analyzing all the sentences including V in the application corpus.

ARIOSTO_LEX is a lexical learning system based on collocational analysis. The input knowledge to ARIOSTO_LEX are syntactic pairs and triples (verb-direct object V_N, subject verb N_V, verb-preposition-noun V_prep_N, etc.), augmented with high level semantic tags. Semantic tags are very high level (for example, all verbs are ACTs or STATEs), since we don't want to beg the question of lexical acquisition. They represent a sort of a-priori primitive knowledge of the domain, which is a psychologically plausible hypothesis, as mentioned in Section 7.1.1. Semantic tags are assigned manually for the Italian domains (legal and commercial, hereafter LD and CD), while WORDNET tags have been used for an English domain (remote sensing, hereafter RSD).

In short, the algorithms works as follows. First, collocations extracted from the application corpus are clustered according to the semantic *and* syntactic tag[4] of one or both the co-occurring content words. The result are what we call *clustered association data*. For example, V_prep_N(*sell,to,shareholder*) and V_prep_N(*assign,to,taxpayer*), occurring with frequency $f1$ and $f2$ respectively, are merged into a unique association V_prep_N(*ACT,to,HUMAN_ENTITY*) with frequency $f1+f2$. The statistically relevant conceptual associations are presented to a linguist, that can replace syntactic patterns with the underlying conceptual relation (e.g., [ACT]⇒(BENEFICIARY)⇒[HUMAN_ENTITY]). These *coarse grained selectional restrictions* are later used for a more refined lexical acquisition phase. We have shown in [Basili *et al.*, 1992] that in sub languages there are many unintuitive ways of relating concepts to each other, that would have been very hard to find without the help of an automatic procedure.

Then, for each content word w, we acquire all the collocations in which it participates. We select among ambiguous patterns using a

---

[4] We did not discuss of syntactic tags for brevity. Our (not-so) shallow parser detects productive pairs and triples like verb subject and direct object (N_V and V_N, respectively), prepositional triples between non adjacent words (N_prep_N, V_prep_N), etc.

preference method described in [Basili *et al.*, 1993a]. The detected collocations for a word *w* are then generalized using the coarse grained selectional restrictions acquired during the previous phase. For example, the following collocations including the word *measurement* in the RSD: N_prep_N(*measurement,from,satellite*), N_N(*radar, measurement*) and N_prep_N(*measurement,from,antenna*) let the ARIOSTO_LEX system learn the following selectional restriction:

```
[INSTRUMENTALITY] <= (INSTRUMENT) <= [MEASUREMENT]
```

where INSTRUMENTALITY is a WORDNET category for the nouns *radar, satellite,* and *antenna,* and *instrument* is one of the conceptual relations used. Notice that *the use of conceptual relations is not strictly necessary,* though it adds semantic value to the data. One could simply store the syntactic subcategorization of each word along with the semantic restriction on the accompanying word in a collocation, e.g., something like: *measurement*: ([N_prep_N1 *from*, N1_N], INSTRUMENTALITY(N1)). It is also possible to cluster, for each verb or verbal noun, all the syntactic subcategorization frames for which there is an evidence in the corpus. In this case, lexical acquisition is entirely automatic.

In Figure 7.1 we show one of the screen out of ARIOSTO_LEX. The word shown is *measurement,* very frequent in the RSD, as presented to the linguist. Three windows show, respectively, the lexical entry that ARIOSTO_LEX proposes to acquire, a list of accepted patterns for which only one example was found (lexical patterns are generalized only when at least two similar patterns are found), and a list of rejected patterns. The linguist can modify or accept any of these choices. Each acquired selectional restriction is represented as follows:

```
pre_sem_lex
   (word,
    conceptual_relation,
    semantic tag,
    direction,
    SE,
    CF)
```

The first four arguments identify the selectional restriction and the direction of the conceptual relation, i.e.:

```
[measurement]->(OBJ)->[PROPERTY]
```
(measurement of reflectivity, temperature etc.)

Figure 7.1
Lexical entry for the word *measurement* in the remote sensing domain (RSD)

$$[\texttt{measurement}] \texttt{->} (\texttt{INSTRUMENT}) \texttt{->} [\texttt{INSTRUMENTALITY}]$$
(measurement from satellite, aircraft, radar)

SE and *CF* are two statistical measures of the *semantic expectation* and *confidence* of the acquired selectional restriction (see the aforementioned papers for details). ARIOSTO_LEX provides the linguist with several facilities to inspect and validate the acquired lexicon, such as examples of phrases from which a selectional restriction was derived, and other nice gadgets. For example, the central window in Figure 7.1 (opened only on demand) shows the Conceptual Graph of the acquired entry.

Getting back to our verb clustering problem, it is easily seen that, using the thematic knowledge on verbs extracted by ARIOSTO_LEX, we can represent the thematic roles of a verb v in a sentence as a feature-vector:

$$v/(R_{i_t} : Cat_{j_t}) \quad i_t \in I, j_t \in J, t = 1, 2, \ldots, n \tag{7.2.1}$$

In (7.2.1), R_{i_t} are the thematic roles (AGENT, INSTRUMENT etc.) and Cat_{j_t} are the conceptual types of the words to which v is related semantically. For example, the following sentence in the CD:

> "... la ditta produce beni di consumo con macchinari elettromecca-nici.." ("... the company produces goods with electromechanical machines..")

originates the instance:

```
produce / (AGENT:       HUMAN_ENTITY,
            OBJECT:      GOODS,
            INSTRUMENT:  INSTRUMENTALITY )
```

In the RSD, the sentence:

> "... the satellite produced an image with high accuracy"

originates the instance:[5]

```
produce / (MANNER:      PROPERTY,
            THEME:       COGNITIVE_CONTENT,
            INSTRUMENT:  INSTRUMENTALITY )
```

The ambiguities are resolved using a probability-based criterion, as mentioned above. Notice also that the same syntactic components (*with + noun*) in the two sentences play entirely different semantic roles (*with(=INSTRUMENT) machines* and *with (=MANNER) accuracy*), and vice versa, the same semantic roles (INSTRUMENT: INSTRUMENTALITY) are played by different syntactic components (*produce with machines* and *satellite produces*). This further demonstrate that syntactic similarity cannot be used as a clue for semantic similarity.

Semantic similarity is instead strongly suggested by the observation of verb configurations, in which words of the same conceptual type play the same roles.

The categorization process must capture this similarity among local meanings of verbs.

---

[5] Notice that we used WORDNET tags only later in our work, when we analyzed an English domain, since WORDNET is not currently available in Italian. In our previous papers, our manually assigned label in the CD was MACHINE rather than INSTRUMENTALITY, but the two classes are clearly the same.

7.2.2 Cluster representation

The representation of verb clusters follows the scheme adopted in COB-WEB. Each target class is represented by the probability that its members (i.e. verbs) are seen with a set of typical roles. Given the set $\{R_i\}_{i \in I}$ of thematic roles and the set $\{Cat_j\}_{j \in J}$ of conceptual types, a target class C for our clustering system is given by the following

$$C = \langle c_C, [x]_{ij}, V_C, S_C \rangle \tag{7.2.2}$$

or equivalently by

$$\langle c, [x]_{ij}, V, S \rangle \tag{7.2.3}$$

A class is represented in COBWEB by the matrix $[x]_{ij}$, showing the distribution of probability among relations (R_i) and conceptual types (Cat_j). The additional parameters V_C and c_C are introduced to account for multiple instances of the same verb in a class. c_C is the cardinality (i.e. the number of different instance members of C, and V_C is the set of pairs $\langle v, v\sharp \rangle$ such that it exists at least one instance

$$v/(R_j : Cat_j)$$

classified in C, and $v\sharp$ is the number of such instances. Finally, S_C is the set of C subtypes. The definitions of the *empty class* (7.2.4) and of the *top node* of the taxonomy (7.2.5) follows from (7.2.2)

$$\langle 0, [x]_{ij}, \{\emptyset\}, \{\emptyset\} \rangle \qquad \text{with } x_{ij} = 0 \text{ for each } i, j \tag{7.2.4}$$

$$\langle N_{\text{tot}}, [x]_{ij}, V, S \rangle \tag{7.2.5}$$

where N_{tot} is the number of available instances in the learning set, and V is the set of verbs with their absolute occurrences.

Special type of classes are those in which only a verb has been classified, that we will call singleton classes. A *singleton class* is a class $C = \langle c, [x]_{ij}, V, S \rangle$ for which $\text{card}(V) = 1$. It will be denoted by $\{v\}$ where v is the only member of (whatever its occurrences) C. For a singleton class it is clearly true that $S = \{\emptyset\}$. Note that a singleton class is different from an instance because any number of instances of the verb v can be classified in $\{v\}$.

7.2.3   Measuring the utility of a classification

As remarked before, a useful property of concept formation algorithms, with respect to agglomerate statistical approaches, is the use of formal methods that guide the classification choices.

Quantitative approaches to model human choices in categorization have been adopted in psychological models of conceptual development. In her seminal work, [Rosch, 1978] introduced a metrics of preference, the *category cue validity*, expressed by the sum of expectations of observing some feature in the class members. This value is maximum for the so-called *basic level* categories. A later development, used in COBWEB, introduces the notion of *category utility*, derived from the application of the Bayes law to the expression of the predictive power of a given classification. Given a classification into K classes, and with P denoting probability, the *category utility* is given by:

$$\sum_{k=1}^{K} P(C_k) \sum_{ij} P(attr_i = val_j | C_k)^2 \tag{7.2.6}$$

In COBWEB, a hill climbing algorithm is defined to maximize the category utility of a resulting classification. The following expression is used to discriminate among conflicting clusters:

$$\frac{\sum_{k=1}^{K} P(C_k) \sum_{ij} P(attr_i = val_j | C_k)^2 - \sum_{ij} P(attr_i = val_j)^2}{K} \tag{7.2.7}$$

The clusters that maximize the above quantity provide the system with the capability of deriving the best predictive taxonomy with respect to the set of i attributes and j values. This evaluation maximizes infra-class similarity and intra-class dissimilarity. The notion of category utility adopted in COBWEB, however, does not fully cope with our linguistic problem. As remarked in the previous section, multiple instances of the same entity are not considered in COBWEB. In order to account for multiple instances of a verb, we introduced the notion of *mnemonic inertia*. The mnemonic inertia models an inertial trend attracting a new instance of an already classified verb in the class where it was previously classified. It balances the pattern-based clustering criterium of the category utility with a head-based criterium.

Given the incoming instance $v/(R_i : Cat_j)$ and a current classification in the set of classes C_k, for each k the mnemonic inertia is modelled by:

$$\mu_k(v) = \sharp_v/c_k \tag{7.2.8}$$

where $\sharp_v$ is the number of instances of the verb v already classified in C_k and c_k is the cardinality of C_k.

(7.2.8) expresses a fuzzy membership of v to the class C_k. The more instances of v are classified into C_k, the more future observations of v will be attracted by C_k. A suitable combination of the mnemonic inertia and the category utility provides our system with generalization capabilities along with the "conservative" policy of leaving different verb instances separate. The desired effect within the data is that slightly different usage's of a verb are classified in the same cluster, while remarkable differences result in different classifications.

The global measure of category utility, used by the CIAULA algorithm during classification, can now be defined. Let $v/(R_i : Cat_j)$ be the incoming instance, C_k be the set of classes, and let $cu(v, k)$ be the category utility as defined in (7.2.7). The measure m, given by

$$\mu(v, k) = \nu\, cu(v, k) + (1 - \nu)\, \mu_k(v) \qquad \nu \in [0, 1] \tag{7.2.9}$$

expresses the *global utility* of the classification obtained by assigning the instance v to the class C_k. (7.2.9) is a distance metrics among instances and classes.

7.2.4   The incremental clustering algorithm

The algorithm for the incremental clustering of verb instances follows the approach used in COBWEB. Given a new incoming instance I and a current valid classification $\{C_k\}_{k \in K}$, the system evaluates the utility of the new classification obtained by inserting I in each class. The maximum utility value corresponds to the best predictive configuration of classes. A further attempt is made to change the current configuration (introducing a new class, merging the two best candidate for the classification or splitting the best classes in the set of its son) to improve the predictivity. The main difference with respect to COBWEB, due to the linguistic nature of the problem at hand, concern the procedure to evaluate the utility of a temporary classification and the MERGE operator, as it applies to singleton classes. The description of the algorithm is given in Figure 7.2. According to (7.2.9), the procedure $G\_UTILITY(x, I, C, Top, \nu)$ evaluates the utility of the classification as a combination of the category utility and the inertial factor introduced in (7.2.8).

```
Input:        Top  root node of the current taxonomy,
              I, Unclassified verb semantic instance,
              v(I), verb head of the instance I.
Output:       An exhaustive conceptual classification of the incoming instances.
Variables:    C, P, S, N, M    classes of the taxonomy,
              x, p, s, n, m, q    measures of global utility of a classification.


CIAULA( Top, I, v)
        IF Top is a terminal
        THEN
                IF Top is the singleton {v(I)}
                THEN            INCORPORATE(Top, I)
                ELSE            NEW_TERMINAL(Top, I)
                                INCORPORATE(Top, I)
        ELSE
                INCORPORATE(Top, I)
                FOR EACH subtype C of Top
                                     G_UTILITY(x, I, C, Top, v)
                Let:    p    the best score x for classifying I in the class P
                        s    the second best score x for classifying I in the class S
                        n    the score x for classifyng I in a new node N, subtype of Top
                        m    the score x of classifying I in node M, merge between P and S
                        q    the score x in classifying I in a classification obtained removing P from the
                             current level and picking up the set of its son to the previous P level

                IF p is the highest score
                THEN CIAULA( P, I, v)
                ELSE IF n is the highest score
                        THEN   initialize N with values shown by I
                ELSE IF m is the highest score
                        THEN MERGE( M, P, S, Top, I)
                                CIAULA( M, I, v)
                ELSE IF q is the highest score
                THEN SPLIT( P, Top)
                        CIAULA( Top, I, n)
                END
```

Figure 7.2
The algorithm for conceptual clustering of verbs

Figure 7.3 shows graphically the difference between the standard MERGE operation, identical to that used in COBWEB, and the elementary MERGE between two singleton classes, as defined in CIAULA.

Figure 7.4 shows the probability matrix of two clusters in the legal domain. In Figure 7.4a the cluster is very high-level (Level 1, under the top node), hence the matrix is more sparse. Figure 7.4b shows a lower level cluster (Level 3), for which all clustered instances have been

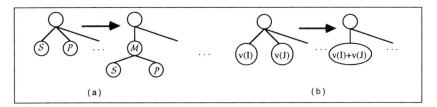

Figure 7.3
Merge (a) vs. elementary merge (b)

observed within the same pattern:

```
verb / ( OBJECT:      AMOUNT,
           RECIPIENT:  HUMAN_ENTITY)
```

as in *"effettuare un pagamento alla banca"* (*"to make a payment to the bank)."*

7.3   Basic Level Categories

The algorithm has been tested against our three corpora. For each corpus, we run several experiments with 1000–3000 examples of 100–300 verbs. Upon a careful analysis of the clusters obtained from each domain, the resulting classifications were judged in general quite expressive, and semantically biased from the target linguistic domains, a part from some noise due parsing errors.[6] However, the granularity of the description of the final taxonomy is too fine, to be usefully imported in the type hierarchy of a NLP system. Furthermore, the order of presentation of the different examples strongly influences the final result.[7] In order to derive reliable results we must find some invariant with respect to the presentation order. An additional requirement is to define some objective measure of the quality of the acquired classification, other than the personal judgment of the authors.

In this section we define a measure of the class *informative power*, able to capture the most relevant levels of the hierarchy. The idea is to extract from the hierarchy the *basic level classes*, or classes that are repository of the most relevant lexical information about their members. We define

---

[6] Parsing errors however are considerably reduced by the use of corpus-based PP-attachment disambiguation methods, and by the use of semantic tags, that increase statistical plausibility

[7] This is an inherent problem with concept formation algorithms

```
Class:   2134    Father class: 0
Cardinality: 114 (23 - 0.20) Level:  1  Tau: 0.07 Omega: 0.20

             A    D    RE   G    HE   AE   S    RE   TE   P    AM   Q    M
 AGEN:    0.00 0.03 0.02 0.00 0.02 0.03 0.00 0.00 0.01 0.01 0.06 0.00 0.00
  AFF:    0.31 0.02 0.03 0.03 0.02 1.00 0.14 0.00 0.02 0.01 0.01 0.00 0.00
 FI_S:    0.08 0.00 0.00 0.00 0.00 0.00 0.00 0.00 0.00 0.00 0.00 0.00 0.00
 MANN:    0.07 0.02 0.00 0.00 0.00 0.00 0.00 0.00 0.00 0.00 0.03 0.01 0.02
 FI_D:    0.15 0.00 0.00 0.00 0.00 0.05 0.00 0.00 0.00 0.00 0.00 0.00 0.00
 FI_L:    0.01 0.05 0.01 0.01 0.01 0.00 0.00 0.00 0.00 0.00 0.03 0.00 0.00
  REF:    0.00 0.08 0.00 0.00 0.00 0.00 0.00 0.00 0.00 0.00 0.00 0.00 0.00
  REC:    0.00 0.00 0.00 0.00 0.00 0.00 0.00 0.00 0.00 0.00 0.00 0.00 0.00
CAUSE:    0.01 0.00 0.00 0.00 0.00 0.00 0.00 0.00 0.00 0.00 0.00 0.00 0.00
  LOC:    0.00 0.00 0.00 0.00 0.00 0.00 0.00 0.00 0.00 0.03 0.00 0.00 0.00

Heads:
 - ricorrere (occ 23)    - effettuare (occ 21)  - considerare (occ 15)
 - dichiarare (occ 14)   - applicare (occ 12)     - eseguire (occ 11)
 - riguardare (occ 9)    - derivare (occ 6)       - allegare (occ 6)
 - annotare (occ 4)      - dire (occ 3)           - ammettere (occ 2)
 - pretendere (occ 2)    - emettere (occ 2)       - corrispondere (occ 2)
 - disporre (occ 2)      - omettere (occ 2)       - approvare (occ 1)
 - costruire (occ 1)     - ritenere (occ 1)       - porre (occ 1)
 - comprendere (occ 1)   - trarre (occ 1)

                              ( a )

Class:   3446    Father class: 408
Cardinality: 12 (7 - 0.58) Level:  3  Typicality: 1.00 Omega: 0.58
             A    D    RE   G    HE   AE   S    RE   TE   P    AM   Q    M
 AGEN:    0.00 0.00 0.00 0.00 0.00 0.00 0.00 0.00 0.00 0.00 0.00 0.00 0.00
  AFF:    0.00 0.00 0.00 0.00 0.00 0.00 0.00 0.00 0.00 0.00 1.00 0.00 0.00
 FI_S:    0.00 0.00 0.00 0.00 0.00 0.00 0.00 0.00 0.00 0.00 0.00 0.00 0.00
 MANN:    0.00 0.00 0.00 0.00 0.00 0.00 0.00 0.00 0.00 0.00 0.00 0.00 0.00
 FI_D:    0.00 0.00 0.00 0.00 0.00 0.00 0.00 0.00 0.00 0.00 0.00 0.00 0.00
 FI_L:    0.00 0.00 0.00 0.00 0.00 0.00 0.00 0.00 0.00 0.00 0.00 0.00 0.00
  REF:    0.00 0.00 0.00 0.00 0.00 0.00 0.00 0.00 0.00 0.00 0.00 0.00 0.00
  REC:    0.00 0.00 0.00 0.00 1.00 0.00 0.00 0.00 0.00 0.00 0.00 0.00 0.00
CAUSE:    0.00 0.00 0.00 0.00 0.00 0.00 0.00 0.00 0.00 0.00 0.00 0.00 0.00
  LOC:    0.00 0.00 0.00 0.00 0.00 0.00 0.00 0.00 0.00 0.00 0.00 0.00 0.00

Heads:
 - applicare (occ 5)     - corrispondere (occ 2)    - distribuire (occ 1)
 - effettuare (occ 1)    - derivare (occ 1)         - dichiarare (occ 1)
 - eseguire (occ 1)

                              ( b )
```

Legenda of conceptual relations: AGEN = AGENTIVE, AFF = AFFECTED, FI_S = FIGURATIVE SOURCE, MANN = MANNER, FI_D = FIGURATIVE DESTINATION, FI_L = FIGURATIVE LOCATION, REF = REFERENCE, REC = RECIPIENT, CAUSE = CAUSE, LOC = LOCATION. *Legenda* of semantic tags: A = ACT, HE = HUMAN ENTITY, D = DOCUMENT, AM = AMOUNT, G = GOODS, RE = REAL ESTATE, S = STATUS, TE = TEMPORAL ENTITY, AE = ABSTRACT ENTITY, Q = QUALITY, M = MANNER.

Figure 7.4
Example of clusters produced by CIAULA at levels 1 (a) and 3 (b)

basic level classes of the classification those bringing most predictive and stable information with respect to the presentation order.

The notion of basic level classes has been introduced in [Rosch, 1978] (Section 7.1.1). What is a basic-level class for verbs? A formal definition for these more representative classes, able to guide the intuition of the linguist in the categorization activity has been attempted, and will be discussed in the next section.

7.3.1 Formalizing the notion of basic level categories

The information conveyed by the derived clusters, $C = \langle c, [x]_{ij}, V, S \rangle$, is in the distributions of the matrices $[x]_{ij}$, and in the set V. Two examples may be helpful at distinguishing classes that are more selective, from other more vague clusters.

Let $C1$ be a singleton class, with $C1 = \langle 1, [x1], V1, \{\emptyset\} \rangle$. $c = 1$ clearly implies that $[x1]$ is binary. This class is highly *typical*, as it is strongly characterized by its only instance, but it has no generalization power. Given, for example, a class $C1 = \langle 10, [x2], V2, S \rangle$ for which the cardinality of a $V2$ is 10, and let $[x2]$ be such that for each couple $\langle i, j \rangle$ for which $x2_{ij} \neq 0$, it follows $x2_{ij} = 1/10$. This class is scarcely typical but has a *strong generalization power*, as it clusters verbs that show no overlaps between the thematic roles they are represented by. We can say that typicality is signaled by high values of roles-types probabilities (i.e. $x_{ij} = P((R_i : Cat_j) \mid C)$) while the generalization power ω of a class $C = \langle c, [x]_{ij}, V, S \rangle$, is related to the following quantity:

$$\omega = card(V)/c \tag{7.3.10}$$

To quantify the typicality of a class $C = \langle c, [x]_{ij}, V, S \rangle$, the following definitions are useful. Given a threshold $\alpha \in [0, 1]$, the *typicality* of C is given by:

$$\tau_C = \frac{\sum_{i,j \in T_C} x_{ij}}{card(T_C)} \tag{7.3.11}$$

where T_C is the *typicality set* of C, i.e. $\{i, j\} \mid x_{ij} > \alpha$.

DEF (Basic-level verb category): Given two thresholds $\gamma, \delta \in [0, 1]$, $C = \langle c, [x]_{ij}, V, S \rangle$ is a *basic-level category* for the related taxonomy iff:

$$\omega < \gamma \quad \textit{(generalization power)} \tag{7.3.12}$$

$$\tau_C > \delta \qquad \textit{(typicality)} \tag{7.3.13}$$

Like all the classes derived by the algorithm of Section 7.2.4, each basic-level category $C = \langle c, [x]_{ij}, V, S \rangle$ determines two fuzzy membership values of the verb v included in V. The *local membership* of v to C, $\mu_1 C_{(v)}$, is defined by:

$$\mu_1 C_{(v)} = \sharp_v / \max\{\sharp \mid \langle w, \sharp_w \rangle \in V\} \tag{7.3.14}$$

The *global membership* of v to C, $\mu_2 C_{(v)}$, is:

$$\mu_2 C_{(v)} = \sharp_v / n_v \tag{7.3.15}$$

where n_v is the number of different instances of v in the learning set. (7.3.14) depends on the contribution of v to the distribution of probabilities $[x]_{ij}$, i.e. it measures the adherence of v to the prototype. (7.3.15) determines how typical is the classification of v in C, with respect to all the observations of v in the corpus. Low values of the global membership are useful at identifying instances of v that are likely to be originated by parsing errors.

Given a classification T of extended sets of linguistic instances, the definition of basic-level category earlier identifies all the basic-level classes. Repeated experiment over the two corpora demonstrated that these classes are almost invariant with respect to the presentation order of the instances.

7.3.2   Linguistic analysis

We derived the basic level categories for the three domains, and we studied the effect of changing the parameters v, γ and δ. Though we could empirically determine an optimal range for each parameter, the final choice depends upon the domain. The problem is that, except for verbs that are used in a very narrow, technical sense in each domain, the thematic structure of verbs is variegated and poorly overlapping. Hence small variations in the values of γ and δ critically affect the shape of the derived clusters. One can get small clusters (2-3 instances) of highly similar verbs, or larger clusters with partially overlapping verb patterns. The best compromise depends upon the sublanguage and its variability.

Appendix 1 shows all the basic level categories derived from a small learning set, named DPR633, that belongs to the legal corpus. CIAULA receives in input 293 examples of 30 verbs. The reason for showing DPR633 rather than an excerpt of the results derived from the full corpus is that there was no objective way to select among the over 300 basic level classes. In the Appendix, the relatively low values of μ_1 and μ_2 are due to the small example set, rather than to errors in parsing, as remarked in the previous section. Of course, the basic-level classes extracted from the larger corpora exhibit a more striking similarity among their members, indicated by highest values of global and local membership. An example of two clusters extracted from the whole legal corpus was shown in Figure 7.4.

The example shown in the Appendix 1 is, however, "good enough" to highlight some interesting property of our clustering method. Each cluster has a semantic description, and the degree of local and global membership of verbs give an objective measure of the similarity among cluster members. It is interesting to observe that the algorithm classifies in distinct clusters different verb usage's. For example, the cluster 4 and the cluster 6 classify two different usage's of the verb *indicare*, e.g., *indicare un'ammontare (to indicate an amount)* and *indicare un motivo (to specify a motivation)*, where *"ammontare"* is a type of AMOUNT(AM) and *"motivo"* is a type of ABSTRACT_ENTITY (AE).

The two clusters 13 and 14 capture the physical and abstract use of *eseguire*, e.g., *eseguire un'opera(to build a building)*(=REAL_ESTATE) vs. *eseguire un pagamento (to make a payment*(=AMOUNT,ACT)).

The clusters 3 and 6 classify two uses of the verb *tenere*, i.e. *tenere un registro (to keep a record*(=DOCUMENT) vs. *tenere un discorso (to hold a speech*(=ABSTRACT_ENTITY)). Many other (often domain-dependent) examples are reflected in the derived classification.

Appendix 2 shows the basic level clusters derived from an excerpt of the remote sensing domain. Many verbs in this domain are used in a rather technical sense. For example, *contribute* in class 1488 is found in patterns like *"the modification*(=ACT) *contributes to ... by smoothing* (=ACT) *the ratio...,"* i.e. the same pattern of verbs like *correlate, calculate,* and *estimate.* etc, which more intuitively would be considered "similar."

Examples of ambiguous verbs are often found even in this domain. For example, the verb *observe* in class 1988 is found in the sense of *"to observe a correlation, property* (=COGNITIVE_CONTENT),"* while in class 351 the same verb has the pattern *" to observe an area, a territory* (=LOCATION) etc.

7.4   Summary

To summarize, we believe that CIAULA has several advantages:

1. The derived clusters have a semantic description, namely the predicted *thematic roles* of its members.
2. The clustering algorithm incrementally assigns instances to classes, evaluating its choices on the basis of a formal criterium, *the global utility*.
3. The defined measures of typicality and generalization power make it possible to select the basic-level classes of a hierarchy, i.e. those that are repository of most lexical information about their members. These classes demonstrated substantially stable with respect to the order of presentation option, i.e. the predicted thematic roles of its members.
4. It is possible to discriminate different usage's of verbs, since verb instances are considered individually.

The hierarchy, as obtained by CIAULA, is not usable *tout court* by a NLP system, however class descriptions and basic-level categories are very useful at addressing the intuition of the linguist, since they suggest many interesting and subtle categories that may hold in a specific language domain.

Appendix 1:
Basic level classes derived from the DPR633 Corpus

List of semantic tags in the Legal Domain:

A = ACT; HE = HUMAN ENTITY; D = DOCUMENT; AM = AMOUNT; G = GOODS; RE = REAL ESTATES; S = STATUS; TE = TEMPORAL ENTITY; AE = ABSTRACT ENTITY; Q = QUALITY; M = MANNER.

Figure 7.5
Basic level classes derived from the DPR633 Corpus

Appendix 2:
Basic level classes derived from the Remote Sensing Corpus

List of WORDNET semantic tags in the Remote Sensing Domain:

A = ACT, HUMAN ACTION; HE = PERSON, INDIVIDUAL; O = ORGANIZA-
TION; CGN = CONTENT, COGNITIVE CONTENT; Art = ARTIFACT, ARTICLE;
SD = SCIENCE, SCIENTIFIC DISCIPLINE; TP = TIME PERIOD, AMOUNT OF
TIME; INS = INTRUMENTALITY; Loc = LOCATIONS; PR = PROPERTY; NO =
NATURAL OBJECT; ABS = ABSTRACTION; ATTR = ATTRIBUTE.

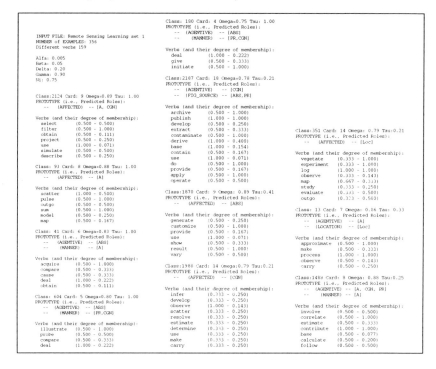

Figure 7.6
Basic level classes derived from the Remote Sensing Corpus

8 Distinguished Usage

Scott A. Waterman

8.1 Introduction

Recently, some implementors of NLP systems have been moving away from using conventional syntactic parsing methods, instead adopting a variety of *pattern based* approaches for complex understanding tasks such as the Message Understanding Conferences [MUC-4, 1992], [MUC-5, 1993] and the ARPA-sponsored TIPSTER project. These pattern-based systems are characterized by short and fairly specific lexically indexed patterns which are used to specify the relation between strings in the source text and particular entries in a problem-dependent knowledge representation. The patterns are variously represented by regular expression strings [Cowie *et al.*, 1993], small sets of limited-context grammar rules [Lehnert *et al.*, 1991], finite-state automata [Hobbs and Appelt, 1992], and other suitable schemes.

This one-level process or pattern matching substitutes for a conventional two-level process of a full syntactic parse followed by semantic interpretation.

With considerably less time and development effort (notably demonstrated by [Lehnert *et al.*, 1991], [Hobbs and Appelt, 1992]), these systems achieve performance comparable to more standard systems that rely heavily on full syntactic analysis [Hobbs *et al.*, 1990], [Grishman *et al.*, 1992]. However, because these pattern-based systems are still viewed as linguistically ungrounded and somewhat *ad hoc*, formal work in the application and acquisition of lexical patterns has lagged system development. In most current systems, patterns are produced through tedious hand analysis of text [Lehnert *et al.*, 1991], [Cowie *et al.*, 1993], [Hobbs and Appelt, 1992], while system coverage of the text material is gained either through extensive linguistic knowledge on the part of the researcher (in judging appropriate pattern generalizations), or by generating and testing massive numbers of patterns.

One exception to this tedious hand analysis is Lehnert's work [Lehnert *et al.*, 1992], in which machine learning techniques are used to infer possible patterns for extraction. While this *AutoSlog* technique has dramatically reduced system development time, the inference techniques used are weak in the sense that they cannot identify new phenomena that may have linguistic or practical relevance. Further, they use only sparse linguistic information, and provide no means of generalizing patterns across semantic domains.

8.1.1 A theoretical framework

By relating lexical pattern-based approaches to a lexical semantic framework, such as the Generative Lexicon theory [Pustejovsky, 1991], my aim is to provide a basis through which pattern-based understanding systems can be understood in more conventional linguistic terms. Within such a framework, methods for pattern acquisition can be studied and developed, while the effectiveness of patterns, in terms of functionality and agreement with linguistic theory, can be assessed.

My main contention is that such a framework can be developed by viewing the lexical patterns as structural mappings from text to denotation in a compositional lexical semantics, blurring the distinction between syntactic and semantic analysis, and obviating the need for separate syntactic and semantic processing systems. This interpretation follows directly from an appeal to functional semantic principles, and from their theoretical relation to syntactic properties. In the framework I present, patterns indexed to individual words relate semantic interpretations to lexical constraints, in a manner dictated by the lexical items in context and their configuration. The interpretation of large constructions is made possible by matching the mutual constraints of multiple words as they appear together. This interpretive mechanism could be realized as a lexically indexed semantic grammar, implemented in a parsing formalism such as LTAGs [Schabes *et al.*, 1988], link grammars or slot grammars. In such a system, the interpretations of single words are dictated by the constraints of context, and these constraints are combined for multiple words to provide a consistent interpretation for phrasal and sentential constructions.

8.1.2 Pattern acquisition

The approach to lexical pattern acquisition outlined here seeks to automatically separate the various modes in which a lexical item is used.

These *modes of use* are distinguished on the basis of context cues — the presence (or absence) of particular lexical items and members of syntactic classes correlated with their various configurations in the context of the term under study. The distinguishing cues for these modes are defined *inductively* from a large set of example usage of the term. Because the distinctions are based on syntactic behavior theoretically related to semantic variance, these modes of use should also provide semantically relevant distinctions.

Once this sort of automatic classification of modes has been performed, it is up to the linguistically knowledgable researcher or system user to relate each to the practical semantic representation. Because the acquisition process is necessarily disconnected from the real world semantics of the language, this sort of interpretive labeling must be made in a semantically grounded manner (i.e., by the researcher). However, because a relevant classification has already been made by automatic means, the task is much simplified. If we divide lexicon development into stages of identifying relevant syntactic and semantic categories, classifying the lexical items, and attaching to each item its appropriate semantics, the first two have been performed automatically. The third, I would argue, can not be automated without a truly intelligent machine; the in-depth world knowledge required to provide the semantic interpretation of language is available only to an agent operating in the world.

Related work describing automatic lexical acquisition rarely attempts to focus on identifying the multiple uses of a single term, instead only classifying words against other words [Schütze, 1993a], [Basili *et al.*, 1993d], [Pereira *et al.*, 1993]. Other work, primarily dealing with acquiring subcategorization frames [Brent, 1991a], [Ushioda *et al.*, 1993] is similar in flavor to the present work, but searches for occurrences of a fixed set of previously identified syntactic patterns, rather than inducing them from the textual structure.

These and other works describing corpus techniques for deducing lexical structure [Pustejovsky, 1992], [Pustejovsky and Anick, 1988] and semantically marked selectional frames [Grishman and Sterling, 1992] also suggest that lexical/semantic patterns can be induced from corpora, but do not directly apply to the generation of distributed pattern-based systems.

8.2   Information Extraction

The recent Message Understanding Conferences (MUCs) and ARPA TIPSTER project have posed a complex and fairly specific problem in text understanding. The problem given is that of creating semantic *templates* or *frames* to correspond to newswire and newspaper articles about a particular subject. The expressiveness of the templates is restricted and somewhat skeletal, capturing the bare facts of the text, and not its complete meaning. Hobbs [Hobbs and Appelt, 1992] has argued effectively that the problem is not one of full text understanding, but specifically one of *information extraction* — many types of information, such as speaker attitude, intensional constructs, facts not relevant to the chosen domain, etc., are not required. Only a representation-specific set of domain information is the target for extraction, while other non-pertinent information may be ignored.

These types of systems provide a useful groundwork for the study of text interpretation systems because of the relative lack of difficulty in representing and manipulating the resulting knowledge structures. Although denotational structures for the type of factual information required in extraction can be quite complex, they are still far more tractable than representations of speaker attitude, opaque contexts, or intensional constructions.

For example, in the ongoing TIPSTER project, information in only two specific domains is to be extracted — one domain is joint ventures and business ownership, the other the microelectronics industry. The domains are further restricted by the particular hierarchy of predicate types used in the knowledge representation. Each domain has a set of *templates* (a particular database object implementation) which rigidly define what types of facts and relations from the text are representable.

8.2.1   Mapping — extraction : text $\mapsto$ KR

These information extraction tasks, as a subset of text understanding tasks, can be viewed as *mapping problems*, in which the problem is to find the proper representation, in terms of templates, for the source text. One needs to find the mapping from the strings of the source text to a problem-dependent knowledge representation scheme.

The template knowledge representation used in the TIPSTER/MUC tasks is based on a frame-like system commonly known as the *entity-*

relation, or ER, model.

The ER model codes information as multi-place *relations*. Typically, each type of relation has a fixed number of arguments, each of which is an *entity* in the model. Entities can either be *atomic* — in the case of TIPSTER, atoms can be strings from text or items from a predetermined hierarchy of types — or they can be *composite*, referring to other relational structures.

Objects referenced in text often participate in more than one relationship. For example, the direct object of a sentence will often be the subject of a subordinate clause, either explicitly, or through a pronominal reference. In a strict ER model, two atoms, each denoting this direct object, would have to be used, once for each clause. By a slight extension, atoms in the ER model can be generalized to objects which can take multiple references. Thus, no real atoms appear in relations, but only references to atoms, or to other relations. This model is often termed an *object-oriented* model, but because of the overloading of that name in so many fields, I prefer to call these models *reference-relation* models. The important extension from the more standard model is that everything is accessible by reference, and that atomic structures are not singularly bound into one relation.

8.3 Functionality in Lexical Semantics

The structure of the denotational representation is important not only for its expressiveness, but also in its relationship to the structure of the language it is to be derived from. If one takes the stand that the surface structure of language is not arbitrary, but rather depends heavily on semantic constraints stemming from the concepts and relations that are conveyed through its use, then the form of these concepts becomes highly important. An accurate model of these relations and constraints will have a benefit in implying and constraining both their appearance in the language, and the possible styles of semantic representation.

Many, if not most, theories used in computational linguistics today assume some degree of *functionality* in language, with corresponding structures at the syntactic and semantic levels. This assumption is so pervasive that it can be difficult to separate the syntactic and semantic descriptions. Even purely syntactic theories exhibit this phenomenon:

words are said to act as operators, or to take arguments, when what is really meant is that they appear in particular syntactic constructs. For example, a syntactic theory such as CCG [Steedman, 1986] uses terms like 'function application' and 'function combination' to refer to the behavior of lexical items, whereas the theory is a proof-theoretic analysis of syntax. The only function application available on theoretical grounds here is at a metasyntactic-level — that of applying combinators to derive categories from other categories. By positing functional behavior to the lexical items and categories themselves, one implicitly attributes meaning to them.

These functional concepts are not directly applicable to the symbols used in a language, but apply only in a semantic domain, a world of ideas and relations. This vocabulary of functional structure has its most recent origins in mathematical descriptions of meaning, such as predicate logic and the lambda calculus. That fact that accepted grammatical theories of language (e.g., CFG, LFG, CCG, HPSG, GB) have co-opted this vocabulary, and assume a parallel functional structure, should be clear evidence that these functional semantic structures have parallels in syntax.

8.3.1   Semantic constraints on language

If semantic constraints play such a role in determining syntactic properties, through what mechanisms do they operate? This is really one of the fundamental questions of linguistics, and one in which a enormous amount of effort has been expended. With the deference due to such an enterprise, I will attempt to outline what I see as the three major sorts of semantic mapping mechanism that have been explored: categorical, morphological, and structural.

All three mechanisms assume some degree of functionality in the treatment of composition; that is, terms can have semantic roles associated with them that are expected to take fillers from the surrounding context. The roles here are objects or relations that are semantically associated with the lexical entry — semantic constituents that can be integrated with the meaning of the term. An object reference such as 'chair' implies the concept of sitting, and of a sitter. 'Cooperation' implies the notion of participant, which itself implies an event to participate in. A verb such as 'eat' has associated with it an eater and something being eaten. It is obvious that not all of these associations are always realized lexically. It is the manner and degree to which these associated roles are and can be expressed that is controlled by the three following constraint mechanisms.

Categorical constraints   These specify the semantic or functional class of the arguments for a lexical entry. In order to fill the role, the argument must satisfy these class restrictions. In our simple 'eat' example, the filler of the EATER role must be capable of eating. In existing lexical systems, this information, when given for verbs, is often expressed as the role labels of subcategorization frames. The type of the argument itself can be expressed in a number of ways; e.g., in a feature-based class system, it might be +ANIMATE or +CONSUMER or some such equivalent.

This kind of categorical constraint is not limited to verbs; other forms project semantic category constraints as well. Adverbs, loosely speaking, are a class that take events as arguments. Many nouns take relational arguments as well, although it may be less obvious. *Brother*, for example, needs a person to be the brother of, as in *my brother*, or *Joe's brother*.

The category information of the role fillers needed to match these constraints can be present in a number of forms. It may be found implicitly in the semantic denotation of the filler (as with *Joe*), or it can be explicitly provided through morphology (see below) or through *functional typing*. This sort of category identification moderates role filling through secondary functional terms, which accept the ultimate filler and force a particular interpretation of it. In English, the prepositions are used primarily in this capacity, taking nominal arguments and *coercing* them to match the roles provided by higher level structure. For instance, directional terms such as *west* or *left* can take a reference argument, which is logically a location. Terms often used as fillers for this argument, however, don't have a usual location interpretation. Their interpretation is moderated by the role assignment and implicit type assignment behavior of the prepositions: 'west *of* the house,' 'left *from* the tree.' This behavior is part of a larger family of type shifting mechanisms, called *type coercion* [Pustejovsky, 1991], in which the expected or available role types force a particular interpretation of the filler.

Morphological constraints   These specify the relation between the available realizations of a lexical entry and the various possible subsets of its meaning. While the core meaning of an entry is fixed, certain common properties, e.g., number, time reference, etc., are more variable. These peripheral semantic properties can be fixed through the choice of morphological form.

Morphological constraints also play a large part in determining what role in some relation a lexical item is allowed to fill. In this *case marking*, morphology is used to indicate how this lexical item relates to the semantic roles being required by a higher level structure.

Morphological variations span a wide range of consistency: they can be relatively uniform across the lexicon, as in the case of tense and number variation, or can be completely idiosyncratic.

Structural constraints   These determine the ordering and configurational structure of the arguments. These constraints determine how the realizations of the roles of the relation denoted by a lexical item may be appear relative to one another and to the entry. Global word ordering (SVO, SOV, etc.) is a high level manifestation of these constraints. Some terms have more individual constraints: the genitive marker *'s* in English takes its single argument to the left; the two arguments to a conjunction appear to either side. No entry seems to constrain the realizations of its arguments to a particular numbers of words, so we may assume that this configurational specificity does not work at the level of the lexical unit, but rather at the level of the semantic unit. Phrasal items, whose semantics have been encapsulated as a single concept, are the items over which the configurations are specified.

None of these constraint mechanisms is inviolable; nor are they independent. The interactions between the three often displays strange variability, especially where they interact heavily. In English, for example, there is little morphological marking of roles, and structural and categorical constraints seem to bear the burden of relational assignment. However, when role assignments are made explicitly by functional type casting, as when prepositional phrases are used as arguments, positional constraints can be overridden. In a heavily case-marked language such as Latin, however, we see far less dependence on the structural constraints, as the role/filler correspondence has already been made through morphological constraints, and word order can be more variable.

There is an immediate parallel between the semantic specification of function/argument structure and the specification of the reference-relation representations: the function is analogous to the predicate relation, while the arguments are the referenced components of the relation. In computational linguistic models, this sort of functional semantics has proved very useful in providing a mechanism for deriving frame-like denotations when processing language (predicate logic and unification frames, two of the more popular denotation schemes, are both subsets of the general relational models). In fact, it is often the case that the relations of the models are the same as the semantic relations specified by the language. (Whether this is because of a desire for representational efficiency or for other reasons I leave unexplored.)

8.4   Integrating Syntactic with Semantic Constraints

Because these three type of interpretation constraints interact so heavily, a mechanism that explicitly examines the degree of specificity in argument *position* and in argument *type*, and especially their interaction with one another in use, should be better able to achieve the goals of interpretation; that is, to relate the text to a particular denotation.

Theoretical approaches to lexical semantics have begun to incorporate this merging of syntactic and semantic description. The incorporation of argument structure or selectional frames is a large step in this direction. While the notion of argument structure is usually applied only to verbs, some theories, such as the generative lexicon theory (GL), extend the idea to include *all* lexical categories [Pustejovsky, 1991]. For the purposes of this discussion, we can consider the GL lexicon to have a three-part representation of these lexical constraints associated with every term:

1. **Semantic structure** which provides the relational structure denoted by the entry. This includes categorical constraints for fillers, and default values for unspecified fillers. These categorical constraints and relational structure are contained in the *qualia* description of the entry. These constraints are used both in deriving expectations for the syntactic form of arguments, and in *coercing* ambiguous or polysemous arguments into the required types.
2. **Appearance information** which indicates how this entry can appear at the symbol level, including morphology.

3. **Cospecification** which relates the possible fillers of the semantic structure to various realization forms, including argument configuration and syntactic realization information. These constraints can be specified much like regular expressions, and can provide varying degrees of 'fit' to the syntax.

It is easy to see how a theoretical approach such as this, based on these lexical constraints, could be operationalized in an understanding system. Using a lexically indexed system, the configurational constraints (cospecifications) of each term could be expanded against the context of that term in order to find a structural match. This match, which is essentially a parse of the context, would then be tested for consistency with the semantic constraints, to find whether there is an interpretation of each of the structural components matching the appropriate semantic type constraints. Perhaps various alternate configurations would have to be tested against the various possible interpretations of the term, but once this is done, a complete interpretation of the word in context has been formed.

This system, which by conjoining argument type and positional information avoids making a distinction between separate syntactic and semantic analysis, would be a *pattern system*. This system has been implemented, in part, in the DIDEROT information extraction system [Cowie *et al.*, 1993].

8.5 Patterns

Pattern-based understanding systems combine syntactic and semantic processing through the use of *patterns*. Patterns consist of lexically indexed syntactic templates that are matched to text, in much the same way as are regular expressions, along with type constraints on substrings of the match. Portions of the syntactic template are referenced to the semantic representation of the lexical item, so that text found matching these portions of the pattern must also have denotations consistent with the corresponding semantic roles.

These patterns can be thought of as lexically indexed local grammar fragments, annotated with semantic relations between the various arguments and the knowledge representation. In the most general system, the units of matching could range from single lexical items to phrasal components or variables with arbitrary type constraints. The variables in the pattern can be mapped directly into the knowledge representation, or, through type constraints, used as abstract specifications on the syntax. In general, the pattern matching system is a local phenomenon, which doesn't seek to create a global syntactic analysis. However, because of typing constraints interacting between multiple patterns, global structures and long-distance phenomena can be observed.

8.5.1   DIDEROT, a pattern example

For example, in the DIDEROT project [Cowie *et al.*, 1993], a pattern is represented as a GL structure (GLS) which gives the syntactic context along with mappings from text variables to a predicate logic knowledge representation. A typical set of patterns used to extract joint-venture events, indexed here from the word 'establish,' is given in figure 8.1.

The cospecification information is contained here in the `cospec` field. The index variable 'self' is used to refer to an appearance of any of the morphological forms of 'establish.' These forms are given in the `syn(...)` field. Other parts of the `cospec` are either literals, such as 'venture' or 'agreement,' which must match the text exactly, or variables (A1, A2, A3...). The `args` field indicates how argument variables should be realized syntactically. A1 and A2 here must be `type(np)`, where np designates a heuristic class of noun phrases. The last element of the cospec, '*,' is a Kleene star over all tokens — anything or nothing may appear in this position.

The semantic structure of the entry is given in `template_semantics` a field which specifically relates the arguments which match the appearance template (the `cospec`) to the relational semantic of the knowledge representation. The argument variables are restricted to a semantic *type path*, such as `[code_2,joint_organ]`, given in the `qualia` field. The type path establishes a region in a type hierarchy which must contain the type of the argument [Pustejovsky and Boguraev, 1993].

Because of the difficulty and expense of deriving patterns, GLSs could not be produced for every term of importance in DIDEROT. Rather, large segments of the lexicon are statically typed in a sublexicon less intricate than the GLS lexicon. When the GLS is applied to text, the matching of argument variables is accomplished either by calls to GLSs of the appropriate type, or by the invocation of small heuristic grammars. These small grammars combine the type information of their constituents to

```
gls(establish,
  syn(...),
  args([arg1(A1,
        syn([type(np)]),
        qualia([formal([code_2,organization])])),
      arg2(A2,
        syn([type(np)]),
        qualia([formal([code_2,joint_organ])])),
      arg3(A3,
        syn([type(np),morph([establish,etablished,...])]),
        qualia([formal([code_2,organization])])))]),
  qualia([formal(tie_up_lcp)]),
  cospec([
    [A1,*,self,*,A2,*,with,A3],
    [A1,and,A3,*,self,*,A2],
    [A1,together,with,A3,*,self,*,A2],
    [A2,is,to,be,self,*,with, A3],
    [A1,*,signed,*,agreement,*,self, A2],
    [A1,*,self,*,joint,venture,A2,with,A3],
    [A2,was,self,with,A3]]),
  types(tie_up_verb),
  template_semantics(pt_tie_up,
      tie_up([A1,A3],A2,_,existing,_))).
```

Figure 8.1
A GLS for 'establish'

match the constraints of the governing GLS.

These subgrammars are used especially for proper name recognition. Both company names and human names are matched using small grammars based on part-of-speech tags and the sublexicon typing. Some company names are keyed from semantic indicators such as 'Corp.' and 'Inc.,' while many human and place names are identified from a large fixed name lexicon.

Overall, other pattern-based systems operate in much the same manner, varying somewhat in details concerning the amount of machinery for pattern-matching, and the richness of the typing systems.

8.6   The Current State of Pattern Acquisition

The TIPSTER and MUC projects have provided a wealth of knowledge about the difficulty of building pattern-based systems. The hardest and most time-consuming task involved is certainly the acquisition of patterns, which is still done primarily by tedious hand analysis. Working backwards from the *key* templates (hand generated knowledge representations of texts as interpreted by the project sponsors), one can, by careful reading of the text, usually find those segments of text which correspond to the representation entries. Although the key templates are originally created by a researcher doing a careful reading, the correspondence between text segments and the key templates has not been recorded, making the process error prone and leaving the text open for reinterpretation. The next step, that of correlating the text with the representation and deriving a pattern which captures the relation, is the most tedious and difficult part of the task. Typing constraints for each class of predicate must be remembered by the researcher performing the task, and interactions between patterns must be identified and analyzed for possible interference.

At least two of the systems used in the MUC and TIPSTER projects used some automatic acquisition techniques. The *Autoslog* component of the CIRCUS system [Lehnert *et al.*, 1992] attempted to find valid patterns from a pre-parsed input, using an inference mechanism derived by matching new text against previously filled templates. Even though the patterns are produced from single occurrences of matches, so that any one pattern is unlikely to generalize, the system achieved surprising performance through shear coverage. This system reduced the pattern lexicon development time by hundreds of ours.

In the DIDEROT system, two levels of automatic pattern construction were used. First, information from structured dictionary entries [Boguraev and Briscoe, 1989a], [Wilks *et al.*, 1990b] was used to derive moderately effective, but fairly unspecific lexical patterns. Further pattern acquisition was performed by automating concordance studies to find syntactic patterns which were statistically relevant over many uses of a term. The techniques presented here are an outgrowth of this work on inducing patterns from examples found in corpus.

8.7 Structural Similarity Clustering

The pattern systems described here attempt to relate the use of terms in context to corresponding denotations. One of the major assumptions made here, as well as in all algorithmic computational linguistic systems, is one of *consistency* of use and meaning — that a term, or any linguistic structure, used in a particular fashion will give rise to the same denotation today as it will tomorrow. The goals of any grammar induction or lexical semantic acquisition problem are to define those particulars — to find the distinguishing features of the usage as they relate to the features of the denotation.

The approach given here focuses only on the *structural* features of usage and denotation. By classifying features relevant to the text-to-denotation mapping, the aim is to provide a vocabulary and mechanism for deriving and evaluating interpretation procedures.

The reason for this focus stems from the nature of the available data. Raw text is abundant — consider the hundreds of megabytes of text available through newswire services, through email and USENET, or through reference corpora. This raw text gives direct information about the *structural* constraints a term is subject to — how it appears relative to other terms. It does not offer information as readily for semantic or morphological forms of lexical knowledge. To build a database of sense tagged, or even simply phrase-bracketed text requires enormous amounts of manpower not available to the average lexical researcher. This considerations limit us to investigating only the structural aspects of the corpus data.

One method for investigating these structural interactions is that of classifying their uses into categories which have some *structural similarity*. This similarity can be defined either in syntactic or semantic terms. In terms of the function-argument structure or reference-relation representations, words with similar type ambiguities and similar argument number are described as being syntactically similar, while differing in interpretation. On the other side, categories with similar functional or relational type are said to have similar semantics, even though their functional properties within the language (number and typical realization of arguments) might differ considerably.

This work provides a step in forming a vocabulary of categorical (semantic) and structural (syntactic) classes through which we can describe the constraints acting between words. Classification methods for both lexical and semantic structure are outlined here. As I have already mentioned, however, semantic data is hard to come by, and it would be more practical to limit the study to the lexical structure only. An experimental implementation of the lexical approach is presented in the latter sections of the chapter.

8.7.1 Acquiring lexical structure

Without considering its semantics, the use of a word can be expressed solely by its lexical environment, or context. Grammar-driven systems as well as pattern systems achieve their performance by relying on the expected structural properties of the language. If one can capture the consistencies and paradigms in the usage of a word in explicit terms of the similarities and common structural properties of the lexical environment in which that word appears, then one has a description of its structural constraints associated with it. This is, of course, what traditional systems do with grammar rules which dictate what structures, and with what other terms, a word may be used. Using a lexicalized grammar helps to make this relationship explicit, but it exists in all grammars.

From the acquisition point of view, however, we are presented with a very lexicalized version of the data. To study a word's usage, all we need do is observe the literal context in which it is used. Of course, some suitable representation of that context is needed. Partial parse trees, as in LTAGs, would be perhaps ideal, but the data we are presented with contains no parse or bracketing information.

Instead, we can form a description using the data we have — the identity and position of the surrounding lexical items. Using this, we can form a probabilistic description of what structure we expect to find in context. Given enough data, we might be able to form distinct categories of what that context looks like.

For example, the simplest probabilistic description of a context would have, for each position preceding and following the item, a distribution of the likelihood of occurrence of every other word (see fig. 8.2). This is very similar in style to n-gram models, which are used along with Markov models of language (see e.g., [Baker, 1975]). The primary difference here is that n-gram models are primarily used to predict a single item of a sequence after having observed $n - 1$ items, whereas a context

$$\cdots \quad \begin{bmatrix} p(\alpha_2{=}w_1) \\ p(\alpha_2{=}w_2) \\ \vdots \\ p(\alpha_2{=}w_3) \end{bmatrix} \begin{bmatrix} p(\alpha_1{=}w_1) \\ p(\alpha_1{=}w_2) \\ \vdots \\ p(\alpha_1{=}w_3) \end{bmatrix} \quad k \quad \begin{bmatrix} p(\beta_1{=}w_1) \\ p(\beta_1{=}w_2) \\ \vdots \\ p(\beta_1{=}w_3) \end{bmatrix} \begin{bmatrix} p(\beta_2{=}w_1) \\ p(\beta_2{=}w_2) \\ \vdots \\ p(\beta_2{=}w_3) \end{bmatrix} \quad \cdots$$

Figure 8.2
A simple probabilistic representation of the context about k.

description such as this is used to predict the n items surrounding the one of primary interest.

A lexicon which used these context vectors to encode the structural constraints would have many context vectors for each entry. Each vector would capture one of the *modes of use* of the term — one of the principle categories of context in which it is used. Since the structural constraints of an entry are dictated by its meaning, the term would have a separate interpretation in each of the different modes. In the pattern lexicon presented earlier (fig. 8.1), these separate modes of use are represented crudely by regular expressions in the `cospec` field. Each mode is given a separate mapping from its components to the relational semantic structure of the entry.

To acquire such a lexicon, a collection of usage would be analyzed in order to pick out these natural classes of context. Since they are defined purely in terms of the lexical environment, the collection would have to be fairly large in order to observe enough occurrences of similar structure to ensure statistical relevance.

These similarities of context would be determined by the structural similarities of their component strings of words. The presence and relative ordering of identical words, words belonging to the same structural similarity classes, or phrasal components, recursively defined in terms of context types, would be the environment features necessary for determining these classes.

Groups of contexts could be organized into context types based on these similarity measures, with group membership determined by similarity. The contexts could be assembled into a hierarchical structure, in which groups of high similarity combine to form higher-order clusters encompassing the structural features of their component groups.

Word classes could be defined inductively on this tree of context types by classifying words according to the sets of context types in which they have appeared. The hierarchy of context types and word classes encodes the specificity of the relation to the category. Lower levels of the hierarchy have strict context constraints, while higher levels, combining the classes beneath them, place looser constraints on context patterns. By studying the lexical context classes in relation to the semantic properties of the terms, we could illuminate those features of context which correlate with more general semantic properties as well as those which are idiosyncratic to the individual entries.

An experimental method for performing these sorts of classification is presented in the later part of this chapter, using string edit distance as a metric of similarity, and agglomerative clustering techniques to provide the classification structure.

8.7.2   Semantic structure

In an analogous way, if denotations were available for a sufficiently large quantity of text, the relational structure of the denotations, as it relates to the text could be classified purely from their structural properties. This would give a method for inducing the categorical constraints that go hand-in-hand with the structural constraints given above, but also for inducing the relational structure of the denotations themselves. In exactly the same manner as for context classes, relation predicates could be grouped hierarchically based on similarity of structural features. The features one could use to derive predicate classes include predicate arity, specificity, argument types, and structure depth, as well as a semantic type hierarchy or lattice defined for specific domain.

The large databases of parallel text and denotations that would be necessary for this are certainly not as widely available as text corpora for study. Representations would have to be generated by hand. However, the work in template filling and analysis contributed by the research community to the TIPSTER effort has shown that deriving a sufficient volume is not out of the question.

As with lexical structure, this classification of predicate structure would allow to identify properties generic to all denotation, as well as ones idiosyncratically related to individual terms. It would also provide a mechanism for creating a hierarchy of predicate types, from those which are very specific in their structure and categorical constraints, to ones more loosely constrained and adaptable to circumstance.

8.7.3   Integration

The natural integration of these two lines of study would result in a vocabulary of semantic and lexical classes that would enable the correlation of the lexical structure of a text with its denotational structure, and the derivation of structural mappings between the two.

As an example of the benefits this integration might give to understanding systems, and of how such a structural acquisition system might operate, consider the following example, from the TIPSTER/MUC-5 domain:

Imagine a researcher developing the domain-dependent vocabulary for an extraction system. Assume that the system has a classification of the structural properties of general text, and has also a type hierarchy for general and domain-specific representations.

The researcher has annotated a short segment of text with its interpretation in the problem domain. (See fig. 8.3). In the figure, the indices relate segments of text to their corresponding denotations. SMALL CAPS are used in the denotation to indicate known quantities in the domain specific type hierarchy; mixed case is used for unknown types.

Now that the researcher has provided a connection between text and denotation, the system can use the classifications of context and relation types as a vocabulary to describe the structural mapping. For instance, it is now known that 'IBM,' and also 'Motorola,' which may have been unknown terms, can act as AGENT arguments, and specifically, as the AGENT arguments of a DEVELOPMENT predicate. The system is also given the information that "devices" can act as a PRODUCT within certain relationships, as can "tools."

This annotated text also informs the system that the phrase "is jointly developing" can sit within this particular structured context of phrasal units, and that it bears a certain relationship to the DEVELOPMENT predicate. If this relationship can be correlated with other examples of "developing" mediating a similar context to a DEVELOPMENT predicate, then the system can infer a more general mapping between "developing" within this sort of context and the DEVELOPMENT predicate.

Assuming the system has already acquired a domain-independent encoding of the co-agentive functionality of 'with,' now there is evidence specifically that DEVELOPMENT allows this behavior, and that a configuration giving that interpretation can be generalized as:

$[_A[_B\text{IBM}]_B$ is jointly developing $[_C$practical X-ray tools for $[_D$the manufacture of $[_G\text{devices}]_G$ $[_E$based on 0.25 micron or small geometries$]_E]_D]_C$ with $[_F\text{Motorola}]_F]_A$.

DEVELOPMENT $_A$
{
   AGENT:
   "IBM"$_B$
   "Motorola"$_F$
{
   PRODUCT:
   "tools"$_C$
   {
     TYPE:
     X-RAY
     {
       USE:
       MANUFACTURE$_D$
       {
         PRODUCT:
         "devices"$_G$
         {
           FEATURE_SIZE:
           0.25 μM$_E$

Figure 8.3
A segment of text, marked against a predicate interpretation

$$[A_1 \ldots \text{PRODUCT with } A_2]$$

This knowledge can augment both the entry for 'with' and the mapping structures for DEVELOPMENT relations.

Once the system has been provided with enough text-denotation pairs particular to the domain, it may, relying more heavily on inferred structural knowledge, postulate a general mapping for the word "is," relating the syntactic pattern $[\text{ARG}_1$ is 'X' $\text{ARG}_2 \ldots]$ to a predicate structurelike:

$$
\begin{array}{l}
\text{X-PRED} \\
\{ \quad \text{ARG}_1 \\
\{ \quad \text{ARG}_2
\end{array}
$$

(where the word 'X' is correlated with the predicate X-PRED). This general mapping for 'is' could be used to postulate a correlation between 'developing' and DEVELOPMENT.

Still, one could hope to build a system such as this only through the development of a catalog and vocabulary of structural descriptions.

8.8   Lexical Clustering Using Edit Distance

In order to create a catalog of lexical structural descriptions, one needs a method for comparing and classifying the strings of words that make up the contexts. One method for judging the similarity between strings of lexical items (tokens) is the *edit distance* formulated by Levenshtein [Levenshtein, 1966]. This is a similarity measure based on the minimum number of token insertions, deletions, and substitutions (mutations) required to transform one string into another. A generalization of this edit distance can be made by assigning differing weights to insertions of particular tokens or classes of tokens, and by also assigning weights to token substitution pairs. Straightforward computational methods for finding the edit distance between two strings [Sellers, 1974], [Wagner and Fisher, 1974] have been used on a variety of problems in biology, genetics, speech and handwriting analysis [Sankoff and Kruskal, 1983], as well as in syntactic analysis of formal languages [Lu and Fu, 1977]. (For a good introduction with applications to many domains, see [Sankoff and Kruskal, 1983].)

To demonstrate the generalized edit distance, consider the two strings:

the path that is the path
the way that is not the way

The first string can be transformed into the second by a number of insertion, deletion, and substitution operations. Substitutions are commonly counted as two operations, since they give the same effect as a deletion-insertion combination. In this example, 'not' could be inserted; 'path' could be substituted by 'way,' then the second 'path' deleted at the end, then 'way' inserted; 'that' could be deleted then reinserted, and then 'not' inserted; etc. Many different sequences lead to the same result, but there will be a minimum number of operations required for the transformation.

After a short inspection, we could expect a minimum of 5 operations in this case — two for each change from 'path' to 'way,' and one for the insertion of 'not.'

This distance measure can be generalized to compensate for different similarities between types of tokens. For instance, if one decides that 'way' and 'path' are more similar to each other than either is, say, to 'is' or 'the,' then it would be good to have the substitution of 'path'–'way' amount to less than the possible substitution 'path'–'is.' To accomplish this, a *cost* can be associated with each operation, perhaps even a different cost for each sort of insertion or substitution. Then a transformation of *minimum cost,* rather than minimum operations, can be defined. If one makes the simple assumption that a substitution costs no more than the corresponding deletion-insertion pair, then this minimum cost can be shown to obey metric properties, and defines the *generalized edit distance* between the two strings, with larger distances corresponding to less similar strings.

There is a straightforward method for computing edit distance. In a prime example of dynamic programming, the edit distance is computed for every pair of initial substrings of the two strings under study, with results for shorter substrings combining to give results for longer substrings.

More explicitly, let our two strings be $A = (a_0, a_1, \ldots, a_m)$ and $B = (b_0, b_1, \ldots, b_n)$, where a_i is the ith token in string A, starting with token 1. We let the first component of the the string, a_0, be a *null token,* representing an empty position into which we can insert.

Define also the initial substring $A_i = (a_0, a_1, \ldots, a_i)$ of a string to be the first i tokens, including the null token at the beginning.

The computation starts by assigning $D(A_0, B_0) = 0$, the cost of transforming a_0 to b_0, the null token to itself. Each subsequent step in the computation proceeds with the simple rule:

$$D(A_i, B_j) = \min \begin{cases} D(A_i, B_{j-1}) + D_{\text{insert}}(b_j) \\ D(A_{i-1}, B_j) + D_{\text{insert}}(a_i) \\ D(A_{i-1}, B_{j-1}) + D_{\text{substitute}}(a_i, b_j) \end{cases}$$

where $D_{\text{insert}}(x)$ is the cost for inserting x, and $D_{\text{substitute}}(x, y)$ is the cost of substituting x for y.

Starting with $D(0, 0)$, one can fill each $D(i, j)$ in a table, ending at $D(m, n)$, the edit distance between the two strings. The table is filled from upper left to lower right, as each entry is computed from its upper, leftward, and diagonal neighbors using the minimum rule above. Figure 8.4 gives this table for the example strings.

A ————————————→

B		–	the	path	that	is	the	path
–	0	1	2	3	4	5	6
the	1	0	1	2	3	4	5
way	2	1	2	3	4	5	6
that	3	2	3	2	3	4	5
is	4	3	4	3	2	3	4
not	5	4	5	4	3	4	4
the	6	5	6	5	4	3	4
way	7	6	7	6	5	4	5

Figure 8.4
Dynamic programming for edit distance ('–' is the null token)

8.8.1 String alignments

As a by-product of the edit distance computation, one can create an *alignment* of the two strings. This alignment matches the elements of the two sequences in linear order and shows the correspondence between tokens and substrings of the two matched strings. An alignment can be generated directly from the table created in the edit distance computation by following the path of minima chosen during the computation from the upper left corner to the lower right. Rightward travel along this path corresponds to insertion of a token from string A, downward travel to tokens from string B, and diagonal paths to substitutions. (Multiple minimum paths may result, giving alternate but equivalent alignments.)

The alignment created from our two example strings (figure 8.5) gives the correspondence between the tokens of the two initial strings. From the figure, it is easy to see the structural similarities of the two strings.

–	the	path	that	is	–	the	path
–	the	way	that	is	not	the	way

Figure 8.5
A string alignment table

Alignments can be created for sets of more than two strings. These can be expressed in terms of extended alignment tables, with added rows corresponding to the additional strings. These alignment tables could further be abstracted to probabilistic descriptions of the sequences, like that in figure 8.2. This type of representation has also been used for describing and classifying typical sequences of base-pairs in RNA sequences [Chan and Wang, 1991].

8.9 Context Clustering

A simple clustering technique was chosen which would produce a hierarchical classification of contexts with similar structural properties. In this approach, contexts judged most similar in terms of a generalized edit distance were grouped into clusters. This technique is similar to some methods used in automatic grammar induction [Lu and Fu, 1977].

Clustering was chosen over grammar induction or other abstract techniques for the simple reason that the result is more easily explained from the data. The resultant groupings indicate exactly which data contribute, and alignments can help to determine the exact nature of the contribution. Grammar induction techniques give results so far abstracted from the data that analysis is often unclear.

The clustering procedure used was the group average method, a variety of agglomerative hierarchical clustering often used in biological and genetic studies in numerical taxonomy [Anderberg, 1973]. The technique is *agglomerative* in that groups of increasing size are built from smaller groups. It is *hierarchical* in that each the members of a cluster retain their pre-existing cluster organization, as opposed to a flat structure in which the origins of cluster members are not retained.

The hierarchy produced by the clustering algorithm is useful in judging similarity in a variety of ways. Comparing the clusters at one similarity level with those groups either above or below in the hierarchy gives a good indication of which properties are responsible for the indicated level similarity. Properties of the data may become apparent due to their uniform presence (or absence) at a given level in the hierarchy.

8.9.1 Locality in the edit distance

There is a degree to which purely configurational (syntactic) considerations are local in nature. Syntactic well-formedness and syntactic interactions are properties and behaviors that seem to have a high locality of effect. The presence of phrasal constituents in almost every syntactic theory is evidence of the degree to which this belief is held — phrasal boundaries mark the limits of local syntactic interactions for most word classes. Only some word classes, such as verbs and event-denoting nouns, seem to affect the placement and configuration of more distant constituents. Most word types seem to affect (and, conversely, are affected by) primarily the configuration in their immediate vicinity.

In order to highlight the locality of these configurational effects, the edit distance used in the experiments was modified so as to decrease the importance of token distance from the keyword. One would like to weight near tokens more heavily, but without ignoring the contributions of distant ones. A window function (sometimes called a step function) would be simplest, but would only count near tokens and completely discount far ones. A linear dropoff function would be able to include contributions of all tokens, but because some strings are very long, it would necessitate a slow dropoff if even the very distant tokens were to contribute to the measure.

In the end, a geometrically decreasing weight function was chosen, due to its useful properties:

- Near tokens are weighted more heavily than far tokens.
- All tokens in the string still contribute to the distance measure.
- A *half power* distance can be defined, which helps in the understanding and analysis of the results.

The half power distance is the distance for which the tokens on one side (those near the keyword) account for half of the total possible edit distance, while those on the other side (farther from the keyword) account for the remainder. This helps give a more intuitive reading for the resulting distance, with an effective *window* around the keyword which can be treated equally with the remainder of the string.

The implementation of this geometric dropoff requires only a small change to the original dynamic programming algorithm for edit distance. The table-filling rule becomes:

$$D(A_i, B_j) = \min \begin{cases} D(A_i, B_{j-1}) + L^{i+j} \times D_{\text{insert}}(b_j) \\ D(A_{i-1}, B_j) + L^{i+j} \times D_{\text{insert}}(a_i) \\ D(A_{i-1}, B_{j-1}) + L^{i+j} \times D_{\text{substitute}}(a_i, b_j) \end{cases}$$

where L is the *locality factor*, which is defined in terms of the half power distance, P_h: $L = \frac{1}{2}^{1/P_h}$, so that $L^{P_h} = \frac{1}{2}$.

8.9.2   Problem-specific weights

While it would be ideal to perform the analysis using only perfect equality of lexical items as a criterion, both the number of contexts required for useful generalization, and the computational cost of performing such experiments are prohibitive. In order to make the test procedures tractable in these experiments, lexical items were not treated uniformly as purely lexical tokens. The input was first divided into word classes based on standard part-of-speech classification, and edit distance costs were assigned on the basis of those classes.

The text was initially tagged using a stochastic part-of-speech tagger [Meteer *et al.*, 1991b]. The 48 tag types used were divided into 12 equivalence classes (verbs, nouns, determiners, adjectives, etc.) in order to simplify weight assignment. To give members of a given class a higher self-similarity, intra-class substitutions were assigned lower cost than inter-class substitutions. Perfect lexical equality was still accorded a cost of zero.

These particular classes were chosen on the basis of general linguistic knowledge with respect to the underlying functional aspects of the theory. It is hoped that in later analyses, untagged text can be used in the system from end to end, with context type and word classifications coming as a result of the pattern clustering scheme.

8.10   Context Method Results

The context clustering algorithm described above was run using a variety of different lexical items. Two examples are given to provide a basis of comparison with other methods in grammar induction and selectional frame acquisition. Another example illustrates applications of the similarity clustering technique in acquiring domain-specific lexicons.

199 occurrences of *of*, 197 of *without* and 150 of *joint* were chosen randomly from the 1988 *Wall Street Journal* [WSJ, 1988], part-of-speech tagged, and clustered using the localized edit distance and the group average clustering method. The half-power distance used was 6. Be-

of	the	asahan	authority	,
of	the		dealer	,
of	the gross	national	product	,
of	the old		one	−
of	the proposed		actions	,

Figure 8.6
of: the [MOD] NOUN DELIMITER

of	the code	's	spirit
of	the dollar	's recent	rise
of	the company	's quarterly	dividend
of	the president-elect	's favorite	phrases

Figure 8.7
of: the N's NP

cause of processing constraints, only the right-hand side of each lexical environment was used in the clustering. In order to achieve clusters of equal significance correlating both sides of the context, without assuming some intrinsic cross-correlation, the sample size would need to be increased dramatically. (Even though such cross-correlation *can* be safely assumed, it is even safer to study each side independently before making such claims.)

The results shown are alignment tables of the highest-similarity significant clusters formed in each case. Although the clustering algorithm produces a hierarchical categorization, the flat-grouping tables are easier to examine in this limited space.

8.10.1 Prepositional arguments

The prepositional keyword *of* was used to test whether the method could extract general noun-phrase structure (NPs being the usual right-hand complement of *of*). Clusters representing the expected short NP patterns, such as [DET N], [DET Adj N], and [DET N-plural] were generated.

Two of the more interesting low level clusters are illustrated in figures 8.6 and 8.7. Figure 8.7 is a cluster which groups genitive NPs as the argument to *of*. Figure 8.6 illustrates phrasal delineation by punctuation, promising perhaps that the method could also derive the syntactic phrase-structuring properties and conventional uses of punctuation.

Another test was run with the prepositional keyword *without*, again to test the for NP structure, and to illustrate semantic subtyping of the

without	a significant	correction
without	a significant	retreat
without	a proper	hearing
without	a legislative	vote
without	a	bone

without	any		coattails
without	any		results
without	any		authorization whatsoever
without	any	congressional	authorization
without	any prior regulatory		approval

Figure 8.8
without: [a|any] EVENT-NOMINAL

without	raising	tax	rates
without	raising		taxes
without	hurting		customers
without	telling		them
without	recognizing		it
without	borrowing		money
without	using	installment	notes

without	taking	a	strike
without	fomenting	a	revolution
without	complying	with federal	disclosure

without		putting	up any	cash
without		buying	any	shares
without	ever	entering	the	courthouse
without	bail	pending	a	hearing

Figure 8.9
without: Xing Y

arguments. Most of the argument clusters found were phrases denoting an event or action, either with a nominal event head (figure 8.8), or with a participial phrase (figure 8.9).

The clustering for *without* also revealed as significant the idiomatic expression 'without admitting or denying X,' where X is a term carrying negative connotations (figure 8.10).

without	admitting	or	denying		wrongdoing
without	admitting	or	denying	any	wrongdoing
without	admitting	or	denying		guilt
without	admitting	or	denying	the	allegations

Figure 8.10
without: admitting or denying X

joint	bid
joint	effort
joint	appearances
joint	appearance
joint	ventures
joint	venture
joint	chiefs

Figure 8.11
joint: cooperative

joint	venture	of	enron		corp	and	sonat	inc
joint	venture	of	sammis		corp	and	transamerica	corp
joint	venture	of	general	motors	corp	and	allied-signal	inc

Figure 8.12
joint: venture of X CORP and Y INC

8.10.2   Domain-specific vocabulary: joint

A trial using an exemplary word from the TIPSTER domain was also run, to test whether the method could extract paradigmatic use carrying semantic information. The word *joint* was selected because of its semantic relatedness to the cooperative nature of the business tie-up events (the domain of the TIPSTER task), and because of its observed heavy use in relevant context. 150 occurrences of *joint* were taken randomly from the same corpus, and clustered using the same techniques as for *of* and *without*.

The simplest clusters for *joint* are of the form 'joint X,' where X is a group behavior or a group (figure 8.11). This kind of semantic collocation information can also be derived through statistical bi-gram analysis [Hindle and Roth, 1991], [Pustejovsky, 1992].

The phrasal clusters produced by the method, however, cannot be obtained with bi-gram methods. Figures 8.12, 8.13 and 8.14 illustrate clusters of paradigmatic usage of *joint* in the business reporting domain.

joint	venture		with	bp	america		inc
joint	venture		with	icn	pharmaceuticals		inc
joint	venture		with	aaa	development		corp
joint	venture		with	komori	printing	machinery	co
joint	venture	agreement	with	pt	astra	international	inc
joint	venture		with	french	publisher	hachette	sa

Figure 8.13
joint: venture with X INC.

joint	venture of dow	chemical co	, detroit	,
joint	venture of dow	chemical co	in midland , mich ,	
joint	venture of landmark land	corp , carmel	, calif ,	

	and corning glass	works	corning , n	y
	and corning glass	works in corning , n	y
	and ranieri wilson co	new york

Figure 8.14
joint: venture of X CO. LOCATION$_x$ and Y CO. LOCATION$_y$

These clusters reflect the semantic collocations that can be expected to appear with *joint*. The appearance of these clusters shows that such paradigmatic use is derivable by purely structural lexical methods.

The more structured clusters shown here for *joint* (figures 8.12, 8.13, and 8.14) give patterns with direct applicability to information extraction systems. In fact, these patterns were derived previously through other techniques and are currently used in the DIDEROT system to trigger extraction of joint venture events.

8.11   Conclusion

This chapter has presented a linguistic framework in which to view the use of pattern-based extraction systems for text understanding. The framework is based on the functional aspects of denotational lexical semantics, treating the lexical and semantic components of an expression as mutual constraining parts, each imposing constraints on the structure of the other.

The viewpoint, along with the form of the source data, leads to an investigation of the lexical-semantic interaction in terms of a classification of lexical structural properties. The two ends of the spectrum can be analyzed separately, bringing independent structural classifications to bear on the analysis of the interaction.

Methods were outlined for creating classifications of this sort, to create hierarchical descriptions of context and predicate types, which form a descriptive vocabulary for analyzing the interaction of lexical and semantic properties in use.

Experiments were performed on structural clustering of lexical context, using a localized edit distance as a measure of similarity. The results show that structure clustering can derive the lexical information required for identifying and characterizing diverse modes of use.

Future directions   Obviously, the current level of these techniques is not sufficient to automatically create patterns mapping lexical structure to semantic denotations. What they do show, however, is that edit-distance clustering is a useful technique for extracting the syntactic portions of such patterns — from a set of less than 200 contexts in each case we see significant clusters, identical to patterns used in an existing extraction system. Further work is needed in order to fold the semantic mapping into the clustering process. Metrics are needed for classifying both semantic structure and for the integrated mappings. One solution might be to augment the string edit distance with a predicate-similarity metric based on tree-matching, with the relational structure treated as a tree of predicates and arguments. This combined metric could provide a measure of similarity for classifying the structural mappings themselves.

Much of the community has discussed the need for semantically marked text, much like that in the example of figure 8.3, over which to run machine learning methods such as these. A collection of text with relations explicitly marked out would provide an ideal set of learning examples for the clustering technique shown, and for extension into methods integrating the semantic and syntactic clustering. Because of the cost in analysis time, however, the creation of such a collection is currently unreasonable.

The similarity measure could benefit from further research. As it is given, the edit distance provides no distinction between contiguous substring matches and arbitrary subsequence matching. A measurement for *reversals* — the alternation of a pair AB with BA, for tokens (or substrings) A and B — would be useful, as this sort of swapping is common in natural language. There have been some attempts toward this in the genetics community, but no significant success has been achieved.

Acknowledgments

I would like to thank the editors for their helpful comments on this work, as well as the attendees at the SIGLEX workshop at which it was first presented. This work was funded in part under ARPA contract #MDA904-91-C-9328.

V LEXICAL SEMANTICS FROM CORPUS ANALYSIS

9 Detecting Dependencies between Semantic Verb Subclasses and Subcategorization Frames in Text Corpora

Victor Poznański, Antonio Sanfilippo

9.1 Introduction

There is a widespread belief among linguists that a predicate's subcategorization frames are largely determined by its lexical-semantic properties [Talmy, 1985], [Jackendoff, 1990], [Levin, 1989]. Consider the domain of movement verbs. Following [Talmy, 1985], these can be semantically classified with reference to the meaning components: MOTION, MANNER, CAUSATION, THEME (MOVING ENTITY), PATH AND REFERENCE LOCATIONS (GOAL, SOURCE). Lexicalization patterns which arise from identifying clusters of such meaning components in verb senses can be systematically related to distinct subcategorization frames[1]. For example, the arguments of a verb expressing *directed caused motion* (e.g., *bring, put, give*) are normally a causative subject (agent), a theme direct object (moving entity) and a directional argument expressing path and reference location (goal), e.g.,

(1) Jackie   will bring   a bottle of retsina   to   the party
     CAUSER   THEME   PATH   GOAL

However, a motion verb which is not amenable to *direct external causation* [Levin and Rappaport, 1991], will typically take a theme subject, with the possible addition of a directional argument, e.g.,

(2) The baby crawled (across the room)

Co-occurrence restrictions between meaning components may also preempt subcategorization options; for example, manner of motion verbs in Italian cannot integrate a completed path component and therefore never subcategorize for a directional argument, e.g.,

---

[1] Following [Levin, 1989] and [Sanfilippo, 1994], we maintain that valency reduction processes (e.g., the causative-inchoative alternation) are semantically governed and thus do not weaken the correlation between verb semantics and subcategorization properties.

(3) *Carlo ha camminato a casa
    Carlo walked home

These generalizations are important for NLP since they frequently cover large subclasses of lexical items and can be used both to reduce redundancy and elucidate significant aspects of lexical structure. Moreover, a precise characterization of the relation between semantic subclasses and subcategorization properties of verbs can aid lexical isambiguation. For example, the verb *accord* can be used in either one of two senses: *agree* or *give*, e.g.,

(4) a. The two alibis do not accord
        Your alibi does not accord with his
     b. They accorded him a warm welcome

Accord is intransitive in the *agree* senses shown in (4a), and ditransitive in the *give* sense shown in (4b).

The manual encoding of subcategorization options for each choice of verb subclass in the language is very costly to develop and maintain. This problem can be alleviated by automatically extracting collocational information, e.g., grammar codes, from Machine Readable Dictionaries (MRDs). However, most of these dictionaries are not intended for such processing; their readership rarely require or desire such exhaustive and exacting precision. More specifically, the information available is in most cases compiled manually according to the lexicographer's intuitions rather than (semi-)automatically derived from texts recording actual language use. As a source of lexical information for NLP, MRDs are therefore liable to suffer from omissions, inconsistencies and occasional errors as well as being unable to cope with evolving usage [Atkins *et al.*, 1986], [Boguraev and Briscoe, 1989b], [Atkins and Levin, 1991], [Brent, 1991b]. Ultimately, the maintenance costs involved in redressing such inadequacies are likely to reduce the initial appeal of generating subcategorization lists from MRDs.

In keeping with these observations, we implemented a suite of programs which provide an integrated approach to lexical knowledge acquisition. The programs elicit dependencies between semantic verb classes and their admissible subcategorization frames using machine readable thesauri to assist in semantic tagging of texts.

9.2   Background

Currently available dictionaries do not provide a sufficiently reliable source of lexical knowledge for NLP systems. This has led an increasing number of researchers to look at text corpora as a source of information [Church and Hanks, 1990], [Smajda and McKeown, 1990], [Church et al., 1992], [Brent, 1991b], [Basili et al., 1992]. For example, [Brent, 1991b] describes a program which retrieves subcategorization frames from untagged text. Brent's approach relies on detecting nominal, clausal and infinitive complements after identification of proper nouns and pronouns using predictions based on GB's Case Filter [Rouvret and Vergnaud, 1980] — e.g., in English, a noun phrase occurs to the immediate left of a tensed verb, or the immediate right of a main verb or preposition. Brent's results are impressive considering that no text preprocessing (e.g., tagging or bracketing) is assumed. However, the number of subcategorization options recognized is minimal[2], and it is hard to imagine how the approach could be extended to cover the full range of subcategorization possibilities without introducing some form of text preprocessing. Also, the phrasal patterns extracted are too impoverished to infer selectional restrictions as they only contain proper nouns and pronouns.

Lexical acquisition of collocational information from preprocessed text is now becoming more popular as tools for analyzing corpora are getting to be more reliable [Church et al., 1992]. For example, [Basili et al., 1992] present a method for acquiring sublanguage-specific selectional restrictions from corpora which uses text processing techniques such as morphological tagging and shallow syntactic analysis. Their approach relies on extracting word pairs and triples which represent crucial environments for the acquisition of selectional restrictions (e.g., V_prep_N(*go,to,Boston*)). They then replace words with semantic tags (V_prep_N(PHYSICAL_ACT-to-PLACE)) and compute co-occurrence preferences among them. Semantic tags are crucial for making generalizations about the types of words which can appear in a given context (e.g., as the argument of a verb or preposition). However, Basili et al. rely on manual encoding in the assignment of semantic tags;

---

[2] Brent's program recognizes five subcategorization frames built out of three kinds of constituents: noun phrase, clause, infinitive.

such a practice is bound to become more costly as the text under consideration grows in size and may prove prohibitively expensive with very large corpora. Furthermore, the semantic tags are allowed to vary from domain to domain (e.g., commercial and legal corpora) and are not hierarchically structured. With no consequent notion of subsumption, it might be impossible to identify "families" of tags relating to germane concepts across sublanguages (e.g., PHYSICAL_ACT, ACT: BUILDING, REAL_ESTATES).

9.3 CorPSE: A Body of Programs for Acquiring Semantically Tagged Subcategorization Frames from Bracketed Texts

In developing CorPSE (Corpus-based Predicate Structure Extractor) we followed Basili *et al.*'s idea of extracting semantically tagged phrasal frames from preprocessed text, but we used the *Longman Lexicon of Contemporary English* (LLOCE [McArthur, 1981]) to automate semantic tagging. LLOCE entries are similar to those of learner's dictionaries, but are arranged in a thesaurus-like fashion using semantic codes which provide a linguistically-motivated classification of words. For example, [Sanfilippo and Poznański, 1992] show that the semantic codes of LLOCE are instrumental in identifying members of the six subclasses of psychological predicates described in (5) [Levin, 1989], [Jackendoff, 1990].

(5)

Affect type	Experiencer Subject	Stimulus Subject
Neutral	*experience*	*interest*
Positive	*admire*	*fascinate*
Negative	*fear*	*scare*

As shown in (6), each verb representing a subclass has a code which often provides a uniform characterization of the subclass.

(6)

Code	Group Header	Entries
F1	Relating to feeling	*feel, sense, experience . . .*
F140	Admiring and honouring	*admire, respect, look up to . . .*
F121	Fear and Dread	*fear, fear for, be frightened . . .*
F25	Attracting and interesting	*attract, interest, concern . . .*
F26	Attracting and interesting very much	*fascinate, enthrall, enchant . . .*
F122	Frighten and panic	*frighten, scare, terrify . . .*

Moreover, LLOCE codes are conveniently arranged into a 3-tier hierarchy according to specificity, e.g.,

F Feelings, Emotions, Attitudes and Sensations
  F20-F40 Liking and not Liking
    F26 Attracting and Interesting very much
      fascinate, enthrall, enchant, charm, captivate

The bottom layer of the hierarchy contains over 1500 domain-specific tags, the middle layer has 129 tags and the top (most general) layer has 14. Domain-specific tags are always linked to intermediate tags which are, in turn, linked to general tags. Thus we can tag sublanguages using domain-specific semantic codes (as do Basili *et al.*) without generating unrelated sets of such codes.

We assigned semantic tags to *Subcategorization Frame tokens* (SF tokens) extracted from the Penn Treebank [Liberman and Marcus, 1992], [Santorini, 1991a], [Santorini, 1991b] to produce *Subcategorization Frame types* (SF types). Each SF type consists of a verb stem associated with one or more semantic tags, and a list of its complements, if any. The head of noun phrase complements were also semantically tagged. We used LLOCE collocational information — grammar codes — to reduce or remove semantic ambiguity arising from multiple assignment of tags to verb and noun stems. These three stages are exemplified below.

```
SF token: ((DENY VB)
           (NP (ALIENS NNS))
           (NP (*COMPOUND-NOUN*
                   (STATE NN) (BENEFITS NNS))))

SF type: (("deny" ("C193"-refuse "G127"-reject))
             ((*NP* ("C"-people_and_family))
              (*NP* ("N"-general_and_abstract_terms))))
```

```
Disambiguated SF type: (("deny" ("C193"))
                        ((*NP* ("C"))
                         (*NP* ("N"))))
```

9.3.1 CorPSE's general functionality

CorPSE is conceptually segmented into 2 parts: a *predicate structure extractor*, and a *semantic processor*. The predicate structure extractor takes bracketed text as input, and outputs SF tokens. The semantic processor converts SF tokens into SF types and disambiguates them.

Extracting SF Tokens   The predicate structure extractor elicits SF tokens from a bracketed input corpus. These tokens are formed from phrasal fragments which correspond to a subcategorization frame, factoring out the most relevant information. In the case of verbs, such fragments correspond to verb phrases where the following simplificatory changes have been applied:

- NP complements have been reduced to the head noun (or head nouns in the case of coordinated NP's or nominal compounds), e.g.,

  ```
  ((FACES VBZ) (NP (CHARGES NNS)))
  ```

- PP complements have been reduced to the head preposition plus the head of the complement noun phrase, e.g.,

  ```
  ((RIDES VBZ) (PP IN ((VAN NN))))
  ```

- VP complements are reduced to a mention of the VFORM of the head verb, e.g.,

  ```
  ((TRY VB) (VP TO))
  ```

- clausal complements are reduced to a mention of the complementizer which introduces them, e.g.,

  ```
  ((ARGUED VBD) (SBAR THAT))
  ```

An important step in the extraction of SF tokens is to distinguish passive and active verb phrases. Passives are discriminated by locating a past participle following an auxiliary *be*.

Converting SF Tokens into SF Types   The semantic processor operates on the output of the predicate structure extractor. Inflected words in input SF tokens are first passed through a general purpose morphological analyser [Sanfilippo, 1992] and reduced to bare stems suitable for dictionary lookup. The next phase is to supplement SF tokens with semantic tags from LLOCE using the facilities of the ACQUILEX LDB [Boguraev *et al.*, 1990], [Carroll, 1992] and DCK [Sanfilippo, 1992]; LLOCE tags are associated with verb stems and simply replace noun stems.

The resulting SF structures are finally converted into SF types according to the representation system whose syntax is sketched in (7) where: *stem* is the verb stem, *parts* a possibly empty sequence of particles associated with the verb stem, {A . . . N} is the set of LLOCE semantic codes, *pform* the head of a prepositional phrase, *compform* the possibly empty complementizer of a clausal complement, and *cat* any category not covered by np-, pp-, sbar- and vp- frames.

(7) SF-type   ::= (*stem parts* sem comps)
     sem   ::= ({ A . . . N }*)
     comps   ::= comp*
     comp   ::= ({ np-frame | pp-frame | sbar-frame | vp-frame |
                        cat-frame })
     np-frame   ::= (***NP*** sem)
     pp-frame   ::= (***PP*** *pform* comp)
     sbar-frame ::= (***SBAR*** *compform*)
     vp-frame   ::= (***VP*** *vform*)
     cat-frame ::= (***CAT*** *cat*)

Disambiguating SF Types   The disambiguation module of the semantic processor *coalesces* SF types, and reduces semantic tags when verb stems have several codes.

Coalescing merges SF types with isomorphic structure and identical verb stem, combining the semantic codes of NP-frames, e.g.,

```
(("accord" ("D101" "N226"))
   ((*PP* TO (*NP* ("C")))))
(("accord" ("D101" "N226"))
   ((*PP* TO (*NP* ("G")))))
(("accord" ("D101" "N226"))
   ((*PP* TO (*NP* ("C" "G")))))
                    ⇓
(("accord" ("D101" "N226"))
   ((*PP* TO (*NP* ("C" "G")))))
```

This process can be performed in linear time when the input is lexicographically sorted.

We employ two tag reduction methods. The first eliminates equivalent tags, the second applies syntactico-semantic restrictions using LLOCE grammar codes .

When more than one LLOCE code can apply to a particular entry it may be possible to combine them. For example, the verb *function* is assigned two distinct codes in LLOCE: I28 *functioning and serving*, and N123 *functioning and performing*. Although I- and N-codes may in principle differ considerably, in this case they are very similar; indeed, the entries for the two codes are identical. This identity can be automatically inferred from the *descriptor* associated with semantic codes in the LLOCE index. For example, for a verb such as *accord* where each semantic code is related to a distinct entry, the index gives two separate descriptors, *give* and *agree*, eg:

accord ...
   give *v* D101
   agree *v* N226

By contrast, different codes related to the same entry are associated with the same descriptor, as shown for the entry *function* below.

function ...
   work *v* I28, N123

We exploit the correlation between descriptors and semantic codes in the LLOCE index, reducing multiple codes indexed by the same descriptor to just one. More precisely, the reduction involves substitution of all codes having equal descriptors with a new code which represents the logical conjunction of the substituted codes. This is shown in (8) where "I28+N123" is defined as the intersection of "I28" and "N123" in the LLOCE hierarchy of semantics codes as indicated in (9).

(8)
```
(("function" ("I28" "N123"))
   ((*PP* LIKE (*NP* ("C")))))
                ⇓
(("function" ("I28+N123"))
   ((*PP* LIKE (*NP* ("C")))))
```

(9)

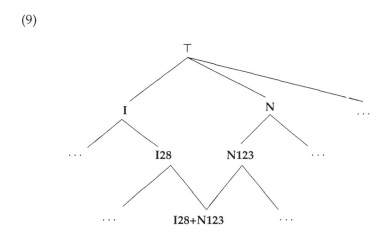

The second means for disambiguating SF types consists of filtering out the codes of verb stems which are incompatible with the type of subcategorization frame in which they occur. This is done by using collocational information provided in LLOCE. For example, the verb *deny* is assigned two distinct semantic codes which cannot be reduced to one as they have different descriptors:

deny . . .
  refuse *v* C193
  reject *v* G127

The difference in semantic code entails distinct subcategorization options: *deny* can have a ditransitive subcategorization frame only in the *refuse* sense, e.g.,

(10) Republican senator David Lock's bill would permanently
  $\left\{ \begin{array}{l} \text{deny (refuse)} \\ \text{*deny (reject)} \end{array} \right\}$ illegal aliens all State benefits

The codependency between semantic verb class and subcategorization can often be inferred by the grammar code of LLOCE entries. For example, only the entry for the *refuse* sense of *deny* in LLOCE includes the grammar code D1 which signals a ditransitive subcategorization frame:

(11)   **C193** *verbs*: **not letting or allowing**
                deny [D1;T1] . . .

       G127 *verbs*: **rejecting** . . .
                deny 1 [T1,4,5;V3] . . . **2** [T1] . . .

Semantic codes which are incompatible with the SF types in which they occur, such as G127 in (12), can thus be filtered out by enforcing constraints between SF type complement structures and LLOCE grammar codes.

(12)   (("deny"("C193" "G127"))
          ((*NP* ("C"))
          (*NP* ("N")))))

To automate this process, we first form a set GC of compatible grammar codes for each choice of complement structure in SF types. For example, the set of compatible grammar codes GC for any SF type with two noun phrase complements is restricted to the singleton set {D1}, e.g.,

(13)   ((*stem sem*)   ⇒ $GC = \{D1\}$
            ((*NP* *sem*)
            (*NP* *sem*)))

A set of 2-tuples of the form (verb-stem-semantic-code, grammar-codes) is formed by noting the LLOCE grammar codes for each semantic code that could apply to the verb stem. If the grammar codes of any 2-tuple have no intersection with the grammatical restrictions GC, we conclude that the associated verb-stem-semantic code is not possible[3]. For example, C193 in the SF type for *deny* in (12) is paired up with the grammar codes {D1;T1} and G127 with {T1,4,5;V3} according to the LLOCE entries for *deny* shown in (11).

Figure (14) illustrates how the relationship between the subcategorization information in extracted verb frames and the grammar codes associated with their verb stems license automatic removal of the semantic code G127, the *reject* sense, from the SF type for ditransitive *deny*. First the use of *deny* in (10) is mapped into an ambiguous SF type using the LLOCE semantic codes. Next, the subcat scheme is mapped into a LLOCE grammar code which filters out incompatible semantic codes

---

[3] This procedure is only effective if the corpus subcategorization information is equally or more precise than the dictionary information. For our corpus, it proved to be the case.

from ambiguous FS types as described above.

(14)

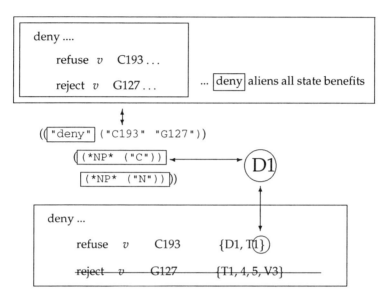

It may appear that there is a certain circularity in our work. We use grammar codes to help disambiguate SF types, but since the corpus could not have been bracketed without some prior grammatical information about these codes, it might be argued that lexical acquisition is limited to a simple restructuring of the information in LLOCE. This picture is inaccurate because our SF types provide collocational information which is not in LLOCE. For example, the SF type shown in (15a) captures the use of *link* in (15b); this subcategorization cannot be inferred from the LLOCE entry where no PP headed by *to* is mentioned.

(15) a. `(("link" NIL ("N"))    ((*NP* ("C"))    (*PP* TO`
        `(*NP* ("B" "N")))))`

   b. The arrest warrant issued in Florida links the attorney to a government probe of the Medhyin drug cartel . . .

Indeed, another possible use for our system would be to provide feedback to an on-line dictionary. We also provide a partial indication of selectional restrictions, i.e., the semantic tags of NP complements. Furthermore, text can be bracketed using techniques such as stochastic and semi-automatic parsing which need not rely on exhaustive lists of subcategorizations.

9.4   Using CorPSE: Emerging Trends and Current Limitations

In testing CorPSE, our main objectives were:

- to assess the functionality of text pre-processing techniques involving automated semantic tagging and lexical disambiguation, and
- to show that such techniques may yield profitable results in capturing regularities in the syntax-semantics interface.

In order to do this, we ran CorPSE on a section of the Penn Treebank comprising 576 bracketed sentences from radio transcripts. From these sentences, CorPSE extracted 1335 SF tokens comprising 1245 active VPs and 90 passives. The SF tokens were converted into 817 SF types. The coalescence process reduced the 817 SF types to 583, which are representative of 346 distinct verb stems. The verb stem of 308 of these 583 SF types was semantically ambiguous as it was associated with more than one semantic tag. In some cases, this ambiguity was appropriate because the semantic codes assigned to the stem were all compatible with the complement structure of their SF type. For example, the verb *call* can occur in either one of two senses, *summon* and *phone*, with no change in subcategorization structure:

(16)   a. Supper's ready, call the kids.
        b. Call me when you land in Paris.

In this case, CorPSE correctly maintains the ambiguity as shown in (17).

```
(17) (("call" ("G"-summon "M"-phone))
     ((*NP* ("C" "J" "N")))))
```

In other cases, the ambiguity was in need of resolution as some of the verb-stem's semantic codes referred to the same LLOCE entry or were incompatible with the complement structure in the SF type (see §9.3.1.3). Disambiguation using semantic tag equivalence reduced the ambiguity of 206 types, totally disambiguating 31 stems. Applying collocation restrictions further reduced 38 stems, totally disambiguating 24 of them.

Taking into account that the amount of data processed was too small to use statistical techniques for disambiguation, the results achieved are very promising: we managed to reduce ambiguity in over half the SF types and totally disambiguated 16 percent, thus providing a unique correspondence between semantic verb class and subcategorization frame in 346 cases. Of the remaining 179 SF frames, 106 had verb stems with two semantic codes, 72 had verb stems with 3-5 semantic codes and the verb stem of one SF type had 6. Needless to say, the number of ambiguous SF types is bound to increase as more texts are processed. However, as we accumulate more data, we will be able to apply statistical techniques to reduce lexical ambiguity, e.g., by computing co-occurrence restrictions between the semantic codes of the verb stem and complement heads in SF types.

The table (18) below summarizes some of the results concerning the correlation of semantic codes and subcategorization options obtained by running CorPSE on the Penn Treebank fragment.

(18)

Code	Occ. #	Rel. Freq.	Ambig %	VP %	SBAR %	PP %
A	4	1	0	0	0	0
B	9	1	44	0	0	3
C	72	9	67	15	0	39
D	57	7	65	16	4	44
E	23	3	83	22	0	57
F	42	5	40	10	2	21
G	132	17	33	7	14	28
H	11	1	82	0	0	27
I	27	3	74	4	0	63
J	68	9	57	12	1	35
K	29	4	69	0	0	48
L	33	4	36	21	3	27
M	130	16	50	2	1	52
N	161	20	44	14	4	35

The first column lists the LLOCE semantic codes which are explained in (19). The second column indicates the number of unique subcategorization occurrences for each code. A major difficulty in computing this relation was the presence of certain constituents as arguments that are usually thought of as adjuncts. For example, purpose clauses and time adverbials such as *yesterday, all day, in March, on Friday* had often been bracketed as arguments (i.e., sisters to a V node). Our solution was to filter out inadequately parsed arguments semi-automatically. Certain constituents were automatically filtered from SF types as their status as adjuncts was manifest, e.g., complements introduced by prepositions and complementizers such as *without, as, since* and *because*. Other suspect constituents, such as infinitive VPs which could represent purpose clauses, were processed by direct query. A second problem was the residual ambiguities in SF types mentioned above. These biased the significance of occurrences since one or more codes in an ambiguous SF type could be inconsistent with the subcategorization of the SF type. A measure of the "noise" factor introduced by ambiguous SF types is given in the third column of (19), where ambiguity rate is computed by dividing the number of codes associated with the same complement structure by the number of occurrences of that code with all complement structures detected in the text.

(19)

Code	Explanation
A	Life & Living Things
B	The Body, its Functions & Welfare
C	People & the Family
D	Building, Houses, the Home, Clothes
E	Food, Drink & Farming
F	Feelings, Emotions, Attitudes & Sensations
G	Thought & Communication, Language & Grammar
H	Substances, Materials, Objects & Equipment
I	Arts & Crafts, Science & Technology, Industry & Education
J	Numbers, Measurement, Money & Commerce
K	Entertainment, Sports & Games
L	Space and Time
M	Movement, Location, Travel & Transport
N	General & Abstract Terms

This ambiguity measure allows the significance of the figures in the second column to be assessed. For example, since the occurrences of "E" instances were invariably ambiguous, it is difficult to draw reliable conclusions about them. Indeed, on referring most of these SF types (e.g., *beat, bolt* and *have*) back to their source texts, the "Food & Drink" connotation proved incorrect. The figures in column 2 were normalised as percentages of the total number of occurrences, the relative frequency, in order to provide a measure of the statistical significance of the results in the remaining columns. We thus conclude that the results for B, E, H, and I are unlikely to be significant as they occur with low relative frequency and are highly ambiguous. The final three columns quantify the relative frequency of occurrence for VP, SBAR and PP complements in SF types for each semantic code.

Although the results are not clear-cut, there are some emerging trends worth considering. For example, the low frequency of VP and SBAR complements with code "M" reflects the relatively rare incidence of clausal arguments in the semantics of motion and location verbs. By contrast, the relatively high frequency of PP complements with this code can be related to the semantic propensity of motion and location verbs to take spatial arguments. The "A" verbs (e.g., *create, live* and *murder*) appear to be strongly biased towards taking a direct object complement only. This might be due to the fact that these verbs involve creating, destroying or manipulating life rather than events. Finally, the overwhelmingly high frequency of SBAR complements with "G" verbs is related to the fact that thought and communication verbs typically involve individuals and states of affairs.

We also found interesting results concerning the distribution of subcategorization options among specializations of the same general code. For example, 23 out of 130 occurrences of "M" verbs exhibited an "NP PP" complement structure; 17 of these were found in SF types with codes "M50-M65" which largely characterize verbs of caused directed motion: *Putting and Taking, Pulling & Pushing*. This trend confirms some of the observations discussed in the introduction. It is now premature to report results of this kind more fully since the corpus data used was too small and genre-specific to make more reliable and detailed inferences about the relation between subcategorization and semantic verb subclass. We hope that further work with larger corpora will uncover new patterns and corroborate current correlations which at present can only be regarded as providing suggestive evidence. Other than using substantially larger texts, improvements could also be obtained by enriching SF types, e.g., by adding information about subject constituents.

9.5   Conclusions

We have provided the building blocks for a system that combines the advantages of free-text processing of corpora with the more organized information found in MRDs, such as semantic tags and collocational information. We have shown how such a system can be used to acquire lexical knowledge in the form of semantically tagged subcategorization frames. These results can assist the automatic construction of lexicons for NLP, semantic tagging for data retrieval from textual databases as well as to help maintain, refine and augment MRDs.

Acknowledgments

Some of the work discussed in this chapter was carried out at the Computer Laboratory in Cambridge within the ACQUILEX project. The Penn-Treebank data used were provided in CD-ROM format by the University of Pennsylvania through the ACL Data Collection Initiative (ACL/DCI CD-ROM I, September 1991). We are indebted to Ian Johnson for helpful comments and encouragement, and to John Beaven and Pete Whitelock for providing feedback on previous versions of this chapter. Also, many thanks to Ann Copestake and Victor Lesk for their invaluable contribution towards mounting LLOCE on the LDB.

10 Acquiring Predicate-Argument Mapping Information from Multilingual Texts

Chinatsu Aone, Douglas McKee

10.1 Introduction

Lexicons for a natural language processing (NLP) system that perform syntactic and semantic analysis require more than purely syntactic (e.g., part-of-speech information) and semantic information (e.g., a concept hierarchy). Language understanding requires mapping from syntactic structures into conceptual representation (henceforth predicate-argument mapping), while language generation requires the inverse mapping. That is, grammatical functions in the syntactic structures (e.g., subject, object, etc.) should be mapped to thematic roles in the semantic structures (e.g., agent, theme, etc.).

In this chapter, we discuss how we acquire such predicate-argument mapping information from multilingual texts automatically (cf. Zernik and Jacobs' work on collecting thematic roles [Zernik and Jacobs, 1990]). As discussed in [Aone and McKee, 1993], the lexicon of our NLP system abstracts the language-dependent portion of predicate-argument mapping information from the core meaning of verb senses (i.e., *semantic concepts* as defined in the knowledge base). We represent this mapping information in terms of cross-linguistically generalized mapping types called *situation types* and word sense-specific *idiosyncrasies*. This representation has enabled us to automatically acquire predicate-argument mapping information, specifically situation types and idiosyncrasies, for verbs in English, Spanish, and Japanese texts.

In the following sections, we first describe how we represent the predicate-mapping information. Then, we discuss how we acquire situation type and idiosyncrasy information automatically from multilingual texts and show some results.

10.2 Predicate-Argument Mapping Representation

Each lexical sense of a verb in our lexicon encodes its default predicate-argument mapping type (i.e., situation type), any word-specific mapping exceptions (i.e., idiosyncrasies), and its semantic meaning (i.e., semantic concept), in addition to its morphological and syntactic information. In the following, we discuss these three levels in detail.

10.2.1   Situation types

Each of a verb's lexical senses is classified into one of the four default predicate-argument mapping types called *situation types*. As shown in Table 10.1, situation types of verbs are defined by two kinds of information: 1) the number of subcategorized NP or S arguments and 2) the types of thematic roles which these arguments should or should not map to.

	# of required NP or S arguments	default thematic roles	prohibited thematic roles
CAUSED-PROCESS	2	Agent Theme	—
PROCESS-OR-STATE	1	Theme	Agent
AGENTIVE-ACTION	1	Agent	—
INVERSE-STATE	2	Goal Theme	Agent

Table 10.1
Definitions of Situation Types

Since this kind of information is applicable to verbs of any language, situation types are language-independent predicate-argument mapping types. Thus, in any language, a verb of type CAUSED-PROCESS (CP) has two arguments which map to AGENT and THEME in the default case (e.g., "kill"). A verb of type PROCESS-OR-STATE (PS) has one argument whose thematic role is THEME, and it does not allow AGENT as one of its thematic roles (e.g., "die"). An AGENTIVE-ACTION (AA) verb also has one argument but the argument maps to AGENT (e.g., "look"). Finally, an INVERSE-STATE (IS) verb has two arguments which map to THEME and GOAL; it does not allow AGENT for its thematic role (e.g., "see"). Examples from three languages are shown in Table 10.2.

Although verbs in different languages are classified into the same four situation types using the same definition, mapping rules which map grammatical functions (i.e., subject, object, etc.) in the syntactic structures[1] to thematic roles in the semantic structures may differ from

---

[1] We use structures similar to LFG's f-structures.

	English	Spanish	Japanese
CAUSED-PROCESS	kill	matar, mirar	korosu, miru
PROCESS-OR-STATE	die	morir	shibousuru
AGENTIVE-ACTION	look	bailar	odoru
INVERSE-STATE	see	ver	mieru

Table 10.2
Situation Types and Verbs in Three Languages

one language to another. This is because languages do not necessarily express the same thematic roles with the same grammatical functions. This mapping information is *language-specific* ([Nirenburg and Levin, 1991]).

The default mapping rules for the four situation types are shown in Table 10.3.

		⇒ English/Spanish	⇒ Japanese
CAUSED-PROCESS	AGENT	(SURFACE SUBJECT)	(SURFACE SUBJECT)
	THEME	(SURFACE OBJECT)	(SURFACE OBJECT)
PROCESS-OR-STATE	THEME	(SURFACE SUBJECT)	(SURFACE SUBJECT)
AGENTIVE-ACTION	AGENT	(SURFACE SUBJECT)	(SURFACE SUBJECT)
INVERSE-STATE	GOAL	(SURFACE SUBJECT)	(SURFACE SUBJECT)
	THEME	(SURFACE OBJECT)	(SURFACE OBJECT)
			(PARTICLE "GA")

Table 10.3
Default Mapping Rules for Three Languages

They are nearly identical for the three languages (English, Spanish, and Japanese) we have analyzed so far. The only difference is that in Japanese the THEME of an INVERSE-STATE verb is expressed by marking the object NP with a particle "-ga," which is usually a subject marker[2] ([Kuno, 1973]).[3] So we add such information to the INVERSE-STATE mapping rule for Japanese. Generalization expressed in situation types has saved us from defining semantic mapping rules for each verb sense

---

[2] There is a debate over whether the NP with "ga" is a subject or object. However, our approach can accommodate either analysis.
[3] The GOAL of some INVERSE-STATE verbs in Japanese can be expressed by a "ni" postpositional phrase. However, as [Kuno, 1973] points out, since this is an idiosyncratic phenomenon, such information does not go to the default mapping rule.

in each language, and also made it possible to acquire them from large corpora automatically.

This classification system has been partially derived from Vendler and Dowty's aspectual classifications [Vendler, 1967], [Dowty, 1979] and the lexicalization patterns of [Talmy, 1985]. For example, all AGENTIVE-ACTION verbs are so-called *activity* verbs, and so-called *stative* verbs fall under either INVERSE-STATE (if transitive) or PROCESS-OR-STATE (if intransitive). However, the situation types are *not* for specifying the semantics of aspect which is actually a property of the whole sentence rather than a verb itself (cf. [Krifka, 1989], [Dorr, 1992], [Moens and Steedman, 1988]). For instance, as shown below, the same verb can be classified into two different aspectual classes (i.e., activity and accomplishment) depending on the types of object NP's or existence of certain PP's.

(1) a. Sue drank wine for/*in an hour.
    b. Sue drank a bottle of wine *for/in an hour.
(2) a. Harry climbed for/*in an hour.
    b. Harry climbed to the top *for/in an hour.

Situation types are intended to address the issue of cross-linguistic predicate-argument mapping generalization, rather than the semantics of aspect.

10.2.2   Idiosyncrasies

Idiosyncrasies slots in the lexicon specify word sense-specific idiosyncratic phenomena which cannot be captured by semantic concepts or situation types. In particular, subcategorized pre/postpositions of verbs are specified here. For example, the fact that "look" denotes its THEME argument by the preposition "at" is captured by specifying idiosyncrasies. Examples of lexical entries with idiosyncrasies in English, Spanish and Japanese are shown in Figure 10.1. As discussed in the next section, we derive this kind of word-specific information automatically from corpora.

10.2.3   Semantic concepts

Each lexical meaning of a verb is represented by a semantic concept (or frame) in our language-independent knowledge base, which is similar to the one described in [Onyshkevych and Nirenburg, 1991]. Each verb

```
(LOOK (CATEGORY . V)
      (SENSE-NAME . LOOK-1)
      (SEMANTIC-CONCEPT #LOOK#)
      (IDIOSYNCRASIES (THEME (MAPPING (LITERAL "AT"))))
      (SITUATION-TYPE AGENTIVE-ACTION))


(INFECTAR
      (CATEGORY . V)
      (SENSE-NAME . INFECTAR-1)
      (SEMANTIC-CONCEPT #INFECT#)
      (IDIOSYNCRASIES (THEME (MAPPING (LITERAL "CON" "DE")))
                      (GOAL (MAPPING (SURFACE OBJECT))))
      (SITUATION-TYPE CAUSED-PROCESS))


(NARU (CATEGORY . V)
      (SENSE-NAME . NARU-1)
      (SEMANTIC-CONCEPT #BECOME#)
      (IDIOSYNCRASIES (GOAL (MAPPING (LITERAL "TO" "NI"))))
      (SITUATION-TYPE PROCESS-OR-STATE))
```

Figure 10.1
Lexical entries for "look," "infectar," and "naru"

frame has thematic role slots, which have two facets, TYPE and MAPPING.
A TYPE facet value of a given slot provides a constraint on the type of
objects which can be the value of the slot. In the MAPPING facets, we have
encoded some cross-linguistically general predicate-argument mapping
information. For example, we have defined that all the subclasses of
#COMMUNICATION-EVENT# (e.g., #REPORT#, #CONFIRM#, etc.) map their
sentential complements (SENT-COMP) to THEME, as shown in Figure 10.2.

10.2.4 Merging predicate-argument mapping information

For each verb, the information stored in the three levels discussed above
is merged to form a complete set of mapping rules. During this merging
process, the idiosyncrasies take precedence over the situation types
and the semantic concepts, and the situation types over the semantic
concepts. For example, the two derived mapping rules for "break"(i.e.,
one for "break" as in "John broke the window" and the other for "break"
as in "The window broke") are shown in Figure 10.3. Notice that the

```
(#COMMUNICATION-EVENT#
    (AKO #DYNAMIC-SITUATION#)
    (AGENT  (TYPE #PERSON# #ORGANIZATION#))
    (THEME  (TYPE #SITUATION# #ENTITY#)
            (MAPPING (SENT-COMP T)))
    (GOAL   (TYPE #PERSON# #ORGANIZATION#)
            (MAPPING (P-ARG GOAL)))))
```

Figure 10.2
Semantic Concept #COMMUNICATION-EVENT#

semantic TYPE restriction and INSTRUMENT role stored in the knowledge
base are also inherited at this time.

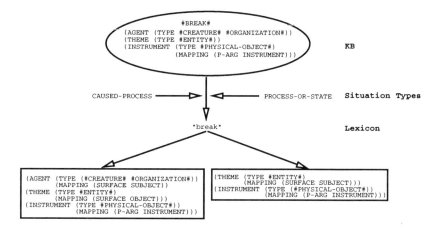

Figure 10.3
Information from the KB, the situation type, and the lexicon all combine to form two
predicate-argument mappings for the verb "break."

10.3   Automatic Acquisition from Corpora

In order to expand our lexicon to the size needed for broad coverage
and to be able to tune the system to specific domains quickly, we have
implemented algorithms to automatically build multilingual lexicons
from corpora. In this section, we discuss how the situation types and
lexical idiosyncrasies are determined for verbs.

Verb	Occs	TR	SA	Predicted ST	Correct ST	Prepositional Idiosyncrasy
suffice	8	0.6250	0.0000	IS	IS	
time	15	0.8333	1.0000	CP IS	CP	
train	20	1.0000	1.0000	CP IS	CP PS	at
wrap	22	0.7222	0.6667	CP IS	CP	up over in with
sort	25	0.4211	1.0000	CP IS AA PS	CP AA	out
unite	27	0.5833	1.0000	CP IS AA PS	CP AA	
transport	28	0.8571	0.6667	CP IS	CP	
sustain	32	0.9062	0.6842	CP IS	CP	
substitute	33	0.7500	0.5000	IS	CP PS	for
target	36	0.7778	0.8000	CP IS	CP	
store	36	0.9091	1.0000	CP IS	CP	on
steal	36	0.9167	0.6667	CP IS	CP	from
shut	36	0.2400	0.5000	IS PS	CP PS	up for
stretch	53	0.5278	0.5000	IS PS	CP PS	over into out from
strip	57	0.7609	0.8571	CP IS	CP	from into of
threaten	58	0.8793	0.4419	IS	CP IS	over
wear	61	0.8033	0.6667	CP IS	IS	over
treat	77	0.8052	0.8000	CP IS	CP	as
terminate	79	0.9726	1.0000	CP IS	CP PS	
weigh	81	0.2069	0.5294	IS PS	CP PS	on with into
teach	82	0.7794	0.6875	CP IS	CP	at
surround	85	0.8000	0.6667	CP IS	CP	
total	97	0.0515	0.2759	PS	CP PS	at
vary	112	0.1354	0.0294	IS PS	CP PS	from over
wait	130	0.1923	1.0000	CP IS AA PS	AA	for up
speak	139	0.1667	0.7500	CP IS AA PS	AA CP	out at up
survive	146	0.4754	0.3846	IS PS	IS PS	
surge	188	0.0182	0.3125	PS	PS	
supply	188	0.7176	0.8571	CP IS	CP	with
sit	199	0.0625	0.7027	AA PS	AA PS	on with at out in
tend	200	0.8594	0.4340	IS	CP IS	
break	219	0.4771	0.5000	IS PS	CP PS	up into out
write	243	0.4637	0.9123	CP IS AA PS	CP AA	off
watch	268	0.7069	0.8462	CP IS	CP	out over
succeed	277	0.5379	0.8899	CP IS AA PS	CP PS	
stay	300	0.2156	0.6604	CP IS AA PS	PS	out up on with at
stand	310	0.2841	0.7237	CP IS AA PS	PS CP AA	up at as out on
tell	368	0.8054	0.8101	CP IS	CP	
spend	445	0.3823	0.8125	CP IS AA PS	CP	on over
support	454	0.8486	0.5370	IS	CP IS	
suggest	570	0.7782	0.5918	IS	CP IS	
turn	852	0.3418	0.5891	IS PS	CP PS	out into up over
start	890	0.3474	0.6221	CP IS AA PS	CP PS	with off out
look	1084	0.1718	0.6520	CP IS AA PS	AA PS	at into for up
think	1227	0.7602	0.9237	CP IS	CP	
try	1272	0.7904	0.8743	CP IS	CP	
want	1659	0.8559	0.8787	CP IS	IS	
use	2211	0.8416	0.7725	CP IS	CP	
take	2525	0.7447	0.5933	IS	CP IS	over off out into

Table 10.4
Automatically Derived Situation Type and Idiosyncrasy Data

Our overall approach is to use simple robust parsing techniques that depend on a few language-dependent syntactic heuristics (e.g., in English and Spanish, a verb's object usually directly follows the verb), and a dictionary for part of speech information. We have used these techniques to acquire information from English, Spanish, and Japanese corpora varying in length from about 25000 words to 2.7 million words.

10.3.1   Acquiring situation type information

We use two surface features to restrict the possible situation types of a verb: the verb's *transitivity rating* (TR) and its *subject animacy* (SA).

The transitivity rating of a verb is defined to be the number of transitive occurrences in the corpus divided by the total occurrences of the verb. In English, a verb appears in the transitive when either:

- The verb is directly followed by a noun, determiner, personal pronoun, adjective, or wh-pronoun (e.g., "John owns a cow.")
- The verb is directly followed by a "that" as a subordinate conjunction (e.g., "John said that he liked llamas.")
- The verb is directly followed by an infinitive (e.g., "John promised to walk the dog.")
- The verb past participle is preceded by "be," as would occur in a passive construction (e.g., "The apple was eaten by the pig.")

For Spanish, we use a very similar algorithm, and for Japanese, we look for noun phrases with an object marker "-wo" near and to the left of the verb. A high transitivity is correlated with CAUSED-PROCESS and INVERSE-STATE while a low transitivity correlates with AGENTIVE-ACTION and PROCESS-OR-STATE. Table 10.4 shows 50 verbs and their calculated transitivity rating. Figure 10.4 shows that for all but one of the verbs that are unambiguously transitive the transitivity rating is above 0.6. The verb "spend" has a transitivity rating of 0.38 because most of its direct objects are numeric dollar amounts. Phrases which begin with a number are not recognized as direct objects, since most numeric amounts following verbs are adjuncts as in "John ran 3 miles." We define a verb's subject animacy to be the number of times the verb appears with an animate subject over the total occurrences of the verb where we identified the subject. Any noun or pronoun directly preceding a verb is considered to be its subject. This heuristic fails in cases where the subject NP is modified by a PP or relative clause as in "The man under the car wore a red shirt." We have only implemented this metric for English. The verb's subject is considered to be animate if it is

Transitivity:

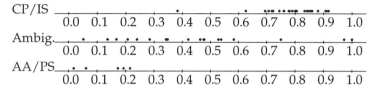

Subject Animacy:

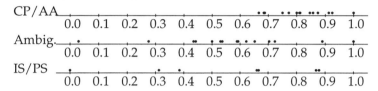

Figure 10.4
This graph shows the accuracy of the Transitivity and Subject Animacy metrics.

any one of the following lexical types.

- A personal pronoun ("it" and "they" were excluded, since they may refer back to inanimate objects.)
- A proper name
- A word under "agent" or "people" in WordNet ([Miller *et al.*, 1990])
- A word that appears in a MUC-4 template slot that can be filled only with humans ([Agency, 1992])

Verbs that have a low subject animacy cannot be either CAUSED-PROCESS or AGENTIVE-ACTION, since the syntactic subject must map to the AGENT thematic role. A high subject animacy does not correlate with any particular situation type, since several stative verbs take only animate subjects (e.g., perception verbs).

The predicted situation types shown in Figure 10.4 were calculated with the following algorithm:

1. Assume that the verb can occur with every situation type.
2. If the transitivity rating is greater than 0.6, then discard the AGENTIVE-

ACTION and PROCESS-OR-STATE possibilities.

3. If the transitivity rating is below 0.1, then discard the CAUSED-PROCESS and INVERSE-STATE possibilities.

4. If the subject animacy is below 0.6, then discard the CAUSED-PROCESS and AGENTIVE-ACTION possibilities.

We are planning several improvements to our situation type determination algorithms. First, because some stative verbs can take animate subjects (e.g., perception verbs like "see," "know," etc.), we sometimes cannot distinguish between INVERSE-STATE or PROCESS-OR-STATE and CAUSED-PROCESS or AGENTIVE-ACTION verbs. This problem, however, can be solved by using algorithms by [Brent, 1991b] or [Dorr, 1992] for identifying stative verbs.

Second, verbs ambiguous between CAUSED-PROCESS and PROCESS-OR-STATE (e.g., "break," "vary") often get inconclusive results because they appear transitively about 50% of the time. When these verbs are transitive, the subjects are almost always animate and when they are intransitive, the subjects are nearly always inanimate. We plan to recognize these situations by calculating animacy separately for transitive and intransitive cases.

10.3.2 Acquiring idiosyncratic information

We automatically identify likely pre/postpositional argument structures for a given verb by looking for pre/postpositions in places where they are likely to attach to the verb (i.e., within a few words to the right for Spanish and English, and to the left for Japanese). When a particular

word	possible clausal complements
know	THATCOMP
vow	THATCOMP, TOCOMP
eat	–
want	TOCOMP
resume	INGCOMP

Table 10.5
English Verbs which Take Complementizers

pre/postposition appears here much more often than chance (based on either Mutual Information or a chi-squared test [Church and Hanks,

verb	MI with "que"
indicar	9.3
señalar	8.7
estimar	8.6
calcular	7.7
precisar	7.7
anunciar	7.7

Table 10.6
Spanish Verbs which Take Complementizers

verb	preposition	MI between verb and prep
luchar	contra	12.4
unir	contra	8.9
vacunar	contra	8.9
cifrar	sobre	9.6
consultar	sobre	9.6
pasar	sobre	8.6
acordar	con	10.8
contar	con	10.3
relacionar	con	9.7
notificar	en	8.7
ocurrir	en	8.0
encontrar	en	7.8

Table 10.7
Spanish Verbs that Take Prepositional Arguments

1990], [Church and Gale, 1991]), we assume that it is a likely argument. A very similar strategy works well at identifying verbs that take sentential complements by looking for complementizers (e.g., "that," "to") in positions of likely attachment. Some English examples are shown in Tables 10.4 and 10.5, and Spanish examples are shown in Tables 10.6 and 10.7. The details of the exact algorithms used for English are contained in [McKee and Maloney, 1992]. Areas for improvement include distinguishing between cases where a verb takes a prepositional arguments, a prepositional particle, or a common adjunct.

10.4   Conclusion

We have automatically built lexicons with predicate-argument mapping information from English, Spanish and Japanese corpora. These lexicons have been used for several multilingual data extraction applications ([Aone *et al.*, 1993a], [Aone *et al.*, 1993b]) and a prototype Japanese-English machine translation system. The algorithms presented here have minimized our lexical acquisition effort considerably.

Currently we are investigating ways in which thematic role slots of verb frames and semantic type restrictions on these slots can be derived automatically from corpora ([Dagan and Itai, 1990], [Hindle and Rooth, 1991], [Zernik and Jacobs, 1990]) so that knowledge acquisition at all three levels of predicate-argument mapping can be automated.

VI MEASURING LEXICAL ACQUISITION

11 Evaluation Techniques for Automatic Semantic Extraction: Comparing Syntactic and Window Based Approaches

Gregory Grefenstette

11.1 Introduction

As more text becomes available electronically, it is tempting to imagine the development of automatic filters able to screen these tremendous flows of text extracting useful bits of information. In order to properly filter, it is useful to know when two words are similar in a corpus. Knowing this would alleviate part of the *term variability* problem of natural language discussed in Furnas *et al.* (1987). Individuals will choose a variety of words to name the same object or operation, with little overlap between people's choices. This variability in naming was cited as the principal reason for large numbers of missed citations in a large-scale evaluation of an information retrieval system [Blair and Maron, 1985]. A proper filter must be able to access information in the text using any word of a set of similar words. A number of knowledge-rich [Jacobs and Rau, 1990], [Calzolari and Bindi, 1990], [Mauldin, 1991] and knowledge-poor [Brown *et al.*, 1992], [Hindle, 1990], [Ruge, 1991], [Grefenstette, 1992b] methods have been proposed for recognizing when words are similar. The knowledge-rich approaches require either a conceptual dependency representation, or semantic tagging of the words, while the knowledge-poor approaches require no previously encoded semantic information, and depend on frequency of co-occurrence of word contexts to determine similarity. Evaluations of results produced by the above systems are often been limited to visual verification by a human subject or left to the human reader.

   In this chapter, we propose gold standard evaluation techniques, allowing us to objectively evaluate and to compare two knowledge-poor approaches for extracting word similarity relations from large text corpora. In order to evaluate the relations extracted, we measure the overlap of the results of each technique against existing hand-created repositories of semantic information such as thesauri and dictionaries. We describe below how such resources can be used as evaluation tools, and apply them to two knowledge-poor approaches.

One of the semantic extraction approaches tested here uses selective natural language processing, in this case the lexical-syntactic relations that can be extracted for each word in a corpus by robust parsers [Hindle, 1983], [Grefenstette, 1994a]. The other approach uses a variation on a classic windowing technique around each word such as was used in [Phillips, 1985]. Both techniques are applied to the same 4 megabyte corpus. We evaluate the results of both techniques using our gold standard evaluations over thesauri and dictionaries and compare the results obtained by the syntactic based method to those obtained by the windowing method. The syntax-based method provides a better overlap with the manually defined thesaurus classes for the 600 most frequently appearing words in the corpus, while for rare words the windowing method performs slightly better for rare words.

11.2   Gold Standards Evaluation

11.2.1   Thesauri

Roget's Thesaurus is readily available via anonymous ftp[1]. In it are collected more than 30,000 unique words arranged in a shallow hierarchy under 1000 topic numbers such as "Existence" (Topic Number 1), "Inexistence" (2), "Substantiality" (3), "Unsubstantiality" (4), ..., "Rite" (998), "Canonicals" (999), and "Temple" (1000). Although this is far from the total number of semantic axes of which one could think, it does provide a wide swath of commonly accepted associations of English language words. We would expect that any system claiming to extract semantics from text should find some of the relations contained in this resource.

By transforming the online source of such a thesaurus, we use it as a gold standard by which to measure the results of different similarity extraction techniques. This measurement is done by checking whether the 'similar words' discovered by each technique are placed under the same heading in this thesaurus.

In order to create this evaluation tool, we extracted a list consisting of all single-word entries from our thesauri with their topic number or numbers. A portion of the extracted *Roget* list in Figure 11.1 shows that

---

[1]For example, in March 1993 it was available via anonymous ftp at the Internet site *world.std.com* in the directory /obi/obi2/Gutenberg/etext91, as well at over 30 other sites.

Roget's	
entry	Topic
...	
abatement	36
abatement	813
abatis	717
abatjour	260
abattis	717
abattoir	361
abba	166
abbacy	995
abbatial	995
abbatical	995
abbatis	717
abbe	996
abbess	996
...	

Macquarie	
entry	subheading
...	
disesteem	036406
disesteem	063701
diseur	022701
disfavour	003901
disfavour	056601
disfavour	063701
disfeature	018212
disfeaturement	018201
disfigure	006804
disfigure	018212
disfigure	020103
disfigured	006803
disfigured	020102
...	

Figure 11.1
Samples from one word entries in both thesauri

abatement appears under two topics: "Nonincrease" (36) and "Discount" (813). *Abbe* and *abbess* both belong under the same topic heading 996 ("Clergy"). The extracted *Roget's* list has 60,071 words (an average of 60 words for each of the 1000 topics). Of these 32,000 are unique (an average of two occurrence for each word). If we assume for simplicity that each word appears under exactly 2 of the 1000 topics, and that the words are uniformly distributed, the chance that two words w_1 and w_2 occur under the same topic is

$$P_{Roget} = 1 - (998/1000)^2,$$

since w_1 is under 2 topic headings and since the chance that w_2 is under any specific topic heading is 2/1000. The probability of finding two randomly chosen words together under the same heading, then, is about 0.4%.

Our measurement of a similarity extraction technique using this gold standard is performed as follows.

> Given a corpus, use the similarity extraction method to derive similarity judgements between the words appearing in the corpus. For each word, take the word appearing as most similar. Examine the human compiled thesaurus to see if that pair of words appears under the same topic number. If it does, count this as a hit.

This procedure was followed on the 4 megabyte corpus described below to test two semantic extraction techniques, one using syntactically derived contexts to judge similarity and one using window-based contexts. The results of these evaluations are also given below.

11.2.2 Dictionary

We also use an online dictionary as a gold standard following a slightly different procedure. Many researchers have drawn on online dictionaries in attempts to do semantic discovery [Sparck Jones, 1986], [Vossen *et al.*, 1989], [Wilks *et al.*, 1990a], whereas we use it here only as a tool for evaluating extraction techniques from unstructured text. We have an online version of *Webster's 7th* available, and we use it in evaluating discovered similarity pairs. This evaluation is based on the assumption that similar words will share some overlap in their dictionary definitions. In order to determine overlap, each the entire literal definition is broken into a list of individual words. This list of tokens contains all the words in the dictionary entry, including dictionary-related markings and abbreviations. In order to clean this list of non-information-bearing words, we automatically removed any word or token

1. of fewer than 4 characters,
2. among the most common 50 words of 4 or more letters in the Brown corpus,
3. among the most common 50 words of 4 or more letters appearing in the definitions of *Webster's 7th*,
4. listed as a preposition, quantifier, or determiner in our lexicon,
5. of 4 or more letters from a common information retrieval stoplist,
6. among the dictionary-related set: *slang, attrib, kind, word, brit, ness, tion, ment.*

These conditions generated a list of 434 stopwords of 4 or more characters which are retracted from any dictionary definition, The remaining words are sorted into a list. For example, the list produced for the definition of the word *administration* is given in Figure 11.2. For simplicity no morphological analysis or any other modifications were performed on the tokens in these lists.

To compare two words using these lists, the intersection of each word's filtered definition list is performed. For example, the intersection between the lists derived from the dictionary entries of *diamond* and

> **ad-min-is-tra-tion** *n.* 1. the act or process of administering 2. performance of executive duties :: <MANAGEMENT> 3. the execution of public affairs as distinguished from policy making 4. a) a body of persons who administer b) <cap> :: a group constituting the political executive in a presidential government c) a governmental agency or board 5. the term of office of an administrative officer or body.
>
> ```
> administer, administering, administrative, affairs,
> agency, board, constituting, distinguished, duties,
> execution, executive, government, governmental,
> making, management, office, officer, performance,
> persons, policy, political, presidential, public, term
> ```

Figure 11.2
Webster definition of "administration," and resulting definition list after filtering through stoplist.

ruby is (*precious, stone*); between *right* and *freedom* it is (*acting, condition, political, power, privilege, right*). In order to use these dictionary-derived lists as an evaluation tool, we perform the following experiment on a corpus.

> Given a corpus, take the similarity pairs derived by the semantic extraction technique in order of decreasing frequency of the first term. Perform the intersection of their respective two dictionary definitions as described above. If this intersection contains <u>two or more</u> elements, count this as a hit.

This evaluation method was also performed on the results of both semantic extraction techniques applied to the corpus described in the next section.

11.3 Corpus

The corpus used for the evaluating the two techniques was extracted from *Grolier's Encyclopedia* for other experiments in semantic extraction. In order to generate a relatively coherent corpus, the corpus was created by extracting only those those sentences which contained the word *Harvard* or one of the thirty hyponyms found under the word *institution* in *WordNet*[2] [Miller *et al.*, 1990], viz. *institution, establishment, charity, religion, . . . , settlement*. This produced a corpus of 3.9 megabytes of text.

11.4   Semantic Extraction Techniques

We will use these gold standard evaluation techniques to compare two techniques for extracting similarity lists from raw text.

The first technique described in [Grefenstette, 1994b] extracts the syntactic context of each word throughout the corpus. The corpus is divided into lexical units via a regular grammar, each lexical unit is assigned a list of context-free syntactic categories, and a normalized form. Then a time linear stochastic grammar similar to the one described in [de Marcken, 1990b] selects a most probable category for each word. A syntactic analyzer based on work done by [Debili, 1982] chunks nouns and verb phrases and create relations within chunks and between chunks. A noun's context becomes all the other adjectives, nouns, and verbs that enter into syntactic relations with it.

As a second technique, more similar to classical knowledge-poor techniques [Phillips, 1985] for judging word similarity, we do not perform syntactic disambiguation and analysis, but simply consider some window of words around a given word as forming the context of that word. We suppose that we have a lexicon, which we do, that gives all the possible parts of speech for a word. Each word in the corpus is looked up in this lexicon as in the first technique, in order to normalize the word and know its possible parts of speech [Evans *et al.*, 1991]. A noun's context will be all the words that can be nouns, adjectives, or verbs within a certain window around the noun. The window that was used was all nouns, adjectives, or verbs on either side of the noun within ten and within the same sentence.

In both cases we will compare nouns to each other, using their contexts. In the first case, the disambiguator determines whether a given ambiguous word is a noun or not. In the second case, we will simply decide that if a word can be at once a noun or verb, or a noun or adjective, that it is a noun. This distinction between the two techniques of using a cursory syntactic analysis or not allows us to evaluate what is

---

[2]WordNet was not used itself as a gold standard since its hierarchy is very deep and its inherent notion of semantic classes is not as clearly defined as in *Roget*

```
    With the arrival of Europeans in 1788 , many Aboriginal
    societies , caught within the coils of expanding white
    settlement , were gradually destroyed .
```

Contexts of nouns extracted after syntactic analysis

```
society catch-SUBJ        arrival european     coil catch-IOBJ
society destroy-DOBJ      socicty aboriginal   settlement whiLe
settlement expand-DOBJ
```

Some contexts extracted with 10 full-word window

```
arrival aboriginal       arrival society      arrival catch
arrival coil             arrival expand       arrival white
arrival settlement       arrival destroy      european arrival
european aboriginal      european society     european catch
european coil            european expand      european white
european settlement      european destroy     society arrival
society european         society aboriginal   society catch
society coil             society expand       society white
society settlement       society destroy      ...
```

Figure 11.3
Comparison of extracted contexts using syntactic and non-syntactic techniques

gained by the addition of this processing step.

Figure 11.3 shows the types of contexts extracted by the selective syntactic technique and by the windowing technique for a sentence from the corpus.

Once context is extracted for each noun, the contexts are compared for similarity using a weighted Jaccard measure footnoteThe Jaccard measure is defined as the number of attributes shared by two objects divided by the total number of unique attributes possessed by both objects. If A is the number of attributes shared by two objects, and B is the number of attributes only appearing with the first object, and C is the number of attributes appearing only with the second object, then the Jaccard measure of similarity between the two objects is $A/(A+B+C)$. This similarity measure yields a value between 0 and 1. The attributes are weighted by taking the log of the attribute frequency with the object multiplied by an inverse entropy measure of the attribute over the corpus. For example, common adjectives have a high entropy and thus lower weights. See [Grefenstette, 1994b]. Here the objects being compared are two nouns, and their attributes are the words found in lexical-syntactic relations to these nouns. [Grefenstette, 1994b]. In order to reduce run time for the similarity comparison, only those nouns

Corpus word	Technique used	
	Syntax	Window
formation	creation	system
work	school	religious
foundation	institution	system
government	constitution	state
education	training	public
religious	religion	century
university	institution	institution
group	institution	member
establishment	creation	government
power	authority	government
creation	establishment	state
state	law	government
program	institution	education
law	constitution	public
year	century	government
center	development	city
art	architecture	science
form	group	life
century	year	religious
member	group	group
part	center	government

Figure 11.4
Sample of words found to be most similar, by the syntactic based technique, and by the window technique, to some frequently occurring words in the corpus

appearing more than 10 times in the corpus were retained. 2661 unique nouns appear 10 times or more. For the windowing technique 33,283 unique attributes with which to judge the words are extracted. The similarity judging run takes 4 full days on a DEC 5000, compared to 3 and 1/2 hours for the similarity calculation using data from the syntactic technique, due to greatly increased number of attributes for each word. For each noun, we retain the noun rated as most similar by the Jaccard similarity measure. Figure 11.4 shows some examples of words found most similar by both techniques.

11.5   Results

The first table, in Figure 11.5, compares the hits produced by the two techniques over *Roget's* and over another online thesaurus, *Macquarie's*,

results over corpus using Window vs. Syntactic Contexts					
	ROGET		MACQUARIE		WEBSTER	
RANK	WINDOW	SYNTAX	WINDOW	SYNTAX	WINDOW	SYNTAX
1-20	25%	50%	15%	40%	55%	50%
21-40	10%	30%	20%	45%	40%	60%
41-60	25%	30%	30%	35%	55%	70%
61-80	15%	30%	20%	30%	45%	65%
81-100	15%	40%	15%	35%	35%	55%
101-200	14%	31%	19%	34%	34%	55%
201-300	21%	29%	20%	30%	29%	34%
301-400	13%	17%	12%	18%	25%	29%
401-500	15%	16%	12%	13%	24%	26%
501-600	13%	11%	10%	15%	19%	16%
601-700	8%	11%	11%	14%	20%	14%
701-800	11%	9%	9%	9%	17%	17%
801-900	17%	6%	13%	7%	25%	12%
901-1000	8%	10%	9%	9%	29%	12%
1001-2000	10.2%	4.9%	11.8%	5.3%	19.2%	6.9%
2001-3000	7.9%	2.4%	7.9%	2.1%	15.2%	5.2%

Figure 11.5
Windowing vs. syntactic percentage of hits for words from most frequent to least

that we had available in the Laboratory for Computational Linguistics at Carnegie Mellon University. This table compares the results obtained from the windowing technique described in preceding paragraphs to those obtained from the syntactic technique, retaining only words for which similarity judgements were made by both techniques.

It can be seen in Figure 11.5 that simple technique of moving a window over a large corpus, counting co-occurrences of words, and eliminating empty words, provides a good hit ratio for frequently appearing words, since about 1 out of 5 of the 100 most frequent words are found similar to words appearing in the same heading in a hand-built thesaurus.

It can also be seen that the performance of the partial syntactic analysis based technique is better for the 600 most frequently appearing nouns, which may be considered as the characteristic vocabulary of the corpus. The difference in performance between the two techniques is statistically significant ($p < 0.05$). The results of a χ^2 test are given in Figure 11.6. Figures 11.7 and 11.8 show the same results as histograms. In these histograms it becomes more evident that the window co-occurrence techniques give more hits for less frequently occurring words, after the 600th most frequent word. One reason for this can be seen by examining the 900th most frequent word, *employment*. Since the windowing technique extracts up to 20 non-stopwords from either

Roget First 600	Syntactic	
	HITS	MISS
WINDOW		
HITS	48	60
MISS	91	401

$$\chi^2 = 6.4$$
$$p < .025$$

Macquarie First 600	Syntactic	
	HITS	MISS
WINDOW		
HITS	42	54
MISS	103	401

$$\chi^2 = 15.3$$
$$p < .005$$

Roget Last 600	Syntactic	
	HITS	MISS
WINDOW		
HITS	2	28
MISS	14	556

$$\chi^2 = 4.6$$
$$p < .05$$

Macquarie Last 600	Syntactic	
	HITS	MISS
WINDOW		
HITS	4	40
MISS	14	542

$$\chi^2 = 12.5$$
$$p < .0005$$

Figure 11.6
χ^2 results comparing syntactic and windowing hits in man-made thesauri

side, there are still 537 context words attached to this word, while the syntactically-based technique, which examines finer-grained contexts, only provides 32 attributes.

Figure 11.9 shows the results of applying the less focused dictionary gold standard experiment to the similarities obtained from the corpus by each technique. For this experiment, both techniques provide about the same overlap for frequent words, and the same significantly stronger showing for the rare words for the windowing technique.

11.6   Conclusion

In this chapter we presented a general method for comparing the results of two similarity extraction techniques via gold standards. This method can be used when no application-specific evaluation technique exists and provides a relative measurement of techniques against human-generated standard semantic resources. We showed how these gold standards could be processed to produce a tool for measuring overlap between their contents and the results of a semantic extraction method. We applied these gold standard evaluations to two different semantic extraction techniques passed over the same 4 megabyte corpus. The

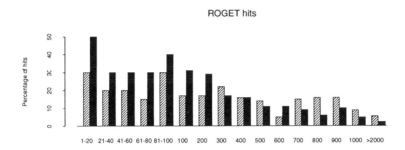

Figure 11.7
Comparison of hit percentage in *Roget's* using simple 10-word windowing
technique(clear) vs. syntactic technique(black). The y-axis gives the percentage of hits
for each group of frequency-ranked terms.

syntax-based technique produced greater overlap with the gold standards derived from thesauri for the characteristic vocabulary of the
corpus, while the window-based technique provided relatively better
results for rare words.

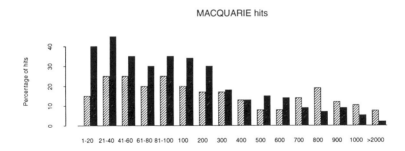

Figure 11.8
Comparison of hits in *Macquarie's* using simple 10-word windowing technique(clear) vs.
syntactic technique(black). The y-axis gives the percentage of hits for each group of
frequency-ranked terms.

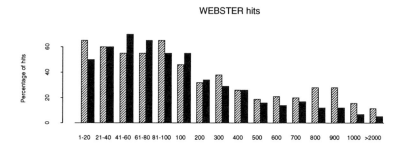

Figure 11.9
Comparison of hit percentage in *Webster's* using simple 10-word windowing technique
(hashed bars) vs. syntactic technique (solid bars). The y-axis gives the percentage of hits
for each group of frequency-ranked terms.

This dichotomous result suggests that no one statistical technique is
adapted to all ranges of frequencies of words from a corpus. Everyday
experience suggests that frequently occurring events can be more finely
analyzed than rarer ones. In the domain of corpus linguistics, the same
reasoning can be applied. For frequent words, finer grained context
such as that provided by even rough syntactic analysis, is rich enough
to judge similarity. For less frequent words, reaping more though less
exact information such as that given by windows of N words provides
more information about each word. For rare words, the context may
have to be extended beyond a window, to the paragraph, or section, or
entire document level, as Crouch (1990) did for rarely appearing words.

Acknowledgments

This research was performed under the auspices of the Laboratory for
Computational Linguistics (Carnegie Mellon University) directed by
Professor David A. Evans.

Bibliography

[Aberdeen *et al.*, 1992] J. Aberdeen, D. Connolly J. Burger, S. Roberts, and M. Vilain. Description of the alembic system as used in MUC-4. In *Proceedings of the Fourth Message Understanding Conference (MUC-4)*, pages 215–222, 1992.

[Agency, 1992] Defense Advanced Research Projects Agency. Proceedings of fourth message understanding conference (muc-4). Morgan Kaufmann Publishers, San Mateo, CA, 1992.

[Alshawi, 1987] Hiyan Alshawi. Processing dictionary definitions with phrasal pattern hierarchies. *American Journal of Computational Linguistics*, 13(3):195–202, 1987.

[Alshawi, 1991] Hiyan Alshawi. *The Core Language Engine*. MIT Press, Cambridge, MA, 1991.

[Amir, 1993] Elan Amir. Carta: A network topology presentation tool. Project report, UC Berkeley, 1993.

[Amsler, 1989] Robert A. Amsler. Research towards the development of a lexical knowledge base for natural language processing. *SIGIR Forum*, (1–2):123, 1989.

[Anderberg, 1973] Michael R. Anderberg. *Cluster Analysis for Applications*. Academic Press, New York, 1973.

[Anick and Pustejovsky, 1990] Peter Anick and James Pustejovsky. An application of lexical semantics to knowledge acquisition from corpora. In *Proceedings of the 13th International Conference on Computational Linguistics*, pages 7–12, Helsinki, Finland, 1990.

[Aone and McKee, 1993] Chinatsu Aone and Doug McKee. Three-level knowledge representation of predicate-argument mapping for multilingual lexicons. In *Proceedings of AAAI Spring Symposium on* Building Lexicons for Machine Translation, 1993.

[Aone *et al.*, 1992] C. Aone, D. McKee, S. Shinn, and H. Blejer. Description of the SOLOMON system as used for MUC-4. In *Proceedings of the Fourth Message Understanding Conference (MUC-4)*, pages 259–267, 1992.

[Aone *et al.*, 1993a] Chinatsu Aone, Hatte Blejer, Sharon Flank, Douglas McKee, and Sandy Shinn. The murasaki project: Multilingual natural language understanding. In *Proceedings of ARPA Human Language Technology Workshop*, Princeton, NJ, 1993.

[Aone *et al.*, 1993b] Chinatsu Aone, Sharon Flank, Paul Krause, and Doug McKee. SRA: Description of the SOLOMON system as used for MUC-5. In *Proceedings of the Fifth Message Understanding Conference (MUC-5)*, 1993.

[Atkins and Levin, 1991] Beryl T. Atkins and Beth Levin. Admitting impediments. In Uri Zernik, editor, *Lexical Acquisition: Using On-Line Resources to Build a Lexicon*. Lawrence Erlbaum Associates, Hillsdale, NJ, 1991.

[Atkins *et al.*, 1986] Beryl T. Atkins, Judy Kegl, and Beth Levin. Explicit and implicit information in dictionaries. In Advances in Lexicology, *Proceedings of the Second Annual Conference of the Centre for the New OED*, University of Waterloo, Ontario, 1986.

[Atkins, 1987] B.T.S. Atkins. Semantic id tags: Corpus evidence for dictionary senses. In *Proceedings of the 3rd Annual Conference of the University of Waterloo Centre for the New Oxford English Dictionary*, pages 17–36, Waterloo, Ontario, 1987.

[Atkins, 1991] B.T.S. Atkins. Building a lexicon: The contribution of lexicography. *International Journal of Lexicography*, 4(3), 1991. B. Boguraev (ed.): Special issue on computational lexicons.

[Atwell, 1987] Eric Atwell. Constituent-likelihood grammar. In Roger Garside, Geoffrey Leech, and Geoffrey Sampson, editors, *The Computational Analysis of English: A Corpus-Based Approach*, pages 57–65. Longman, London and New York, 1987.

[Baker, 1975] Janet K. Baker. Stochastic modeling for automatic speech understanding. In D. R. Reddy, editor, *Speech Recognition*. Academic Press, 1975.

[Baker, 1979] C. Baker. Syntactic theory and the projection problem. *Linguistic Enquiry*, 10:533–581, 1979.

[Barnett *et al.*, 1990] Jim Barnett, Kevin Knight, Inderjeet Mani, and Elaine Rich. Knowledge and natural language processing. *Communications of the ACM*, 3(8):50–71, August 1990.

[Basili *et al.*, 1992] Roberto Basili, Maria-Teresa Pazienza, and Paola Velardi. Computational lexicons: The neat examples and the odd exemplars. In *Proceedings of the 3rd Conference on Applied Natural Language Processing*, Trento, Italy, 1992.

[Basili *et al.*, 1993a] Roberto Basili, Maria-Teresa Pazienza, and Paola Velardi. Semiautomatic extraction of linguistic information for syntactic disambiguation. Applied Artificial Intelligence, 1993.

[Basili *et al.*, 1993b] Roberto Basili, Maria-Teresa Pazienza, and Paola Velardi. What can be learned from raw texts? *Journal of Machine Translation*, 8:147–173, 1993.

[Basili *et al.*, 1993c] Roberto Basili, Maria-Teresa Pazienza, and Paola Velardi. Acquisition of selectional patterns. *Journal of Machine Translation*, 8:175–201, 1993.

[Basili *et al.*, 1993d] Roberto Basili, Maria-Teresa Pazienza, and Paola Velardi. Hierarchical clustering of verbs. In *Acquisition of Lexical Knowledge from Text, Proceedings of the SIGLEX Workshop*, 1993.

[Becker, 1975] Joe Becker. The phrasal lexicon. In *Proceedings of the First International Conference on Theoretical Issues in Natural Language Processing (TINLAP-1)*, pages 60–63, Cambridge, MA, 1975. ACM.

[Berry, 1992] Michael W. Berry. Large-scale sparse singular value computations. *The International Journal of Supercomputer Applications*, 6(1):13–49, 1992.

[Blair and Maron, 1985] D.C. Blair and M.E. Maron. An evaluation of retrieval effectiveness. *Communications of the ACM*, 28:289–299, 1985.

[Boguraev and Briscoe, 1989a] Branimir Boguraev and Ted Briscoe, editors. *Computational Lexicography for Natural Language Processing*. Longman, London and New York, 1989.

[Boguraev and Briscoe, 1989b] Branimir Boguraev and Ted Briscoe. Utilising the LDOCE grammar codes. In Branimir Boguraev and Ted Briscoe, editors, *Computational Lexicography for Natural Language Processing*. Longman UK Limited, London, England, 1989.

[Boguraev and Levin, 1990] Branimir Boguraev and Beth Levin. Models for lexical knowledge bases. In *Proceedings of 6th Annual Conference of the University of Waterloo Centre for the New Oxford English DIctionary and Text Research*, pages 65–78, Waterloo, Ontario, 1990.

[Boguraev *et al.*, 1990] Branimir Boguraev, Ted Briscoe, John Carroll, and Ann Copestake. Database models for computational lexicography. In *Proceedings of the IV-th International Congress on Lexicography (EURALEX)*. Biblograph, Barcelona, Spain, 1990.

[Boguraev, 1991a] Branimir Boguraev. Building a lexicon: The contribution of computers. *International Journal of Lexicography*, 4(3), 1991. Special issue on computational lexicons.

[Boguraev, 1991b] Branimir Boguraev, editor. *Special issue on computational lexicons. International Journal of Lexicography*, 4(3). Oxford University Press, Oxford, UK, 1991.

[Brachman and Schmolze, 1985] R. Brachman and J. Schmolze. An overview of the KL-ONE knowledge representation system. *Cognitive Science*, 9, 1985.

[Brent, 1991a] Michael R. Brent. Automatic acquisition of subcategorization frames from untagged text. In *Proceedings of the 29th Annual Meeting of the ACL*, 1991.

[Brent, 1991b] Michael R. Brent. Automatic semantic classification of verbs from their syntactic contexts: An implemented classifier for stativity. In *Proceedings of the 29th Annual Meeting of the ACL*, Berkeley, CA, 1991.

[Brown *et al.*, 1990] Peter Brown, John Cocke, Steven Della Pietra, Vincent Della Pietra, Frederick Jelinek, John Lafferty, Robert Mercer, and Paul Roossin. A statistical approach to machine translation. *Computational Linguistics*, 16(2):177–184, 1990.

[Brown *et al.*, 1992] Peter F. Brown, Vincent J. Della Pietra, Peter V. deSouza, Jenifer C. Lai, and Robert L. Mercer. Class-based n-gram models of natural language. *Computational Linguistics*, 18(4):467–479, 1992.

[Byrd, 1989] Roy Byrd. Discovering relationships among word senses. In *Proceedings of the 3rd Annual Conference of the University of Waterloo Centre for the New Oxford English*

Dictionary, pages 67–80, Oxford, England, 1989.

[Calzolari and Bindi, 1990] Nicoletta Calzolari and Remo Bindi. Acquisition of lexical information from a large textual italian corpus. In *Proceedings of the 13th International Conference on Computational Linguistics*, Helsinki, Finland, 1990.

[Carroll, 1985] John M. Carroll. *What's in a Name?* Freeman and Company, New York, NY, 1985.

[Carroll, 1992] John Carroll. The ACQUILEX lexical database system: System description and user manual. Technical report 253, University of Cambridge, Cambridge, UK, 1992. In *The (Other) Cambridge ACQUILEX Papers*.

[Chan and Wang, 1991] S.C. Chan and A.K.C. Wang. Synthesis and recognition of sequences. *IEEE Trans. on Pattern Analysis and Machine Intelligence*, 13(12):1245–1255, 1991.

[Chomsky, 1982] Noam Chomsky. *Lectures on Government and Binding*. Foris Publications, Dordrecht, The Netherlands, 1982.

[Church and Gale, 1991] Kenneth Church and William Gale. Concordances for parallel text. In *Proceedings of the 7th Annual Conference of the University of Waterloo Centre for the New OED and Text Research: Using Corpora*, Waterloo, Ontario, 1991.

[Church and Hanks, 1990] Kenneth Church and Patrick Hanks. Word association norms, mutual information and lexicography. *Computational Linguistics*, 16(1):22–29, 1990.

[Church et al., 1992] Kenneth Church, William Gale, Patrick Hanks, and Donald Hindle. Using statistics in lexical analysis. In Uri Zernik, editor, *Lexical Acquisition: Using On-Line Resources to Build a Lexicon*. Lawrence Erlbaum Associates, Hillsdale, NJ, 1992.

[Church, 1988] Kenneth Church. A stochastic parts program and noun phrase parser for unrestricted text. In *Proceedings of the 2nd Conference on Applied Natural Language Processing*, pages 136–143, Austin, TX, 1988.

[CLR, 1994] CLR. Consortium for lexical research, new mexico state university, 1994.

[Coates-Stephens, 1992a] Sam Coates-Stephens. *The Analysis and Acquisition of Proper Names for Robust Text Understanding*. Unpublished PhD dissertation, City University, London, UK, 1992.

[Coates-Stephens, 1992b] Sam Coates-Stephens. The analysis and acquisition of proper names for the understanding of free text. *Computers in the Humanities*, 1992.

[Cohen et al., 1989] R. M. Cohen, T.P. McCandless, and E. Rich. A problem-solving approach to human-computer interface management. In *Proceedings of the Workshop on Blackboard Systems, IJCAI-89*, Detroit, MI, 1989.

[Cowie et al., 1992] Jim Cowie, Louise Guthrie, Yorick Wilks, James Pustejovsky, and Scott Waterman. Description of the *mucbruce* system as used for MUC-4. In *Proceedings of the Fourth Message Understanding Conference (MUC-4)*. Morgan Kaufmann, 1992.

[Cowie et al., 1993] Jim Cowie, Louise Guthrie, James Pustejovsky, Takahiro Wakao, Jin Wang, and Scott Waterman. The DIDEROT information extraction system. In *Proceedings of the First Conference of the Pacific Association for Computational Linguistics*, Vancouver, 1993.

[Crouch, 1990] C. J. Crouch. An approach to the automatic construction of global thesauri. *Information Processing and Management*, 26(5):629–640, 1990.

[Dagan and Itai, 1990] Ido Dagan and Alon Itai. Automatic acquisition of constraints for the resolution of anaphora references and syntactic ambiguities. In *Proceedings of the 13th International Conference on Computational Linguistics*, Helsinki, Finland, 1990.

[Dahl and Ball, 1987] D. Dahl and C.N. Ball. Reference resolution in PUNDIT. Technical report, Unisys, 1987.

[Damerau, 1964] Fred J. Damerau. A technique for computer detection and correction of spelling errors. *Communications of the ACM*, 7(3):171–176, March 1964.

[de Marcken, 1990a] C. G. de Marcken. Parsing the LOB corpus. In *Proceedings of the 28th Annual Meeting of the ACL*, pages 243–251, Pittsburgh, PA, 1990.

[de Marcken, 1990b] Carl G. de Marcken. Parsing the LOB corpus. In *Proceedings of the 28th Annual Meeting of the ACL*, pages 243–251, Pittsburgh, PA, June 1990.

[Debili, 1982] Fathi Debili. *Analyse Syntaxico-Semantique Fondee sur une Acquisition Au-tomatique de Relations Lexicales-Semantiques.* PhD thesis, University of Paris XI, Paris, France, 1982.

[Deerwester *et al.*, 1990] Scott Deerwester, Susan Dumais, George Furnas, Thomas Landauer, and Richard Harshman. Indexing by latent semantic analysis. *Journal of the American Society for Information Science*, 41(6):391–407, 1990.

[DeRose, 1988] Steven S. DeRose. Grammatical category disambiguation by statistical optimization. *Computational Linguistics*, 14(1):31–39, 1988.

[Dorr, 1992] Bonnie Dorr. A Parameterized approach to integrating aspect with lexical-semantics for machine translation. In *Proceedings of the 30th Annual Meeting of the ACL*, 1992.

[Dowty, 1979] David Dowty. *Word Meaning and Montague Grammar.* Reidel, Dordrecht, 1979.

[Ejerhed, 1988] Eva Ejerhed. Finding clauses in unrestricted text by finitary and stochastic methods. In *Proceedings of the 2nd Conference on Applied Natural Language Processing*, pages 219–227, Austin, TX, 1988.

[Evans *et al.*, 1991] David A. Evans, Steve K. Handerson, Robert G. Lefferts, and Ira A. Monarch. A summary of the CLARIT project. Technical Report CMU-LCL-91-2, Laboratory for Computational Linguistics, Carnegie-Mellon University, Pittsburgh, PA, November 1991.

[Fisher, 1987] D. Fisher. Knowledge acquisition via incremental conceptual clustering. *Machine Learning*, 2, 1987.

[Francis and Kučera, 1982] W. Francis and H. Kučera. *Frequency Analysis of English Usage: Lexicon and Grammar.* Houghton-Mifflin, Boston, MA, 1982.

[Fruchtermann and Rheingold, 1990] T. Fruchtermann and E. Rheingold. Graph drawing by force-directed placement. Technical Report UIUCDCS-R-90-1609, Department of Computer Science, University of Illinois, Urbana-Champagne, IL, June 1990.

[Furnas *et al.*, 1987] George W. Furnas, Tomas K. Landauer, L.M. Gomez, and Susan T. Dumais. The vocabulary problem in human-system communication. *Communications of the ACM*, 30(11):964–971, November 1987.

[Gale *et al.*, 1992] William Gale, Kenneth W. Church, and David Yarowsky. A method for disambiguating word senses in a large corpus. Statistical Research Report 104, AT&T Bell Laboratories, 1992.

[Garside *et al.*, 1987] Roger Garside, Geoffrey Leech, and Geoffrey Sampson, editors. *The Computational Analysis of English: A Corpus-Based Approach.* Longman, Harlow and London, 1987.

[Gennari *et al.*, 1989] J. Gennari, P. Langley, and D. Fisher. Model of incremental concept formation. *Artificial Intelligence*, 1989.

[Grefenstette, 1992a] G. Grefenstette. A new knowledge-poor technique for knowledge extraction from large corpora. In *Proceedings of the 15th Annual International Conference on Research and Development in Information Retrieval ACM/SIGIR*, Copenhagen, Denmark, June 1992. ACM.

[Grefenstette, 1992b] G. Grefenstette. SEXTANT: Exploring unexplored contexts for semantic extraction from syntactic analysis. In *Proceedings of the 30th Annual Meeting of the ACL*, Newark, DE, JuneJuly 1992.

[Grefenstette, 1994a] G. Grefenstette. SEXTANT: Extracting semantics from raw text, implementation details. *Integrated Computer-Aided Engineering*, 6(1), 1994. Special Issue on Knowledge Extraction from Text.

[Grefenstette, 1994b] Gregory Grefenstette. *Explorations in Automatic Thesaurus Discovery.* Kluwer Academic Press, Boston, MA, 1994.

[Grishman and Sterling, 1992] Ralph Grishman and J. Sterling. Acquisition of selectional patterns. In *Proceedings of the 14th International Conference on Computational Linguistics*, 1992.

[Grishman *et al.*, 1992] Ralph Grishman, C. Macleod, and J. Sterling. New York University: Description of the PROTEUS system as used for MUC-4. In *Proceedings of the Fourth Message Understanding Conference (MUC-4)*, 1992.

[Harman, 1993] Donna Harman. An overview of the first TREC conference. In *Proceedings of the 16th Annual International Conference on Research and Development in Information Retrieval ACM/SIGIR*, pages 36–47, Pittsburgh, PA, 1993.

[Hearst, 1991] Marti A. Hearst. Noun homograph disambiguation using local context in large text corpora. In *Seventh Annual Conference of the UW Centre for the New OED and Text Research: Using Corpora*, pages 1–22, Oxford, 1991. UW Centre for the New OED and Text Research.

[Hearst, 1992] Marti A. Hearst. Automatic acquisition of hyponyms from large text corpora. In *Proceedings of the 14th International Conference on Computational Linguistics*, pages 539–545, Nantes, France, July 1992.

[Hearst, 1994] Marti A. Hearst. *Context and Structure in Automated Full-Text Information Access*. PhD thesis, University of California at Berkeley, 1994. (available as Computer Science Division Technical Report).

[Heim, 1981] Irene Heim. *The Semantics of Definite and Indefinite Noun Phrases*. Unpublished Ph.D. dissertation, University of Massachusetts, Department of Linguistics, 1981.

[Hemphill *et al.*, 1990] C. Hemphill, J. Godfrey, and G. Doddington. The ATIS spoken language systems pilot corpus. In *Proceedings of a Speech and Natural Language Workshop*, pages 96–101, Hidden Valley, PA, 1990.

[Hindle and Rooth, 1991] Donald Hindle and Mats Rooth. Structural ambiguity and lexical relations. In *Proceedings of the 29th Annual Meeting of the ACL*, 1991.

[Hindle, 1983] Donald Hindle. User manual for Fidditch. Technical Report 7590–142, Naval Research Laboratory, 1983.

[Hindle, 1990] Donald Hindle. Noun classification from predicate-argument structures. In *Proceedings of the 28th Annual Meeting of the ACL*, pages 268–275, Pittsburgh, PA, 1990.

[Hobbs and Appelt, 1992] Jerry Hobbs and Doug Appelt. SRI International: Description of the FASTUS system used for MUC-4. In *Proceedings of the Fourth Message Understanding Conference (MUC-4)*, 1992.

[Hobbs *et al.*, 1990] Jerry Hobbs, Doug Appelt, and M. Pal. Interpretation as abduction. Technical Report Technical Note 449, SRI International AI Center, Palo Alto, 1990.

[Jackendoff, 1983] Ray Jackendoff. *Semantics and Cognition*. MIT Press, Cambridge, MA, 1983.

[Jackendoff, 1990] Ray Jackendoff. *Semantic Structures*. MIT Press, Cambridge, MA, 1990.

[Jacobs and Rau, 1990] Paul Jacobs and Lisa Rau. SCISOR: Extracting information from on-line news. *Communications of the ACM*, 33(11):88–97, 1990.

[Jacobs, 1988] Paul Jacobs. Relation driven text skimming. Technical report, General Electric Co., 1988.

[Justeson and Katz, 1991] John Justeson and Slava Katz. Co-occurences of antonymous adjectives and their contexts. *Computational Linguistics*, 17(1), 1991.

[Kahaner, 1991] Kahaner. The Kahaner email corpus, 1991.

[Karttunen, 1968] Lauri Karttunen. Discourse referents. In J. McCawley, editor, *Syntax and Semantics*. Academic Press, New York, NY, 1968.

[Katoh *et al.*, 1991] N. Katoh, N. Uratani, and T. Aizawa. Processing proper nouns in machine translation for English news. In *Proceedings of a Conference on Current Issues in Computational Linguistics*, Penang, Malaysia, 1991.

[Keil, 1989] F. Keil. *Concepts, Kinds and Cognitive Development*. MIT Press, Cambridge, MA, 1989.

[Kelly and Stone, 1975] Edward Kelly and Philip Stone. *Computer Recognition of English Word Senses*. North-Holland, Amsterdam, 1975.

[Krifka, 1989] Manfred Krifka. Nominal reference, temporal construction, and quantification in event semantics. In R. Bartsch *et al.*, editor, *Semantics and Contextual*

Expressions. Foris Publications, Dordrecht, 1989.

[Kuno, 1973] Susumu Kuno. *The Structure of the Japanese Language*. MIT Press, Cambridge, MA, 1973.

[Kupiec, 1993] Julian Kupiec. MURAX: A robust linguistic approach for question answering using an on-line encyclopedia. In *Proceedings of the 16th Annual International Conference on Research and Development in Information Retrieval ACM/SIGIR*, Pittsburgh, PA, 1993.

[Lakoff, 1987] George Lakoff. *Woman, Fire and Dangerous Things*. University of Chicago Press, Chicago, IL, 1987.

[Landman, 1986] F. Landman. Pegs and alecs. *Linguistics and Philosophy*, pages 97–155, 1986.

[Leacock et al., 1993] Claudia Leacock, Geoffrey Towell, and Ellen M. Voorhees. Corpus-based statistical sense resolution. In *Proceedings of the ARPA Workshop on Human Language Technology*, 1993.

[Leacock et al., in preparation] Claudia Leacock, Shari Landes, and Martin Chodorow. Comparison of sense resolution by statistical classifiers and human subjects. Cognitive Science Laboratory Report, Princeton University, in preparation.

[Lehnert et al., 1991] Wendy Lehnert, Claire Cardie, D. Fisher, E. Riloff, and R. Williams. University of Massachussetts: MUC-3 test results and analysis. In *Proceedings of the Third Message Understanding Conference (MUC-3)*, pages 223–233, 1991.

[Lehnert et al., 1992] Wendy Lehnert, Claire Cardie, D. Fisher, John McCarthy, Ellen Riloff, and S. Soderland. University of Massachusetts: MUC-4 test results and analysis. In *Proceedings of the Fourth Message Understanding Conference (MUC-4)*, 1992.

[Lenat and Guha, 1990] Doug Lenat and Ramanathan Guha. *Building Large Knowledge-Based Systems*. Addison-Wesley Publishing Company, Reading, MA, 1990.

[Levenshtein, 1966] V. I. Levenshtein. Binary codes capable of correcting deletions, insertions, and reversals. *Cybernetics and control Theory*, 10(8):707–710, 1966.

[Levin and Rappaport, 1991] Beth Levin and Malka Rappaport. The lexical semantics of verbs in motion: The perspective from unaccusativity. In I. Roca, editor, *Thematic Structure: Its Role in Grammar*. Foris Publications, Dordrecht, 1991.

[Levin, 1989] Beth Levin. Towards a lexical organization of English verbs. Unpublished ms., Department of Linguistics, Northwestern University, Evanston, IL, 1989.

[Liberman and Marcus, 1992] Mark Liberman and Mitch Marcus. Very large text corpora: What you can do with them, and how to do it. Proceedings of the 30th Annual Meeting of the ACL, 1992. Tutorial notes.

[Liberman and Walker, 1989] Mark Liberman and Donald Walker. ACL data collection initiative: First release. in FINITE STRING Newsletter, *Computational Linguistics*, 15(4):46–47, 1989.

[Liberman, 1989] Mark Liberman. Panel presentation, Proceedings of the 27th Annual Meeting of the ACL, Vancouver, BC, 1989.

[Liddy et al., 1993a] E.D. Liddy, K. McVearry, W. Paik, E.S. Yu, and M. McKenna. Development, implementation and testing of a discourse model for newspaper texts. In *Proceedings of ARPA Human Language Technology Workshop*, Princeton, NJ, 1993.

[Liddy et al., 1993b] E.D. Liddy, W. Paik, E.S. Yu, and K. McVearry. An overview of DR-LINK and its approach to document filtering. In *Proceedings of ARPA Human Language Technology Workshop*, Princeton, NJ, 1993.

[Lu and Fu, 1977] S. Y. Lu and King Sun Fu. A clustering procedure for syntactic patterns. *IEEE Trans. on Systems, Man, and Cybernetics*, October 1977.

[Luperfoy, 1991] Susann Luperfoy. *Discourse Pegs: A Computational Treatment of Context-Dependent Referring Expressions*. Unpublished Ph.D. dissertation, University of Texas at Austin, Department of Linguistics, 1991.

[MacLean, 1976] Alistair MacLean. *The Golden Gate*. Fawcett Publications, Greenwich, CN, 1976.

[Markowitz et al., 1986] Judith Markowitz, Thomas Ahlswede, and Martha Evens. Semantically significant patterns in dictionary definitions. In *Proceedings of the 24th Annual Meeting of the ACL*, pages 112–119, New York, NY, 1986.

[Masand and Duffey, 1985] Brij M. Masand and Roger D. Duffey. A rapid prototype of an information extractor and its application to database table generation. Working paper, Brattle Research Corporation, 1985.

[Masand *et al.*, 1992] Brij Masand, Gordon Linoff, and David Waltz. Classifying news stories using memory based reasoning. In *Proceedings of the 15th Annual International Conference on Research and Development in Information Retrieval ACM/SIGIR*, pages 59–65, Copenhagen, Denmark, 1992.

[Mauldin, 1989] Michael L. Mauldin. Information retrieval by text skimming. Technical Report CMU-CS-89-193, Carnegie Mellon University, 1989.

[Mauldin, 1991] Michael. L. Mauldin. *Conceptual Information Retrieval: A Case Study in Adaptive Parsing*. Kluwer Academic Publishers, Norwell, MA, 1991.

[McArthur, 1981] Tom McArthur. *Longman Lexicon of Contemporary English*. Longman UK Limited, London, England, 1981.

[McDonald, 1992] David D. McDonald. An efficient chart-based algorithm for partial-parsing of unrestricted texts. In *Proceedings of the 3rd Conference on Applied Natural Language Processing*, pages 193–200, Trento, Italy, 1992.

[McDonald, 1993a] David D. McDonald. Internal and external evidence in the identification and semantic categorization of proper names. In *ACL Workshop on* Lexical Acquisition from Text, pages 32–41, Columbus, OH, June 1993.

[McDonald, 1993b] David D. McDonald. The interplay of syntactic and semantic node labels in partial parsing. In *Proceedings of the 3rd International Workshop on Parsing Technologies*, pages 171–186, Tilburg, The Netherlands, 1993.

[McKee and Maloney, 1992] Doug McKee and John Maloney. Using statistics gained from corpora in a knowledge-based NLP system. In *Proceedings of The AAAI Workshop on Statistically-Based NLP Techniques*, 1992.

[Meteer *et al.*, 1991a] Marie Meteer, Richard Schwartz, and Ralph Weischedel. POST: Using probabilities in language processing. In *Proceedings of the 12th International Joint Conference on Artificial Intelligence (IJCAI-91)*, Sydney, Australia, 1991.

[Meteer *et al.*, 1991b] Marie Meteer, Richard Schwartz, and Ralph Weischedel. Empirical studies in part of speech labelling. In *Proceedings of the 4th DARPA Workshop on Speech and Natural Language*, pages 331–336, 1991.

[Miller and Charles, 1991] George A. Miller and Walter G. Charles. Contextual correlates of semantic similarity. *Language and Cognitive Processes*, 6(1), 1991.

[Miller *et al.*, 1990] George A. Miller, Richard Beckwith, Christiane Fellbaum, Derek Gross, and Katherine J. Miller. Introduction to WordNet: An on-line lexical database. *International Journal of Lexicography*, 3(4):235–244, 1990.

[Miller, 1990] George Miller. Special Issue, WordNet: An on-line lexical database. *International Journal of Lexicography*, 3(4), 1990.

[Minsky, 1975] Marvin Minsky. A framework for representing knowledge. In Patrick Winston, editor, *The Psychology of Computer Vision*. McGraw-Hill, New York, NY, 1975.

[Moens and Steedman, 1988] Marc Moens and Mark Steedman. Temporal ontology and temporal reference. *Computational Linguistics*, 14(2), 1988.

[Morris, 1988] Jane Morris. Lexical cohesion, the thesaurus, and the structure of text. Technical Report CSRI-219, Computer Systems Research Institute, University of Toronto, Toronto, Ontario, 1988.

[Mosteller and Wallace, 1964] Frederick Mosteller and David Wallace. *Inference and Disputed Authorship: The Federalist*. Addison-Wesley, Reading, Massachusetts, 1964.

[MUC-4, 1992] *Proceedings of the Fourth Message Understanding Conference (MUC-4)*, San Mateo, 1992. Morgan Kaufman.

[MUC-5, 1993] *Proceedings of the Fifth Message Understanding Conference (MUC-5)*, San Mateo, 1993. Morgan Kaufman.

[Nirenburg and Levin, 1991] Sergei Nirenburg and Lori Levin. Syntax-driven and ontology-driven lexical semantics. In *Proceedings of an ACL Workshop on Lexical Semantics and Knowledge Representation*, Berkeley, CA, 1991.

[Nirenburg and Raskin, 1987] Sergei Nirenburg and Victor Raskin. The subworld concept lexicon and the lexicon management system. *Computational Linguistics*, 13(3–4), 1987.

[Nirenburg, 1989] Sergei Nirenburg. Knowledge-based machine translation. *Machine Translation*, 4(1), 1989. Special issue on knowledge-based machine translation.

[Norvig, 1992] Peter Norvig. *Paradigms of Artificial Intelligence Programming: Case Studies in Common Lisp*. Morgan Kaufmann, San Mateo, CA, 1992.

[Onyshkevych and Nirenburg, 1991] Boyan Onyshkevych and Sergei Nirenburg. Lexicon, ontology and text meaning. In *Proceedings of an ACL Workshop on Lexical Semantics and Knowledge Representation*, Berkeley, CA, 1991.

[Paik *et al.*, 1993a] W. Paik, E.D. Liddy, E.S. Yu, and M. McKenna. Interpreting proper nouns for information retrieval. In *Proceedings of ARPA Human Language Technology Workshop*, Princeton, NJ, 1993.

[Paik *et al.*, 1993b] Woojin Paik, Elizabeth D. Liddy, Edmund Yu, and Mary McKenna. Interpretation of proper nouns for information retrieval. In *ACL Workshop on* Lexical Acquisition from Text, pages 154–160, Columbus, OH, June 1993.

[Paik, 1993] Woojin Paik. Chronological information extraction system. In *Proceedings of the Dagstuhl Seminar on Summarizing Text for Intelligent Communication*, Dagstugl, Germany, 1993.

[Pereira and Tishby, 1992] Fernando Pereira and Naftali Tishby. Distributional similarity, phase transition and hierarchical clustering. In *Proceedings of AAAI Fall Symposium on* Probabilistic Approaches to Natural Language, Cambridge, MA, October 1992.

[Pereira and Tishby, 1993] F. Pereira and Naftali Tishby. Distributional clustering and ontology acquisition. In *Proceedings of the 31st Annual Meeting of the ACL*, Columbus, OH, June 1993.

[Pereira *et al.*, 1993] Fernando Pereira, Naftali Tishby, and Lillian Lee. Distribution clustering of English words. In *Proceedings of the 31st Annual Meeting of the ACL*, 1993.

[Phillips, 1985] Martin Phillips. *Aspects of Text Structure: An Investigation of the Lexical Organization of Text*. Elsevier, Amsterdam, The Netherlands, 1985.

[Pinker, 1989] Stephen Pinker. *Learnability and Cognition — The Acquisition of Argument Structure*. MIT Press, Cambridge, MA, 1989.

[Pirandello, 1992] Luigi Pirandello. *Novelle Per un Anno*. Editore R. Bemporad, Mondadori, 1992.

[Price *et al.*, 1988] P. Price, W. Fisher, J. Bernstein, and D. Pallett. The DARPA 1000-word resource management database for continuous speech recognition. In *Proceedings of IEEE International Conference on Acoustics, Speech, and Signal Processing*, pages 651–654, New York, NY, 1988.

[Pustejovsky and Anick, 1988] James Pustejovsky and Peter Anick. The semantic interpretation of nominals. In *Proceedings of the 12th International Conference on Computational Linguistics*, 1988.

[Pustejovsky and Boguraev, 1993] James Pustejovsky and Branimir Boguraev. Lexical knowledge representation and natural language processing. *Artificial Intelligence*, 63:193–223, 1993.

[Pustejovsky, 1987] James Pustejovsky. On the acquisition of lexical entries: The perceptual origin of thematic relations. In *Proceedings of the 25th Annual Meeting of the ACL*, Stanford, CA, 1987.

[Pustejovsky, 1991] James Pustejovsky. The generative lexicon. *Computational Linguistics*, 17(4), 1991.

[Pustejovsky, 1992] James Pustejovsky. The acquisition of lexical semantic knowledge from large corpora. In *Proceedings of the 5th DARPA Workshop on Speech and Natural Language*, 1992.

[Radford, 1988] Andrew Radford. *Transformational Grammar*. Cambridge University

Press, CAmbridge, England, 1988.

[Rau, 1991] Lisa F. Rau. Extracting company names from text. In *Proceedings of the 7th Conference on Artificial Intelligence Applications*, pages 189–194, Miami Beach, FL, 1991. IEEE.

[Resnik, 1993a] Philip Resnik. *Selection and Information: A Class-Based Approach to Lexical Relationships*. PhD thesis, University of Pennsylvania, December 1993. (available as Institute for Research in Cognitive Science report IRCS-93-42).

[Resnik, 1993b] Philip Resnik. Semantic classes and syntactic ambiguity. In *Proceedings of the ARPA Workshop on Human Language Technology*, 1993.

[Rosch, 1978] Eleanor Rosch. Principle of categorization. In *Cognition and Categorization*. Lawrence Erlbaum Associates, Hillsdale, NJ, 1978.

[Rouvret and Vergnaud, 1980] A. Rouvret and J.R. Vergnaud. Specifying reference to the subject. *Linguistic Enquiry*, 11(1), 1980.

[Ruge, 1991] Gerda Ruge. Experiments on linguistically based term associations. In *RIAO'91*, pages 528–545, Barcelona, Spain, April 1991.

[Rumelhart *et al.*, 1986] D. E. Rumelhart, G. E. Hinton, and R. J. Williams. Learning internal representations by error propagation. In D. E. Rumelhart and J. L. McClelland, editors, *Parallel Distributed Processing: Explorations in the Microstructure of Cognition, Volume 1: Foundations*, pages 318–363. MIT Press, Cambridge, 1986.

[Salton *et al.*, 1975] G. Salton, A. Wong, and C.S. Yang. A vector space model for automatic indexing. *Communications of the ACM*, 18(11):613–620, 1975.

[Sanfilippo and Poznański, 1992] Antonio Sanfilippo and Victor Poznański. The acquisition of lexical knowledge from combined machine-readable dictionary sources. In *Proceedings of the 3rd Conference on Applied Natural Language Processing*, Trento, Italy, 1992.

[Sanfilippo, 1992] Antonio Sanfilippo. A morphological analyser for English and Italian. Technical report 253, University of Cambridge, Cambridge, UK, 1992. In *The (Other) Cambridge ACQUILEX Papers*.

[Sanfilippo, 1994] Antonio Sanfilippo. Word knowledge acquisition, lexicon construction and dictionary compilation. In *Proceedings of the 54th International Conference on Computational Linguistics*, Kyoto, Japan, 1994.

[Sankoff and Kruskal, 1983] D. Sankoff and J.B. Kruskal, editors. *Time warps, string edits, and macromolecules*. Addison Wesley, Reading, MA, 1983.

[Santorini, 1991a] Beatrice Santorini. Bracketing guidelines for the Penn Treebank project. Ms, University of Pennsylvania, Philadelphia, PA, 1991.

[Santorini, 1991b] Beatrice Santorini. Part-of speech guidelines for the Penn Treebank project. Ms, University of Pennsylvania, Philadelphia, PA, 1991.

[Schabes *et al.*, 1988] Yves Schabes, Anne Abeillé, and Aravind K. Joshi. Parsing strategies with 'lexicalized' grammars: Applications to tree-adjoining grammars. In *Proceedings of the 12th International conference on Computational Linguistics (COLING-88)*, Budapest, 1988.

[Schütze, 1993a] Hinrich Schütze. Part of speech induction from scratch. In *Proceedings of the 31st Annual Meeting of the ACL*, 1993.

[Schütze, 1993b] Hinrich Schütze. Word space. In Stephen J. Hanson, Jack D. Cowan, and C. Lee Giles, editors, *Advances in Neural Information Processing Systems 5*. Morgan Kaufmann, San Mateo, CA, 1993.

[Schwartz, 1989] S. Schwartz. Natural kinds and nominal kinds. *Mind*, pages 182–195, 1989.

[Sellers, 1974] P.H. Sellers. An algorithm for the distance between two finite sequences. *J. Comb. Thy*, A16:253–258, 1974.

[Sidner, 1979] Candace L. Sidner. *Towards a Computational Theory of Definite Anaphora Comprehension in Discourse*. Ph.D thesis, Massachussetts Institute of Technology, Electrical Engineering and Computer Science, 1979.

[Sinclair, 1987a] John Sinclair, editor. *The Collins* COBUILD *English Language Dictionary*.

William Collins Sons and Co. Ltd, London and Glasgow, 1987.

[Sinclair, 1987b] John Sinclair, editor. *Looking Up: An Account of the sc cobuild Project in Lexical Computing*. Collins ELT, London and Glasgow, 1987.

[Slator, 1992] Brian Slator. Using context for sense preference. In Uri Zernik, editor, *Lexical Acquisition: Using On-Line Resources to Build a Lexicon*. Lawrence Erlbaum Associates, Hillsdale, NJ, 1992.

[Smadja, 1992] Frank Smadja. Macrocoding the lexicon with co-occurrence knowledge. In Uri Zernik, editor, *Lexical Acquisition: Using On-Line Resources to Build a Lexicon*. Lawrence Erlbaum Associates, Hillsdale, NJ, 1992.

[Smajda and McKeown, 1990] Frank Smajda and Kathleen McKeown. Automatically extracting and representing collocations for language generation. In *Proceedings of the 28th Annual Meeting of the ACL*, pages 252–259, Pittsburgh, PA, 1990.

[Sparck Jones, 1986] Karen Sparck Jones. *Synonymy and Semantic Classification*. Edinburgh University Press, Edinburgh, Scotland, 1986. (PhD thesis delivered by University of Cambridge in 1964).

[Steedman, 1986] M. Steedman. Combinators and grammars. In R. Oehrle, E. Bach, and D. Wheeler, editors, *Categorical Grammars and Natural Language Structures*. Foris, 1986.

[Stepp and Michalski, 1986] E. Stepp and R. Michalski. Conceptual clustering: Inventing goal-oriented classification of structured objects. In R. Michalski, editor, *Machine Learning: An Artificial Intelligence Approach*, volume 2. Morgan Kaufmann, Inc., 1986.

[Strawson, 1985] P. F. Strawson. On referring. In A.P. Martinich, editor, *The Philosophy of Language*. Oxford University Press, Oxford, England, 1985.

[Svartvik and Quirk, 1980] Jan Svartvik and Randall Quirk. *A Corpus of English Conversation*. Lund Studies in English 56. GWK Gleerup, Lund, 1980.

[Talmy, 1985] Lenard Talmy. Lexicalization patterns: Semantic structure in lexical form. In T. Shopen, editor, *Language Typology and Syntactic Description*, number 3 in Grammatical Categories and the Lexicon. Cambridge University Press, Cambridge, England, 1985.

[Ushioda *et al.*, 1993] Akira Ushioda, David A. Evans, Ted Gibson, and Alex Waibel. The automatic acquisition of frequencies of verb subcategorization frames from tagged corpora. In *Acquisition of Lexical Knowledge from Text, Proceedings of the SIGLEX Workshop*, 1993.

[van Berkel and DeSmedt, 1988] B. van Berkel and K. DeSmedt. Triphone analysis: A combined method for the correction of orthographical and typographical errors. In *Proceedings of the 2nd Conference on Applied Natural Language Processing*, pages 77–83, Austin, TX, 1988.

[Vendler, 1967] Zeno Vendler. *Linguistics in Philosophy*. Cornell University Press, 1967.

[Voorhees *et al.*, 1992] Ellen M. Voorhees, Claudia Leacock, and Geoffrey Towell. Learning context to disambiguate word senses. In *Proceedings of the 3rd Computational Learning Theory and Natural Learning Systems Conference*, Cambridge, 1992. MIT Press.

[Vossen *et al.*, 1989] Piek Vossen, Willem Meijs, and Marianne den Broeder. Meaning and structure in dictionary definitions. In Bran Boguraev and Ted Briscoe, editors, *Computational Lexicography for Natural Language Processing*, pages 171–190. Longman Group UK Limited, London, England, 1989.

[Wagner and Fisher, 1974] R. A. Wagner and M. J. Fisher. The string-to-string correction problem. *J. ACM*, 21:168–173, 1974.

[Walker *et al.*, 1995] Donald Walker, Antonio Zampolli, and Nicoletta Calzolari, editors. *Automating the Lexicon: Research and Practice in a Multilingual Environment*. Oxford University Press, Oxford, England, 1995.

[Webber, 1978] Bonnie Webber. *A Formal Approach to Discourse Anaphora*. Unpublished Ph.D. thesis, Harvard University, Department of Applied Mathematics, 1978.

[Webster and Marcus, 1989] Mort Webster and Mitchell Marcus. Automatic acquisition of the lexical semantics of verbs from sentence frames. In *Proceedings of the 27th Annual Meeting of the ACL*, pages 177–184, Vancouver, BC, 1989.

[Weiss, 1973] Stephen Weiss. Learning to disambiguate. *Information Storage and Retrieval*, 9:33–41, 1973.

[Wilks *et al.*, 1990a] Yorick A. Wilks, Dan C. Fass, Cheng-Ming Guo, James E. McDonald, Tony Plate, and Brian M. Slator. Providing machine tractable dictionary tools. *Journal of Computers and Translation*, 2, 1990.

[Wilks *et al.*, 1990b] Yorick A. Wilks, Dan C. Fass, Cheng-Ming Guo, James E. McDonald, Tony Plate, and Brian M. Slator. Providing machine tractable dictionary tools. *Machine Translation*, 5, 1990.

[Wilks *et al.*, 1992] Yorick A. Wilks, Dan C. Fass, Cheng-Ming Guo, James E. McDonald, Tony Plate, and Brian M. Slator. Providing machine tractable dictionary tools. In James Pustejovsky, editor, *Semantics and the Lexicon*. Kluwer, Dordrecht and Boston, 1992.

[WSJ, 1988] The Wall Street Journal, 1988.

[Yarowsky, 1992] David Yarowsky. Word sense disambiguation using statistical models of Roget's categories trained on large corpora. In *Proceedings of the 14th International Conference on Computational Linguistics*, pages 454–460, Nantes, France, July 1992.

[Yarowsky, 1993] David Yarowsky. One sense per collocation. In *Proceedings of the ARPA Workshop on Human Language Technology*, 1993.

[Zernik and Jacobs, 1990] Uri Zernik and Paul Jacobs. Tagging for learning: Collecting thematic relations from corpus. In *Proceedings of the 13th International Conference on Computational Linguistics*, Helsinki, Finland, 1990.

[Zernik, 1989] Uri Zernik. Lexical acquisition: Learning from corpus by capitalizing on lexical categories. In *Proceedings of the 11th International Joint Conference on Artificial Intelligence (IJCAI-89)*, Detroit, MI, 1989.

Author Index

A

Abeillé, A., 144
Aberdeen, J., 41
Ahlswede, T., 77
Aizawa, T, 72
Alshawi, H., 22, 77
Amir, E., 91
Amsler, R., 46
Anderberg, M., 165
Anick, P., 14, 145
Aone, C., 41, 191, 202
Appelt, D., 143, 146
Atkins, B.T.S., 9, 12, 176
Atwell, E., 11

B

Baker, C., 119
Baker, J., 157
Ball, C., 44
Barnett, J., 48
Basili, R., 124, 127–128, 145, 177
Becker, J., 32
Beckwith, R., 78, 121, 199, 210
Bernstein, J., 6
Berry, M.W., 85
Bindi, R., 77, 205
Blair, D.C., 205
Blejer, H., 41, 202
Boguraev, B.K., 7, 9–10, 14, 153, 155, 176, 181
Brachman, R., 117
Brent, M., 145, 176–177, 200
Briscoe, E.J., 7, 155, 176, 181
Brown, P., 12, 205
Burger, S., 41
Byrd, R., 9

C

Calzolari, N., 7, 77, 205
Cardie, C., 143, 155
Carroll, J.A., 181
Carroll, J.M., 46, 52
Chan, S.C., 165
Charles, W.G., 97
Chodorow, M., 107
Chomsky, N., 120
Church, K.W., 11, 13, 98–99, 101, 177, 200
Coates Stephens, S., 24, 43, 46–48, 72
Cocke, J., 12
Cohen, R.M., 48
Connolly, D., 41

Copestake, A.A., 181
Cowie, J., 22, 41–42, 143, 152–153
Crouch, C.J., 216

D

Dagan, I., 202
Dahl, D., 44
Damerau, F., 54
de Marcken, C.G., 50–51, 210
Debili, F., 210
Deerwester, S., 85
Della-Pietra, S., 12
Della-Pietra, V., 12, 205
den Broeder, M., 208
DeRose, S., 11
DeSmedt, K., 12
Doddington, G., 6
Dorr, B., 194, 200
Dowty, D., 194
Duffey, R.D., 23
Dumais, S.T., 85, 205

E

Ejerhed, E., 11
Evans, D.A., 145, 210
Evens, M., 77

F

Fass, D., 14, 77, 155, 208
Fellbaum, C., 78, 121, 199, 210
Fisher, D., 117, 125–126, 143, 155
Fisher, W., 6
Flank, S., 202
Francis, W., 11
Fruchtermann, T., 91
Fu, K.S., 162, 165
Furnas, G.W., 85, 205

G

Gale, W., 13, 98–99, 101, 177, 200
Garside, R., 11
Gennari, J., 117, 125
Gibson, T., 145
Godfrey, J., 6
Gomez, L.M., 205
Grefenstette, G., 77, 205–206, 210–211
Grishman, R., 143, 145
Gross, D., 78, 121, 199, 210
Guha, R., 6
Guo, C.M., 14, 77, 155, 208
Guthrie, L., 22, 41–42, 143, 152–153

H

Handerson, S.K., 210
Hanks, P., 13, 177, 200
Harman, D., 57
Harshman, R., 85
Hearst, M., 77, 83, 93, 110
Heim, I., 44
Hemphill, C., 6
Hindle, D., 13–14, 122, 170, 177, 202, 205–206
Hinton, G.E., 99, 102
Hobbs, J., 143, 146

I

Itai, A., 202

J

Jackendoff, R., 118, 175, 178
Jacobs, P., 48, 77, 191, 202, 205
Jelinek, F., 12
Joshi, A., 144
Justeson, J., 13

K

Kahaner, 58
Karttunen, L., 44
Katoh, N., 72
Katz, S., 13
Kegl, J., 176
Keil, F., 118
Kelly, E., 109
Knight, K., 48
Krause, P., 202
Krifka, M., 194
Kruskal, J.B., 162
Kučera, H., 11
Kuno, S., 193
Kupiec, J., 73

L

Lafferty, J., 12
Lakoff, G., 118
Landauer, T.K., 85, 205
Landes, S., 107
Landman, F., 44
Langley, P., 117, 125
Leacock, C., 98, 107
Lee, L., 145
Leech, G., 11
Lefferts, R.G., 210
Lehnert, W., 143, 155

Lenat, D., 6
Levenshtein, V.I., 162
Levin, B., 9, 175–176, 178, 193
Liberman, M., 11, 25, 179
Liddy, E.D., 43, 47, 58, 61–62, 67–71
Linoff, G., 77
Lu, S.Y., 162, 165
Luperfoy, S., 44

M

Macleod, C., 143
Maloney, J., 201
Mani, I., 48
Marcus, M., 12, 179
Markowitz, J., 77
Markus, M., 122
Maron, M.E., 205
Masand, B.M., 23, 77
Mauldin, M.L., 48, 205
McArthur, T., 178
McCandless, T.P., 48
McCarthy, J., 143, 155
McDonald, D.M., 32–33, 38, 43, 46–47
McDonald, J.E., 14, 77, 155, 208
McKee, D., 41, 191, 201–202
McKenna, M., 43, 47, 58, 61–62, 67–71
McKeown, K., 177
McVearry, K., 61, 67
Meijs, W., 208
Mercer, R., 12
Meteer, M., 61, 167
Michalski, R., 117
Miller, G., 78, 97–98, 121, 199, 210
Miller, K., 78, 121, 199, 210
Minsky, M., 79
Moens, M., 194
Monarch, I., 210
Morris, J., 93
Mosteller, F., 101

N

Nirenburg, S., 6, 117, 193–194
Norvig, P., 49

O

Onyshkevych, B., 194

P

Paik, W., 43, 47, 58, 61–62, 67–71, 73
Pal, M., 143
Pallett, D., 6
Pazienza, M.T., 124, 127–128, 145, 177

Pereira, F., 122–123, 145
Phillips, M., 206, 210
Pinker, S., 118, 120
Pirandello, L., 125
Plate, T., 14, 77, 155, 208
Poznański, V., 178
Price, P., 6
Pustejovsky, J., 14, 22, 41–42, 77, 143–
    145, 149, 151–153, 170

Q

Quirk, R., 11

R

Radford, A., 43
Rappaport, M., 175
Raskin, V., 117
Rau, L., 22, 49, 61, 72, 77, 205
Resnik, P., 78, 110, 112
Rheingold, E., 91
Rich, E., 48
Riloff, E., 143, 155
Roberts, S., 41
Roossin, P., 12
Rooth, M., 170, 202
Rosch, E., 119, 132, 136
Rouvret, A., 177
Ruge, G., 205
Rumelhart, D., 99, 102

S

Salton, G., 99, 101
Sampson, G., 11
Sanfilippo, A., 175, 178, 181
Sankoff, D., 162
Santorini, B., 179
Schabes, Y., 144
Schmolze, J., 117
Schütze, H., 79, 84, 145
Schwartz, R., 61, 118, 167
Sellers, P.H., 162
Shinn, S., 41, 202
Sidner, C., 44
Sinclair, J., 12
Slator, B.M., 12, 14, 77, 155, 208
Smadja, 12
Smajda, F., 177
Soderland, S., 143, 155
Spärck Jones, K., 208
Steedman, M., 148, 194
Stepp, E., 117
Sterling, J., 143, 145
Stone, P., 109

Strawson, P.F., 46
Svartvik, J., 11

T

Talmy, L., 175, 194
Tishby, N., 122–123, 145
Towell, G., 98, 107

U

Uratani, N., 72
Ushioda, A., 145

V

van Berkel, B., 12
Velardi, P., 124, 127–128, 145, 177
Vendler, Z., 194
Vergnaud, J.R., 177
Vilain, M., 41
Voorhees, E.M., 98, 107
Vossen, P., 208

W

Waibel, A., 145
Wakao, T., 143, 152–153
Walker, D., 7, 11
Wallace, D., 101
Waltz, D., 77
Wang, A.K.C., 143, 152–153, 165
Waterman, T.S., 22, 41–42, 143, 152–153
Webber, B., 44
Webster, M., 12, 122
Weischedel, R., 61, 167
Weiss, S., 110
Wilks, Y., 14, 22, 41–42, 77, 155, 208
Williams, R., 99, 102, 143
Wong, A., 99, 101

Y

Yang, C.S., 99, 101
Yarowski, 101
Yarowsky, D., 82, 98–99, 110, 112
Yu, E.S., 43, 47, 58, 61–62, 67–71

Z

Zampolli, A., 7
Zernik, U., 122, 191, 202

Subject Index

A

abbreviation, 22, 26, 30, 35, 49, 52–54, 208
accuracy, 22, 57–58, 105, 108, 112, 130, 199
  measure, 58
ACQUILEX (project), 180, 190
acquisition, ii, 3–7, 9–14, 16, 72–73, 77, 109, 118–119, 125, 127–128, 143–145, 154–157, 160, 167, 176–177, 185, 191, 196, 202
  lexical, *see lexical acquisition*
  multilingual, *see multilingual texts*
  structural, 160
active verb, *see verb, class, active*
activity verb, *see verb, class, of activity*
agentive-action (activity) verb, *see verb, class, agentive-action*
agglomerative clustering, *see clustering, agglomerative*
alignment, 3, 163–165, 168
  string, *see string alignment*
  table, 164
ambiguity, 23, 25, 29, 33, 42, 47, 55, 112, 121, 124, 130, 156, 179, 186–187
  lexical, 179, 186–188
  measure, 187
  of FS type, 184
  of modifier, 27
  of word, *see word, ambiguous*
  semantic, *see semantic ambiguity*
appositive, 4, 31, 49, 51, 55
  construction, 49
  identifier, 51
  modifier, 51
  phrase, 43, 49, 71
argument structure, 21, 118, 150–151, 156, 200
  of verb, 118
argument type, 152, 159
argument variable, 153
Ariosto (system), 126–129
aspect, 11, 13, 48, 118, 156, 167, 171, 176, 194
aspectual classification, 194
association, 6, 12–13, 84, 91, 93, 95, 127, 148, 206
association information, 77, 79, 95, 127
associational lexical relation, *see lexical relation, associational*
author discrimination, 101
author identification, 101

automatic acquisition of local context, *see local context, automatic acquisition*
automatic classifier, 108
automatic grammar induction, *see grammar, induction, automatic*
automatic sense resolution, *see sense, resolution, automatic*
Autoslog (system), 143–144, 155
average context size, 101

B

Bayesian,
  classifier, 101, 105, 107
  decision system, 98
  decision theory, 99
  method, 105
  response pattern, 105
bi-gram analysis, 170
bilingual corpus, *see corpus, bilingual*
Brown Corpus, 10, 208
business news text, 30
business reporting domain, 170

C

case,
  capitalization-sensitive version of a word, *see word, case, capitalization-sensitive*
  case-neutral version of the word, *see word, case, case-neutral*
  distinction, 107, 110
  marking, 21, 150
categorial grammar, *see grammar, categorial*
categorization,
  mechanism, 118
  principle, 118, 121
categorization information of proper noun, *see proper noun, categorization*
category, 10, 22, 28, 33, 36, 61–62, 64, 67, 70–73, 77, 80–83, 86–88, 91, 93, 117, 119, 124, 126, 128, 132–133, 137, 149, 158, 181, 194–195, 210
  derivation algorithm, 83
  identification, 149
  of proper noun, *see proper noun, categorization*
  primary rank of, *see primary rank, of category*
  semantic, *see semantic category*
  set, 83
  size, 80
  top-most node of, 82

category network, 91
causative-inchoative alternation, 175
CCG (Categorial Constraint Grammar),
    147–148
CFG (Context-Free Grammar), 148
characteristic features,
    for word categorization, 15, 118
characteristic vocabulary,
    of a corpus, 213–215
chart, 28–29, 31–33, 47, 49–50
chi-squared test, 200
chronological proper noun knowledge
    base, 73
CIAULA (system), 125–126, 133–135, 138,
    140
city name, *see name, of city*
class, 3, 14, 27, 32–33, 38, 41, 45, 77, 97,
    102, 118–119, 124, 131–133, 135–
    137, 139–140, 149, 153, 155, 167,
    183, 187
    basic-level, 136, 138, 140
    context, 156, 158–159
    lexical, *see lexical class*
    membership, 119
    predicate, *see predicate, class*
    semantic, *see semantic class*
    singleton, 131, 133, 137
    syntactic, 144–145, 156
    word, *see word, class*
classification,
    algorithm, 88
    aspectual, *see aspectual classification*
    classifier performance, 99, 106
    error, 105
    semantic, *see semantic classification*
closed-class word, *see word, closed-class*
CLR (Consortium for Lexical Research),
    49
cluster, 9, 96, 119, 122, 124–126, 128,
    130–135, 137–140, 158, 165, 167–
    168, 170–172, 175
clustering,
    agglomerative, 159, 165
    context, 165, 167
    hierarchical, 165
    phrasal, *see phrasal clustering*
    structural, 156, 162, 171
    verb, *see verb, cluster*
co-occurrence, 3, 15, 84–85, 95, 98–99,
    106, 110, 127, 175, 177, 187, 205–
    206, 213
    lexical, *see lexical co-occurrence*
    preference, 177
    restriction, 175, 187

statistics, 84, 95
    word, *see word, co-occurrence*
COBWEB (system), 125–126, 131–133
code,
    country category, 67
    grammar, *see grammar, code*
    LLOCE, 179, 181–184, 187
    semantic, *see semantic code*
        domain-specific,
        see domain-specific semantic code
    subject field,
        see SFC (Subject Field Code)
    syntactic, *see syntactic code*
    verb, *see verb, code*
coercion, 149, 151
coherent corpus, *see corpus, coherent*
collocation,
    analysis, 13, 127
    information, 176–177, 179, 183, 185,
    190
    matrix, 85
    restriction, 186
    semantic, *see semantic collocation*
collocational hyponyms, *see hyponymy,
    collocational*
Combine-Confidence function, 50
common noun, 37, 42, 61, 67–68
    expansion database, 67
    group, *see group common noun*
communication verb,
    see verb, class, of communication
company, 14, 22–23, 27–33, 35–37, 42,
    44, 49–50, 52, 57, 64–67, 69–70, 72,
    99, 130, 154
    denotation, 23
    name, *see name, of company*
complement,
    sentential, *see sentential complement*
complement structure, 183, 186–187, 189
compositional lexical semantics,
    see lexical semantics, compositional
compositional structure, 21
compound, 4, 28, 31, 33, 45, 49, 179–180
    name, 28
    nominal, 180
    noun, 49
    number, 33
computational linguistics, 3, 8, 11, 13,
    117, 120, 147, 212, 216
concept, 4, 6, 67, 101–103, 117–119, 125–
    127, 132, 135, 147–148, 150, 177,
    191, 194–195
    formation, 117, 125–126, 132, 135
    algorithm, 125–126, 132, 135

hierarchy, 191
conceptual closeness, 122
conceptual dependency, 205
conceptual graph, 129
conceptual relation, 127–128, 135
conceptual representation, 6, 191
conceptual type, 129–131
conjunction attachment, 50
constraints,
    categorical, 149–151, 159
    lexical, 144, 151–152
    mechanisms, 148, 150
    morphological, 149–150
    semantic, 147–148, 151–152, 171
        typing, 152
    structural, 150, 152, 156–159
content vector, 99, 101–103, 105, 107, 112
    classifier, 101, 105, 112
context, 9, 11, 14–16, 21–24, 26–27, 35–
        38, 42–44, 46–47, 49, 58, 62, 64–65,
        71–72, 77, 82, 85, 88, 97–99, 101–
        103, 105–110, 112–113, 116, 119–
        121, 123, 126, 143–144, 146, 148,
        152–153, 156–160, 162, 165, 167,
        170–172, 177, 205, 207, 210–213,
        215
    cue, 144
    feature, 97
    heuristics, 62, 71
    hierarchical classification, 165
    lexical, see lexical context
    probabilistic description, 157–158
    syntactic, see syntactic context
    type, 158, 167
    vector, 85, 158
    word, see word, context
context-sensitive analysis, 21
context-sensitive rule, 37–38
contextual representation, 15, 97, 113
coreference, 44, 47, 51–52, 54–57
    relation, 57
coreferential information, 49
coreferential mention, see mention
    merging, 55
CorPSE (system), 177–178, 180, 186–187
corpus, 3–5, 9–13, 15–17, 25, 37, 51–52,
        57, 61–62, 72, 79, 84–86, 95, 98–
        99, 101, 103, 107, 110, 117, 121–
        128, 135, 138, 141–142, 145, 155–
        156, 170, 178, 180, 183, 185, 189,
        198, 205, 207–215
    analysis, 13, 15–16, 61–62
        of newspaper text, 62
    bilingual, 98

bracketed, 180
Brown, see Brown Corpus
coherent, 209
data, 156, 189
free text, see free text corpus
generation, 209
legal, 138
linguistics, 215
mining, 37
semantics, 205–211, 213–216
vocabulary, 213
    characteristic, see characteristic vocab-
    ulary, of a corpus
corpus-based linguistics, 117
corpus-based sense resolution, 99
cosine measure, 85–86
cospecification, 151–153, 158
cost, 5, 66, 93, 162–163, 167, 172, 176
country,
    category code,
        see code, country category
    name, see name, of country
coverage, 3, 5, 30, 70, 93, 143, 155, 196
cross-linguistic evidence,
    for category construction, 119

D

decision theory, 99, 101
decision tree, 112
definite noun phrase, 45
delimitation,
    algorithm, 26
    process, 27, 33–35
denotation, 23, 25, 28–30, 32–35, 144,
        149–152, 156, 159–161, 172
denotational lexical semantics,
        see lexical semantics, denotational
denotational structure, 146, 160
deterministic grammar,
        see grammar, deterministic
dictionary, 3–4, 7–10, 12–13, 42, 67, 155,
        180, 183, 185, 196, 208, 214
    definition, 208
    entry, 7, 155, 208
    machine-readable, see MRD (Machine-
        Readable Dictionary)
Diderot (system), 143, 152–153, 155, 171
disambiguation, 4, 15, 82, 97, 105, 135,
        176, 181, 186–187, 210
    algorithm, 82
discourse, 24, 28–29, 34–35, 43–44, 52,
        55, 57, 67, 77
    context, 43
    model, 24, 28–29, 34–35, 43

organization of document content, 67
peg, 43–44, 52–55
referent, 44
representation, 43
  three-tiered model, 43–44
structure, 52
distance, 15, 21, 54, 80, 91, 97, 109, 133,
    152, 159, 161–167, 171–172
  computation, 164
  cost, 167
  edit, *see edit distance*
  measure, 162, 166
  metrics, 133
  semantic, *see semantic distance*
distributional method, 126
distributional similarity, 122
document,
  content, 67
  detection, 61
  filtering, 67
  relevance, 57, 61, 67–68
  representation, 68
  topical structure, *see topical structure*
    of a document
domain, 4–6, 9, 15, 52, 77, 118, 121,
    124, 127–128, 130, 134–135, 138–
    143, 146, 148, 159–162, 167, 169–
    170, 175, 177, 179, 196, 215
  business, *see business reporting domain*
  legal, 121, 124, 134, 141
  limited, 77
  remote sensing, 121, 124, 127–128, 130,
    139, 142
  semantic, *see semantic domain*
domain-specific lexicon, 5, 167
domain-specific semantic code, 179
domain-specific tag, 179
domain-specific vocabulary, 169
DR-LINK (system), 61, 63–64, 67–69, 71–
    73

E

edit distance, 15, 159, 161–167, 171–172
  generalized, 162
  weights, 165, 167
entropy, 211
error rate,
  sense resolution task, 108
evaluation, 16, 55, 57–58, 68, 72, 96, 124,
    132, 204–210, 214
  of semantic extraction,
    application-specific technique, 214
  gold standard,
    see gold standard evaluation

methodology, 208
  tool, 205–206, 208
external evidence,
  for proper name analysis, 14, 20, 22–
    24, 28, 30, 36–37, 46, 49
extraction system, 22, 152, 160, 171–172
  multilingual,
    see multilingual data extraction
  of lexical relations, *see lexical relation,*
    extraction
  pattern-based, 143, 145, 154–155, 171

F

feature vector, 126
feature-based class system, 149
first name, 22, 34, 46, 49, 57, 62, 70
fourgram vector, 84–85
free text corpus, 78, 84
frequent sense, 112
frequent word,
    see word, frequency, frequent
functional concept, 148
functional semantics, 147, 150
functional structure, 148
  semantic, 148
Funes (system), 24, 72

G

gazetteer, 22, 36, 41, 49, 62, 71
  geographical, 41
  IDA, *see IDA gazetteer*
  Tipster, 49, 62
gender information, 49, 55
  of mention, 55
gender slot, 54
generative lexicon,
    see GL (Generative Lexicon)
genre, 43, 57, 79, 189
genus information,
  of proper noun, 72
geographic lexicon, 49
geographical gazetteer,
    see gazetteer, geographical
geographical location name, *see name, of*
    geographical location
geography-related headword, 49
GL (Generative Lexicon), 144, 149, 151,
    153
GLS (GL Structure), 153
gold standard, 16, 205–210, 214
  evaluation, 206
gold standard evaluation, 205–210, 214

grammar, 21–23, 25–28, 30–31, 33–34,
  38, 51, 143–144, 152–154, 156–157,
  165, 167, 176, 179, 182–185, 187,
  210
  categorial, 25
  CCG, see CCG (Categorial Constraint
    Grammar
  CFG, see CFG (Context-Free Grammar
  code, 176, 179, 182–185
  deterministic, 25
  heuristic, 153
  induction, 156, 165, 167
   automatic, 165
  lexicalized, 25, 157
  lexically indexed, see lexically indexed
    grammar
  of names, 38
  semantic, 30–31, 33, 144
grammatical function, 27, 33, 191–192
Grolier's American Academic Encyclopedia, 82, 209
group common noun, 61, 68
group proper noun, 61, 67–68

H

hand-built lexicon, 96
hand-built thesaurus,
  see semantic resource, standard
heuristic internal evidence,
  see internal evidence, for proper name
    analysis, heuristic
hierarchical clustering,
  see clustering, hierarchical
hierarchical categorization, 168
hierarchical structure, 77–79, 158
hierarchy, 62, 77–84, 88, 121, 124, 135,
  140, 146–147, 153, 158–160, 165,
  179, 182, 191, 206, 209
high frequency function word, see word,
  frequency, high
high frequency word,
  see word, frequency, high
honorifics, 43, 49, 54
hypernym, 78
hyponymy, 77, 79–80, 109, 209
  collocational, 109

I

IDA gazetteer, 71
idiom, 45, 169
idiosyncrasy, 191–192, 194–196
inference, 6, 9, 13, 49, 143, 155, 189
  technique, 13, 143

information extraction, 22, 145–146, 152,
  160, 171
  system, 22, 152, 171
information retrieval, 14, 41, 57–58, 60–
  61, 64, 68, 73, 77, 101, 205, 208
  efficiency, 63
  stoplist, 208
  system, 57–58, 61, 68, 101, 205
  task, 64, 73
infrequent word, see word, frequency, low
internal evidence,
  for proper name analysis, 14, 22–23,
    26, 28, 35–38, 46, 49
  definitive, 22
  heuristic, 38
  main source of, 49
intransitive verb,
  see verb, class, intransitive
inverse-state verb,
  see verb, class, inverse-state

J

Jaccard measure, 211

K

knowledge,
  acquisition, 4–6, 10, 12, 73, 176, 202
  base, 4, 6, 9, 43–44, 62, 64, 70–73, 191,
    194–195
  lexical, see lexical knowledge
  representation, 13, 126, 143, 146–147,
    150, 152–153, 155
  semantic, see semantic knowledge
  source, 47–49, 52
knowledge representation,
  entity-relation model, 146–147
  reference-relation model, 147, 150
knowledge source, 47–50, 52, 54–55
knowledge-poor techniques for lexical
  relation extraction, see lexical relation, extraction, knowledge-poor techniques
knowledge-rich techniques for lexical
  relation extraction, see lexical relation, extraction, knowledge-rich techniques
KS, see knowledge source

L

language acquisition, 118–119, 125
LDOCE (Longman Dictionary of Contemporary English), 7, 155
least-square approximation, 85

legal corpus, *see corpus, legal*
legal domain, *see domain, legal*
letter fourgram, 84
   vector, *see fourgram vector*
lexical acquisition, 3–5, 9–13, 16, 127–
   128, 145, 176–177, 185, 202
   automatic, 145
   of collocational information, 177
lexical association information, 95
lexical class, 3, 15, 160
lexical classification,
   hierarchical, 15
lexical co-occurrence, 84, 95
lexical context, 82, 158, 171
lexical database, 98
lexical entry, 67, 128, 148–149
lexical environment, 157–158, 167
lexical equality, 167
lexical functional grammar,
   see LFG (Lexical Functional Gram-
   mar)
lexical information, 5, 9–10, 15, 125, 135,
   140, 171, 176
lexical item, 6, 11, 15, 77–79, 84, 93, 144–
   145, 147, 150, 152, 157, 162, 167,
   176
lexical knowledge, 3–6, 9–10, 12, 119,
   156, 176–177, 190
lexical learning, 117, 127
lexical method,
   structural, *see structural lexical method*
lexical pattern,
   acquisition, 144
lexical relation, 79
   associational, 79
   extraction,
     knowledge-poor techniques, 205, 210
     knowledge-rich techniques, 205
   lexico-semantic, 4, 145, 171, 175
   lexico-syntactic, 29, 205, 211
lexical resource, 62
   Brown Corpus, *see Brown Corpus*
   Grolier's, *see Grolier's American Aca-*
     demic Encyclopedia
   LDOCE,
     see LDOCE (Longman Dictionary of
     Contemporary English)
   LLOCE, *see LLOCE (Longman Lexicon*
     of Contemporary English)
   Macquarie, *see Macquarie's Thesaurus*
   NYT, *see New York Times*
   Penn Treebank, *see Penn Treebank*
   Roget, *see Roget's Thesaurus*

Webster's, *see Merriam-Webster's Col-*
   legiate Dictionary (7th Edition)
Who's News, *see Who's News*
WordNet, *see WordNet*
WSJ, *see Wall Street Journal*
lexical semantics, 8–9, 11, 13, 16, 48, 144,
   147, 151, 156, 171
   compositional, 144
   denotational, 171
lexical structure, 11, 156–157, 159–161,
   172, 176
lexical unit, 15, 150, 210
lexicalization, 14, 175, 194
   pattern, 194
lexicalized grammar,
   see grammar, lexicalized
lexically indexed grammar, 144, 152
lexicon, ii, 3–15, 17, 49, 51–52, 70, 76–79,
   95–96, 117, 120, 123, 129, 144–145,
   150–151, 153–155, 158, 167, 178,
   190–191, 194, 196, 202, 208, 210
   acquisition, ii, 14
   builder, 117, 120
   construction,
     automatic, 73, 190
LFG (Lexical Functional Grammar), 148,
   192
linguistic context, 97
linguistic structure, 156
LLOCE (Longman Lexicon of Contemporary English), 178–187, 190
   collocational information, 179
   entry, 185–186
   grammar code, *see code, LLOCE*
   hierarchy, 182
   index, 182
   semantic code, *see code, LLOCE*
   tag, 180
local context, 15, 43, 97, 109–110, 113
location verb, *see verb, class, of location*

M

machine readable dictionary, *see MRD*
   (Machine-Readable Dictionary)
machine readable thesaurus, 176, 206
machine translation, 3, 5–6, 11, 72, 202
   Japanese-English, 202
Macquarie's Thesaurus, 206, 212–214
magazine article, 93
Markov model of language, 157
measure of semantic distance,
   see semantic distance, measure of
medium frequency word,
   see word, frequency, medium

mention, 14, 41, 44, 47–55, 64, 67, 88, 180
    generation, 47–48
    hypothesis, 50, 52, 54–56
    merging,
        see coreferential mention, merging
Merriam-Webster's Collegiate Dictionary
    (7th Edition), 208
metonymy, 49
mnemonic inertia, 132–133
modes of term use, 144–145, 158, 171
morphological constraint,
        see constraints, morphological
morphology, 3, 5–6, 15, 32, 148–151, 153,
    156, 177, 180, 191, 208
movement verb,
        see verb, class, of movement
MRD (Machine-Readable Dictionary), 5,
    7–9, 13, 176, 190, 208
MUC (Message Understanding Confer-
    ence), 14, 143, 146, 155, 160, 199
multi-word name, 32
multilingual data extraction, 202
multilingual lexicons,
    acquisition from corpora, 196
multilingual texts, 16, 191, 196, 202
    for idiosyncrasy information acquisi-
        tion, 191
    for predicate-argument mapping, 191
    for situation type acquisition, 191
mutual information, 200

N

n-gram, 157
name, *see proper name*
    category, 64
    classification,
        facility, 37
    element, 29, 41–43, 45, 47, 52–53
        database, 41
        heuristic, 52
    grammar, *see grammar, of names*
    identification of, 14, 41, 43–45, 58
        text-driven,
            see text-driven identification of name
        mention, 47, 51, 53
    multi-word, *see multi-word name*
    non-proper, *see non-proper name*
    normalization, 52–53, 55
    of city, 62, 64, 70–71
    of company, 29, 42, 44, 49, 52, 57, 72,
        154
        extraction, 72
    of country, 67, 71
    of geographical location, 45

    of organization, 43, 45, 52
    of person, 41–42, 49, 52, 57, 70, 72
    of place, 45, 49, 52, 154
    pattern, 35
    recognition, 22, 41, 154
        system, 22
    reference,
        semantic theory of,
            see semantic theory of name reference
    spotting, 24, 27
    subtype, 34
    tagger, 58
name reference,
    semantic theory, *see semantic theory of
        name reference*
natural language processing,
    selective, 206
    system, 3, 41
natural type, 118
network,
    layout, 91
    topology, 103
neural network, 99, 102–103, 105, 107
    classifier, 102, 105, 107
New York Times, 45, 57, 85–88
news,
    article, 21, 23, 30, 146
    business, *see business news text*
    column, 37
    corpus, 72
    source, 57–58
    story, 43, 64, 66, 70, 73
newspaper article, *see news, article*
newspaper story, *see news, story*
newswire,
    service, 156
    text, 14, 40, 45, 58
nominal compound,
        see compound, nominal
non-capitalized word,
        see word, case, non-capitalized
non-proper name, 45
noun compound, *see compound, noun*
noun phrase, 24, 33, 35, 45, 48, 61–62,
    67, 71, 153, 177, 179–180, 183, 198
    definite, 45
    identification, 48
noun phrase complement, 179, 183
noun phrase semantics, 43
null token, *see token, null*
NYT, *see New York Times*

O

online dictionary,
    see MRD (Machine-Readable Dictionary)
ontology, 6, 49, 51, 117–119
  semantic lexicon, 51
  shallow, 49
open-class word, *see word, open-class*
organization name,
    see name, of organization

P

parser, *see parsing*
parsing, 3, 11, 22–23, 25–27, 33, 38, 51,
    127, 135, 138, 143–144, 185–186,
    196, 205
  chart, *see chart*
  robust, 6, 15, 196, 205
  shallow, 127
pattern, 3–5, 11, 13, 15, 21, 28, 31, 34–35,
    37, 49, 51, 99, 105–106, 110, 121,
    126–128, 132, 134, 138–139, 143–
    145, 152–158, 161, 167–168, 171–
    172, 175, 177, 189, 194
  acquisition, 144, 154–155
  lexical, 128, 143–144, 152, 155
  phrasal, 177
  system, 143, 152, 155–157
pattern-based extraction system,
    see extraction system, pattern-based
Penn Treebank, 179, 186–187, 190
person name, *see name, of person*
phrasal cluster, 170
phrasal component, 152, 158
phrasal constituent, 24, 165
phrasal delineation, 168
phrasal fragment, 180
phrasal item, 150
phrasal pattern, *see pattern, phrasal*
phrasal unit, 160
phrase,
  bracketing, 62, 71
  structure, 25–26, 32–33, 36, 168
  rule, 25, 32
phrase-bracketed text, 156
place name, *see name, of place*
PNF (Proper Name identification Facility), 22–26, 28–29, 32–38
polysemous word, *see word, polysemous*
polysemy, 98, 105–106
polyword, 32–33, 36
  operation, 32

recognition, 33
rule, 32
pre/postposition, 194, 200
pre/postpositional argument structure,
    200
precision, 14, 47, 57–58, 68–72, 109, 112,
    176
predicate, 15–16, 38, 53, 146, 148, 150,
    153, 155, 159–161, 171–172, 175,
    178, 180, 191–192, 194–196, 202
  class, 159
  logic, 148, 150, 153
  type, 15, 146, 159, 171
predicate structure, 159, 161, 178, 180
  extractor, 178, 180
  corpus-based, 178
predicate-argument mapping, 16, 191–
    192, 194–196, 202
prepositional argument, 168, 200–201
prepositional keyword, 168
prepositional particle, 200
primary rank,
  of category, 91
probabilistic part of speech tagger, 61
probability matrix, 134
process-or-state verb,
    see verb, class, process-or-state
Project Gutenberg, 82, 206
pronominal reference, 147
proper name, 14, 20–27, 30–32, 37–38,
    40–45, 47, 58, 86–87, 95, 98, 154,
    199
  categorization,
    semantic, 14, 20–21
  constituent structure of, 26
  element, 45
  internal structure of, 45–46, 119
  open compound, 45
  semantic classification of, 87
  standard form of, 52
  surface form of, 52
  syntactic environment of, 43
proper noun, 14, 38, 60–73, 87, 105, 177
  boundary identification, 61–62, 69
  categorization, 14–15, 20–23, 36, 62–
    68, 70–73, 119, 132, 136, 168
  feature, 68
  result, 72
  scheme, 62, 70
  system, 63–64, 68–72
  classification, 61–62
  scheme, 61–62, 72
  concept, 67
  expansion, 67

extraction, 68
group, *see group proper noun*
knowledge base, 70–71, 73
matching, 61, 68
partial form of, 65
phrase, 61–62, 71
processor, 61
sentence-initial position, 33
tag, 62
uncommon, 71
proximity measure, 49
psycholinguistics, 15, 117–118, 120, 123–124
punctuation, 26–27, 30–33, 35–36, 101, 103, 107, 109–110, 168

Q

qualia, 151, 153
question-answering system, 73

R

rare word, *see word, frequency, rare*
recall, 14, 47, 57–58, 68, 71, 106, 109, 112
recall/precision threshold, 47
reference resolution, 63
relational model,
    as denotational scheme, 150
relational structure,
    of lexical entry, 147, 151, 159, 172
remote sensing domain,
    see domain, remote sensing
representational efficiency, 150
rewrite rule, 22, 24, 26, 33, 36–37
rigid designator, 29
robust parsing, *see parsing, robust*
Roget's Thesaurus, 82, 120–121, 206–207, 209–210, 212–214
RSD (remote sensing domain),
    see domain, remote sensing

S

SBAR complement, 189
selectional restriction, 4, 43, 109, 124, 126–129, 177, 185
semantic ambiguity, 179
semantic analysis, 3, 144, 152, 191
semantic attribute, 43–44, 47–48
semantic bias, 120
semantic category, 28, 33, 149
semantic class, 14–15, 38, 87, 176, 209
semantic classification, 15, 38, 87

of proper name,
    see proper name, semantic classification of
semantic code, 178–179, 181–184, 186–187
semantic collocation, 170
semantic concept, 191–192, 194–195
semantic constituent, 148, 171
semantic constraint,
    see constraints, semantic
semantic denotation, 149, 172
semantic description, 41, 139–140, 147, 151
semantic discovery, 208
semantic distance, 80, 91
    measure of, 80
semantic domain, 118, 143, 148
semantic extraction, 16, 204–210, 214
semantic function, 45
semantic grammar,
    see grammar, semantic
semantic information, 3, 5, 8, 15, 47–49, 170, 191, 205
semantic interpretation,
    of proper name, 21, 25, 32, 143–145
semantic knowledge, 119
semantic links, 35
semantic marker, 109
semantic model, 14, 23, 27, 29–30, 38
    of proper name, 23
semantic processor, 180–181
semantic relatedness, 84, 170
semantic relation, 4, 150, 152
semantic representation, 15, 84, 145, 147, 152
semantic resource,
    lexical, *see lexical resource*
    standard, 213–214
semantic restriction, 128, 182
semantic role, 130, 148–150, 152
semantic similarity, 85–86, 122, 130
semantic structure, 21, 148, 151, 153, 156, 158–159, 172, 191–192
    functional,
        see functional structure, semantic
semantic tag, 16, 122, 127–128, 135, 141–142, 176–177, 179–181, 185–186, 190, 205
    equivalence, 186
semantic template, 13
semantic term, 156
semantic test, 48
semantic theory of name reference, 45
semantic type restriction, 202

semantic variance, 144
semantic verb class, 16, 174, 176, 183,
    187, 189
semantics, 11, 13, 16, 21, 43, 48, 118, 144–
    145, 147, 150–151, 156–157, 171,
    175, 182, 186, 189, 194, 205–211,
    213–215
  compositional,
    see lexical semantics, compositional
  corpus-based, *see corpus, semantics*
  denotational,
    see denotational semantics
  functional, *see functional semantics*
  lexical, *see lexical semantics*
  noun phrase, *see noun phrase semantics*
  of aspect, 194
sense, 4, 9–10, 15–17, 27, 44, 77–78, 82,
    85, 88, 95, 97–99, 101–103, 105–113,
    117–118, 121–124, 138–139, 143, 156,
    175–176, 178, 183–184, 186, 191–
    195
  disambiguation, 4, 15, 97, 105
  discrimination, 124
  indicator, 112
  resolution, 15, 55, 97, 99, 101–102, 105–
    109, 113
    automatic, 97, 109
  vector, 102, 110, 112
    similarity, 112
    topical, 110
sentence-initial position,
  of proper noun,
    *see proper noun, sentence-initial po-
    sition*
sentential complement, 194, 200
SFC (Subject Field Code), 67
  module, 68
  representation, 67
  vector, 67
SGML (Standard Generalized Markup
    Language), 64
shallow hierarchy, 206
shallow parser, *see parsing, shallow*
shallow syntactic analysis, 177
similarity, 15, 53, 79, 85–86, 101, 112,
    119, 122, 124, 130, 132, 138–139,
    155–156, 158–159, 162, 165, 167–
    168, 171–172, 205–216
  extraction, 207
  judgement, 207
  measure, 158, 162, 172, 211
  predicate, 53
  semantic, *see semantic similarity*
  syntactic, *see syntactic similarity*

Singular Value Decomposition, 85
situation type, 16, 191–196, 198–200
sources of evidence,
  for proper name categorization, 47, 65
  external,
    *see external evidence, for proper name
    analysis*
  internal,
    *see internal evidence, for proper name
    analysis*
Sparser, 21, 23–25, 29–33, 36–37
statistical approach, 122, 125, 132
statistical bi-gram analysis, 170
statistical classifier, 97, 107–108
statistical evidence, 122
statistical measure, 13, 129
statistical methods, 15, 97, 107–108, 126
statistical model, 15, 97, 101–102; 106,
    112
statistical models,
  Bayesian classifier, 101
  compared with human performance,
    106
  content vectors, 101, 112
  neural networks, 102
statistical relevance, 158
statistical significance, 187
statistical technique,
  for disambiguation, 16, 187, 215
statistically-derived information, 96
statistics, 13–16, 23, 50, 77, 84, 95, 97–99,
    101–102, 106–108, 112, 122, 125–
    126, 129, 132, 135, 158, 170, 187,
    189, 215
stative verb, *see verb, class, stative*
step function, 166
stop list, 107, 208
stop word, 101, 103, 110, 208, 213
string alignment, 163–165, 168
structural classification, 171
structural feature, 158–159
structural knowledge, 161
structural lexical method, 170
structural mapping, 144, 160, 172
structural similarity, 155–156, 158
subcategorization, 4, 11, 16, 128, 145,
    149, 174–177, 179–180, 183–187, 189–
    190
  frame, 16, 128, 145, 149, 174–175, 177,
    179–180, 183, 190
  property, 175
subject animacy, 198–199
subject field code, *see SFC (Subject Field
    Code)*

sublanguage, 23, 37, 121, 124, 138, 177,
    179
super-categories, 93–95
surface distribution,
    see distribution, surface
synonym, 77, 89
synset, 77, 79–82
syntactic analysis, 143
    cursory, 210
    partial, 213
    rough, 215
    shallow, *see shallow syntactic analysis*
syntactic analyzer, 210
syntactic behavior,
    of lexical items, 5, 9, 11–12, 144, 147,
        149, 160, 165, 170
syntactic construct, 147
syntactic context, 49, 153, 210, 212
syntactic context of word,
    see word, syntactic context of
syntactic disambiguation, 210
syntactic form, 45, 151
syntactic frame, 122
syntactic head, 45
syntactic interaction, 165
syntactic marker, 109
syntactic parse, *see syntactic analysis*
syntactic pattern, 127, 145, 155, 161
syntactic realization, 151
syntactic relation, 22, 205, 210–211
syntactic similarity, 122, 130
syntactic structure, 13, 97, 107, 119, 191–
    192
syntactic tag, 99, 127
syntactic technique, 205, 211–214
syntactic template, 152
syntactic theory, 147, 165
syntactico-semantic restriction, 182
syntax-semantics interface, 16, 186

T

tagging, 3, 12, 14, 16, 41, 49, 55, 57, 61–
    62, 64–65, 70, 99, 121–122, 127–128,
    130, 135, 141–142, 154, 156, 167,
    176–182, 185–186, 190, 205
    by hand, 57
    of names, 55, 57–58
    part-of-speech, 11, 14, 49, 61–62, 65,
        69–70, 154, 167
    probabilistic,
        see probabilistic part of speech tagger
    semantic, 176, 178, 186, 190
    untagged text, *see text, untagged*
taxonomy, 79–80, 95

technical term, 121
template, 9, 13, 110–113, 146, 152–153,
    155, 159, 199
term variability problem, 205
term-similarity information, 79
terminological knowledge, 117
text,
    business news, *see business news text*
    corpus, 13, 15, 79, 98
    Japanese, 191
    labeling, 77, 87
    lexical structure of, 160
    magazine article, *see magazine article*
    multilingual, *see multilingual text*
    newswire, *see newswire, text*
    sources,
        Brown Corpus, *see Brown Corpus*
        New York Times, *see New York Times*
        Penn Treebank, *see Penn Treebank*
        Wall Street Journal,
            see Wall Street Journal
        Who's News, *see Who's News*
    type, 84
    unit, 47
    unrestricted, 14, 21, 25, 29–30, 41
    untagged, 167, 177
Text Structure, 4, 67–68
    component, 67
    information, 68
text-driven identification of name, 43
thematic feature, 118, 124
thematic role, 15, 118, 124, 126, 129, 131,
    137, 140, 191–192, 194, 199, 202
thematic role slot, 194, 202
thesaurus, 82, 121, 176, 178, 205–207,
    209, 212–214
    classes, 205
    machine-readable,
        see machine readable thesaurus
    Macquarie's,
        see Macquaries's Thesaurus
    Roget's, *see Roget's Thesaurus*
three-tiered model of discourse repre-
    sentation, *see discourse, representa-
    tion, three-tiered model*
time adverbial, 187
Tipster, 14, 49, 57, 61–62, 143, 146–147,
    155, 159–160, 167, 170
    corpus, 57
    gazetteer, *see gazetteer, Tipster*
title, 23, 30, 38, 42, 46–47
    in appositive position, 31, 34
    in pre-head position, 31
    of book, 86

of company, 23, 27
of employment, 28, 34, 42
of film, 88
of musical performance, 88
of person, 27–28, 50
of employment, 37
token, 8, 29, 31, 35, 44, 101–103, 105, 110,
    153, 162–164, 166–167, 172, 179–
    180, 186, 208
    null, 163
    scan, 31
token distance, 166
tokenization, 31–32, 47
tokenizer, 31
topic, 4, 15, 57, 77–78, 80, 82–83, 88–89,
    93, 95, 97–98, 106, 206–207
    assignment, 93
    algorithm, 86–89
    labeling, 77, 82, 89, 93
    main, 77, 82–83, 93
topic assignment, 93
topic labeling, 77–78, 82, 89, 93, 95
topic-specific special term, 89
topical context, 15, 97, 102, 105–106, 108–
    110, 113
topical cue, 108
topical redundancy, 93
topical sense vector,
    see sense, vector, topical
topical structure of a document, 89
transitive verb, see verb, class, transitive
transitivity rating, 198–199
treebank, see Penn Treebank
type,
    coercion, 149
    constraint, 152
    hierarchy, 121, 124, 135, 153, 159–160
        domain specific, 160
    information, 153, 198
    semantic, see semantic type restriction

U

uncertainty, 47, 50
uncommon proper noun,
    see proper noun, uncommon
unification, 54–55, 150
United States Constitution, 83, 93
unknown word, see word, unknown
unrestricted text, see text, unrestricted
untagged text, see text, untagged
upper/lower case distinction, 107

V

valency, 175
    reduction, 175
vector, 67, 84–85, 90, 96, 99, 101–103,
    105, 107, 110, 112, 125–126, 129,
    158, 185
    classifier, 101, 105, 112
    representation, 85
    of word, 85
    similarity, 112
    space,
        model of information retrieval sys-
            tem,
        see information retrieval, system, vec-
            tor space model
    word space, see word, space, vector
verb, 11, 13, 15–16, 30, 43, 49, 64, 116–
    133, 135–140, 148–149, 151, 153,
    158, 165, 167, 174–187, 189, 191–
    196, 198–202, 210
    categorization, 119, 123–124
    class, 16, 116, 118, 125–126, 174, 176,
        183, 187, 189
        active, 180
        agentive-action, 192–194, 198–200
        intransitive, 176, 194, 200
        inverse-state, 192–194, 198–200
        of communication, 189
        of location, 189
        of movement, 175
        process-or-state, 192–195, 198–200
        semantic, see semantic verb class
        stative, 199–200
        transitive, 194, 198, 200
    classification, 116, 118, 125–126
        automatic, 118
    cluster, 116, 119, 124, 126, 129, 131
    code,
        grammar, 182–185
        semantic, 182–184, 186–187
    frame, 184, 194, 202
    instance, 126, 133, 140
    phrase, 180, 210
    semantics, 118, 175
    sense, 175, 191, 193
    stem, 179–181, 183–184, 186–187
    subcategorization, 175–177, 183, 185–
        187, 189
        intransitive,
            see verb, class, intransitive
        transitive, see verb, class, transitive
    surface structure, 122

thematic structure, 138

W

Wall Street Journal, 23, 28, 30, 33, 37, 41, 43, 57, 62, 68, 70, 98, 167
Webster's 7th Edition, *see Merriam-Webster's Collegiate Dictionary (7th Edition)*
weight function, 166
Who's News, 24, 30, 37
window, 16, 85, 101, 128–129, 166, 195, 204, 207, 210–215
  function, 166
word, 3–7, 9, 11–16, 22–28, 30–38, 41–42, 44–50, 52–53, 61–62, 65, 69, 77, 79, 82–86, 88–90, 95–99, 101–103, 105–110, 112–113, 117–130, 144–145, 147, 150, 152–153, 156–158, 161–162, 165, 167, 170, 177–178, 180, 191, 194, 196, 199–200, 205–215
  ambiguous, 23, 82, 113, 210
  case,
    capitalization-sensitive, 31
    case-neutral, 31
    distinction,
      see upper/lower case distinction
    non-capitalized, 26
  categorization,
    automatic, 117
  class, 3, 77, 120, 122–123, 158, 165, 167
  classification, 120, 123, 167
  closed-class, 27, 33
  co-occurrence, 99, 106, 110
  context, 77, 205, 213
  form, 3, 103
  frequency,
    frequent, 16, 107, 213–215
    high, 101–102
    low, 101
    medium, 86
    rare, 16, 205, 214–215
  list, 3, 11–12, 22, 36, 107
  meaning, *see word, sense*
  open-class, 97
  order, 97, 99, 107–108, 150
  polysemous, 97–99, 109
    sense of, 99
  representation, 85
  sense, 9, 15–16, 48, 82, 97, 110, 113, 117, 123, 191, 194
  space, 84, 86, 90
    vector, 84, 90
  stem, 101

syntactic context of, 210
unknown, 30, 32, 34–36, 41–42, 48, 61, 89–90
word categorization, 117, 120
WordNet, 15, 77, 79–82, 84, 86–91, 96, 98, 109–110, 120–121, 127–128, 130, 142, 199, 209–210
WordSpace, 79, 84–86, 89–91, 96
  algorithm, 84
  centroid, 96
  vector, 84, 96
WSJ, *see Wall Street Journal*